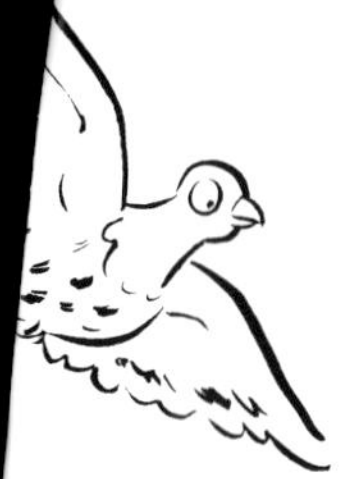

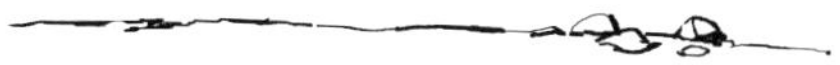

GING
L

BY F

AND COL

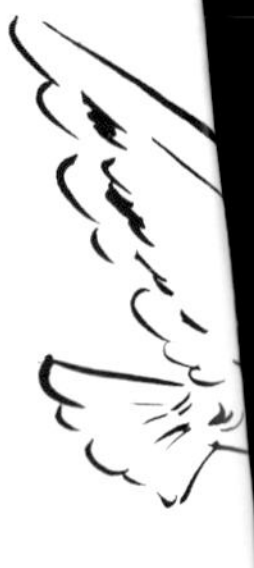

ISBN 978-1-60309-080-3
1. Fiction
2. Mystery
3. Graphic Novels

 Published by Top Shelf Productions, PO Box 1282, Marietta, GA 30061-1282, USA. Publishers: Brett Warnock and Chris Staros. Cover design by Tim Leong. [http://timleong.com/] Production assistance by MaLo Cros. First Printing, May 2011. Printed in Singapore.

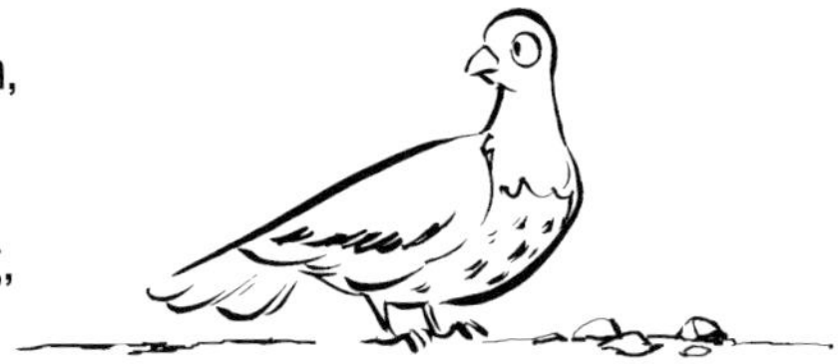

GINGERBREAD GIRL

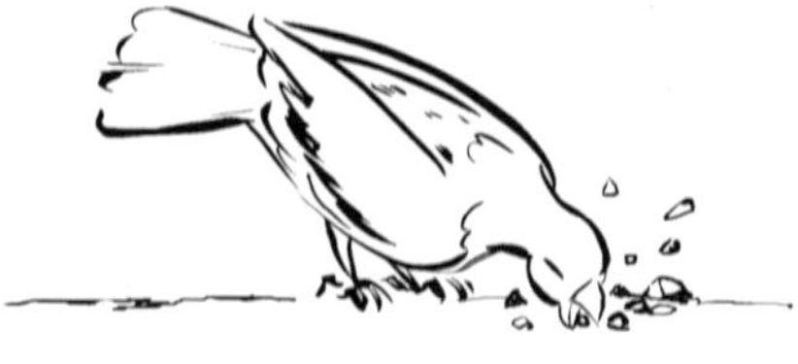

Junior Annah Billips sets a school record for the 100 yard dash at the Pacific Northwest Invitational.

Thomas Greene enjoys a dance with junior Annah Billips.

Jeremy Barton

ce Bickeram

Annahnette Billips

Gin

A day with no classes? Sort of. It's a field trip. Seen here shortly after telling a joke we dare not print, Billips and her

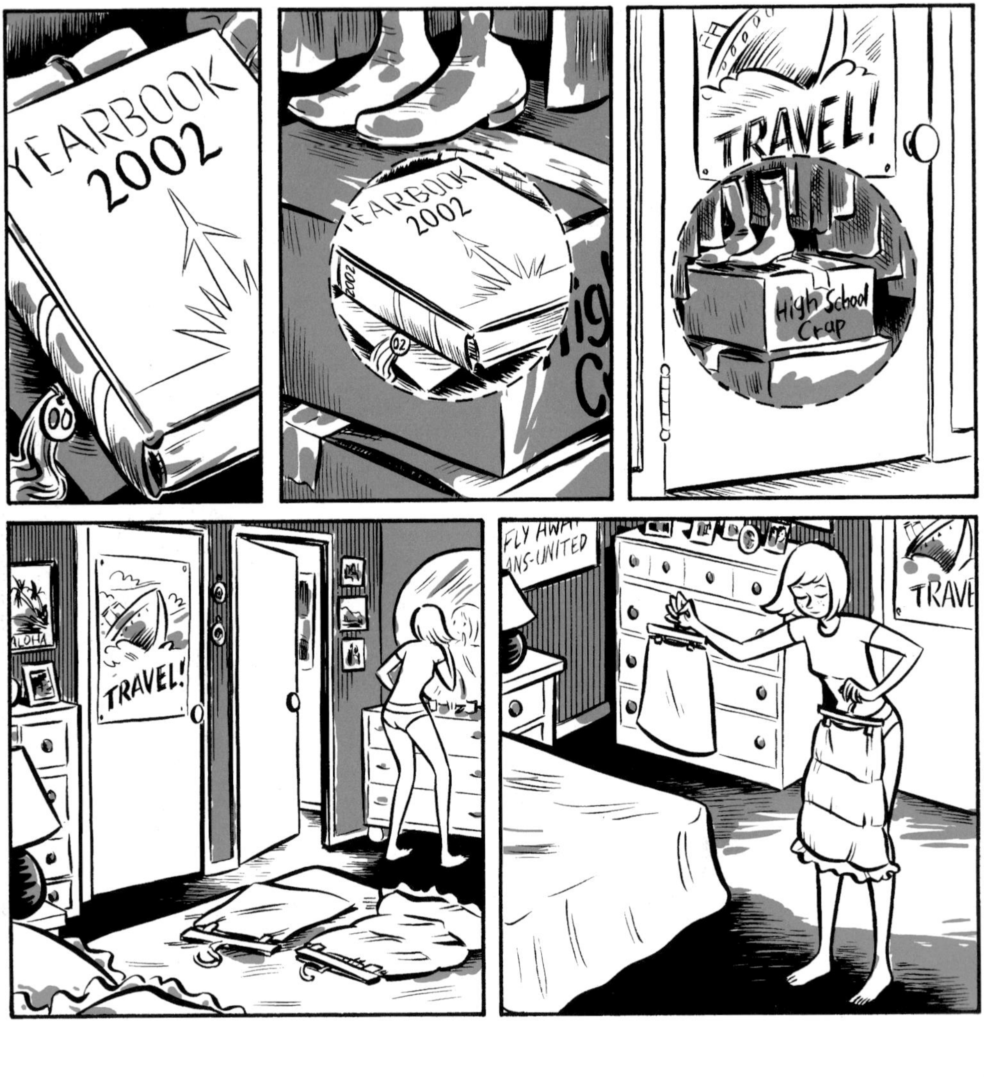
YEARBOOK
2002
YEARBOOK
2002
TRAVEL!
High School
Crap
ALOHA
TRAVEL!

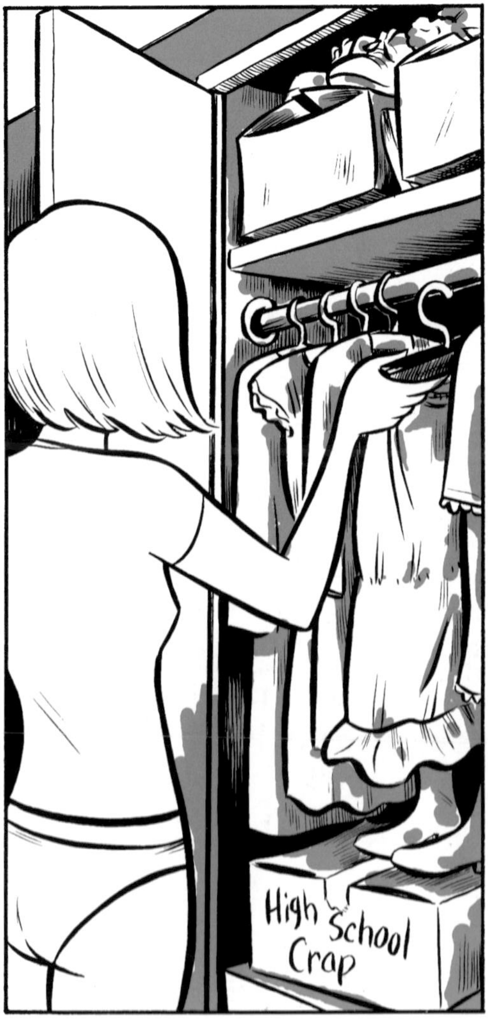
High School Crap

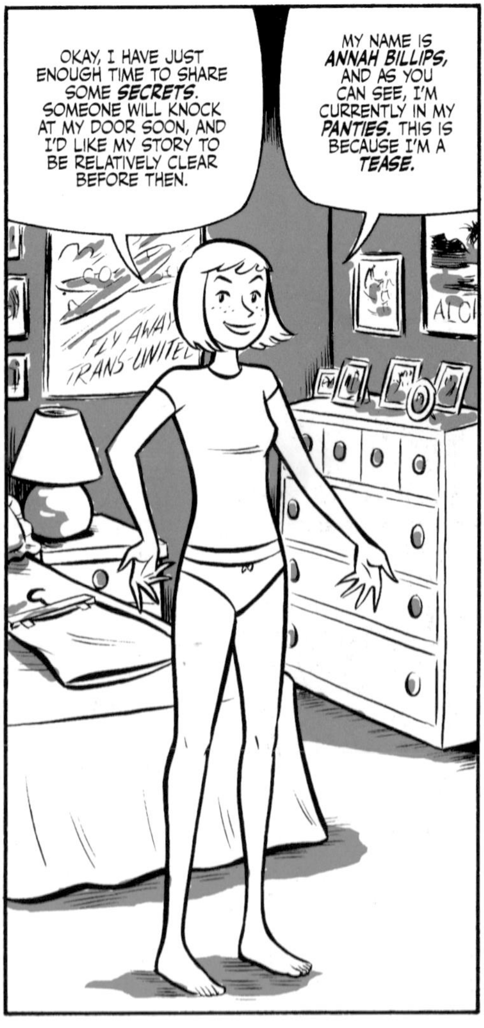
OKAY, I HAVE JUST ENOUGH TIME TO SHARE SOME **SECRETS**. SOMEONE WILL KNOCK AT MY DOOR SOON, AND I'D LIKE MY STORY TO BE RELATIVELY CLEAR BEFORE THEN.
MY NAME IS **ANNAH BILLIPS**, AND AS YOU CAN SEE, I'M CURRENTLY IN MY **PANTIES**. THIS IS BECAUSE I'M A **TEASE**.
FLY AWAY TRANS-UNITED

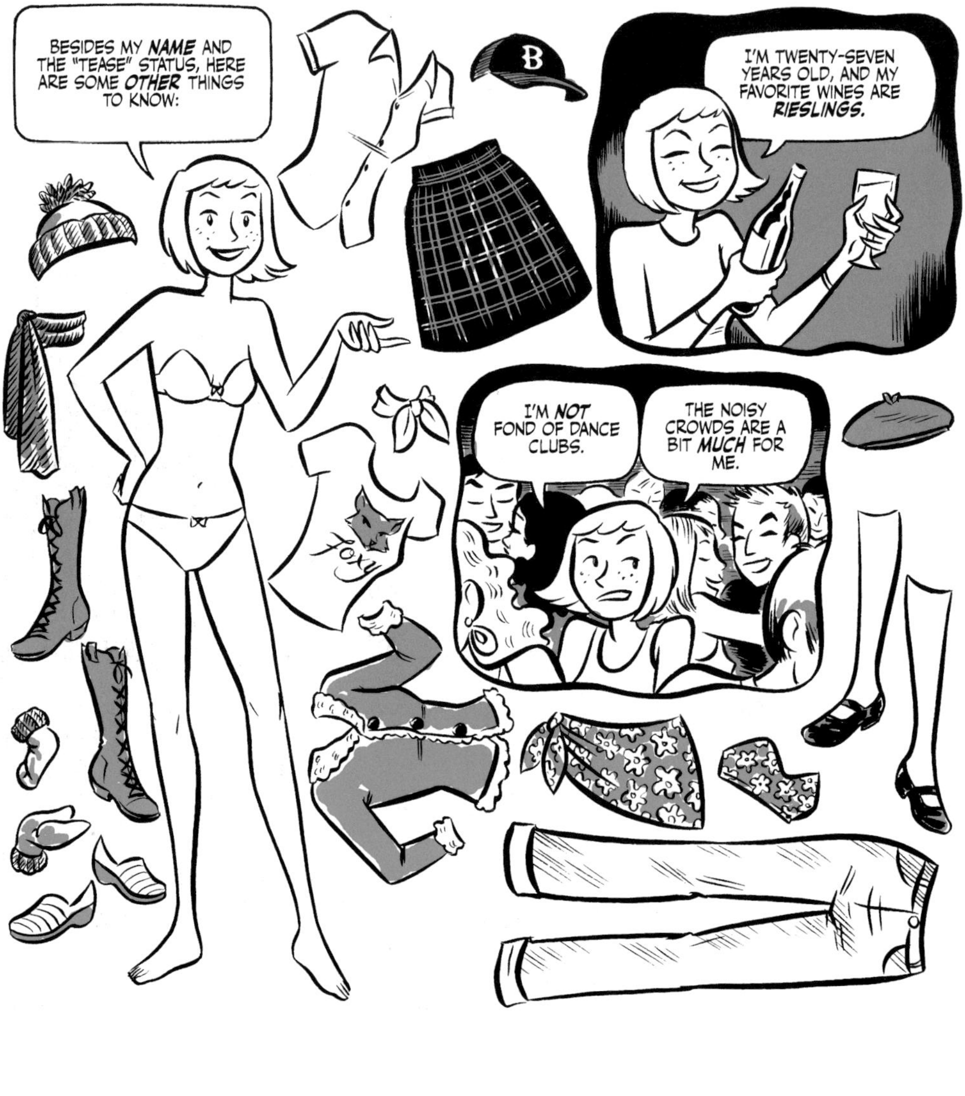
BESIDES MY NAME AND THE "TEASE" STATUS, HERE ARE SOME OTHER THINGS TO KNOW:
I'M TWENTY-SEVEN YEARS OLD, AND MY FAVORITE WINES ARE RIESLINGS.
I'M NOT FOND OF DANCE CLUBS.
THE NOISY CROWDS ARE A BIT MUCH FOR ME.
FOXY

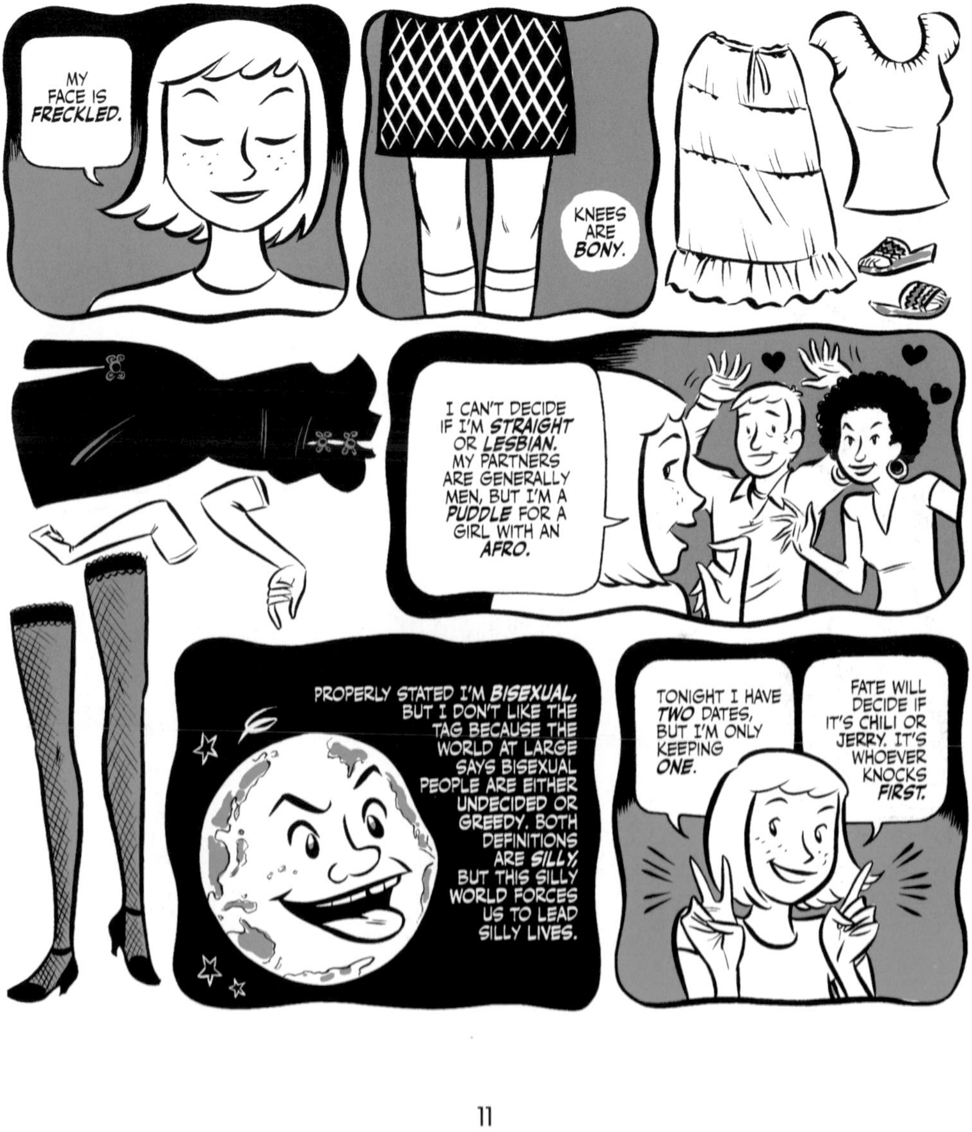
MY FACE IS FRECKLED.
KNEES ARE BONY.
I CAN'T DECIDE IF I'M STRAIGHT OR LESBIAN. MY PARTNERS ARE GENERALLY MEN, BUT I'M A PUDDLE FOR A GIRL WITH AN AFRO.
PROPERLY STATED I'M BISEXUAL, BUT I DON'T LIKE THE TAG BECAUSE THE WORLD AT LARGE SAYS BISEXUAL PEOPLE ARE EITHER UNDECIDED OR GREEDY. BOTH DEFINITIONS ARE SILLY, BUT THIS SILLY WORLD FORCES US TO LEAD SILLY LIVES.
TONIGHT I HAVE TWO DATES, BUT I'M ONLY KEEPING ONE.
FATE WILL DECIDE IF IT'S CHILI OR JERRY. IT'S WHOEVER KNOCKS FIRST.

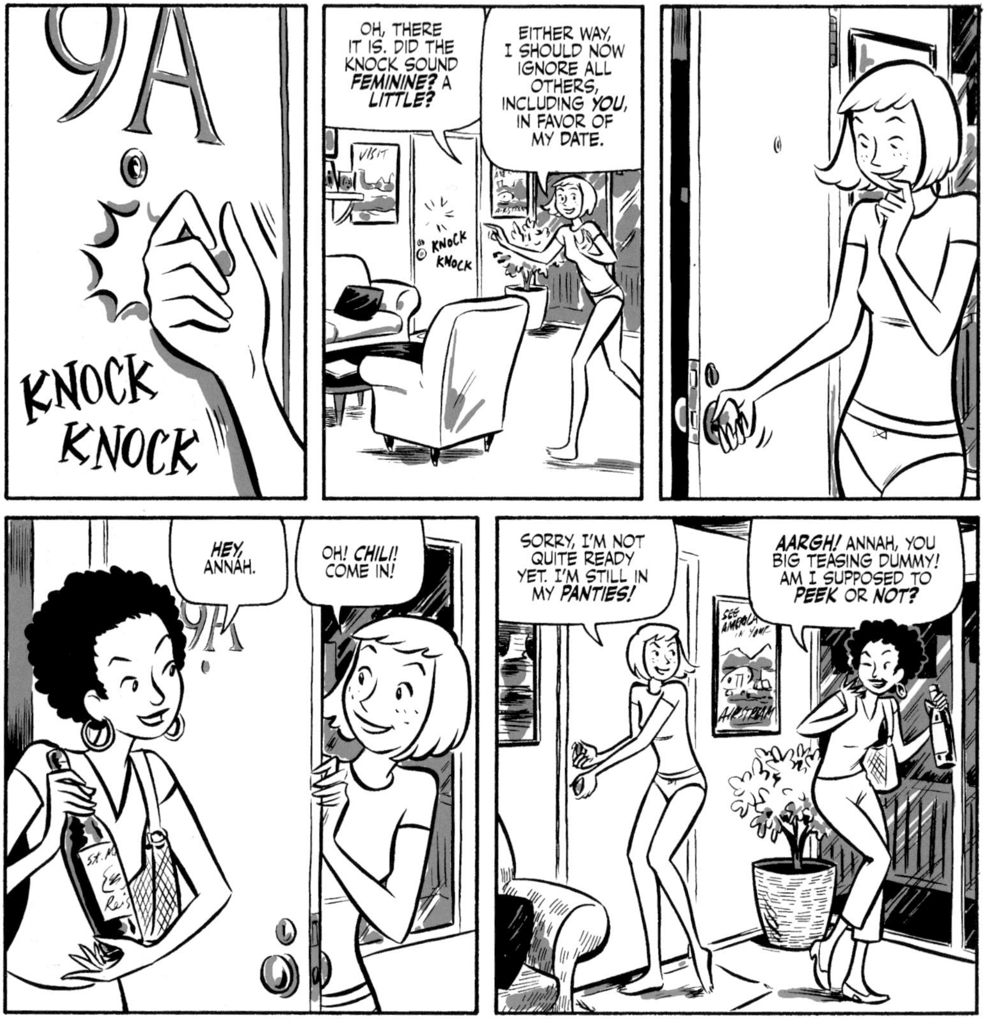
9A
KNOCK KNOCK
OH, THERE IT IS. DID THE KNOCK SOUND *FEMININE?* A *LITTLE?*
KNOCK KNOCK
EITHER WAY, I SHOULD NOW IGNORE ALL OTHERS, INCLUDING *YOU*, IN FAVOR OF MY DATE.
HEY, ANNAH.
OH! *CHILI!* COME IN!
SORRY, I'M NOT QUITE READY YET. I'M STILL IN MY *PANTIES!*
AARGH! ANNAH, YOU BIG TEASING DUMMY! AM I SUPPOSED TO *PEEK* OR *NOT?*

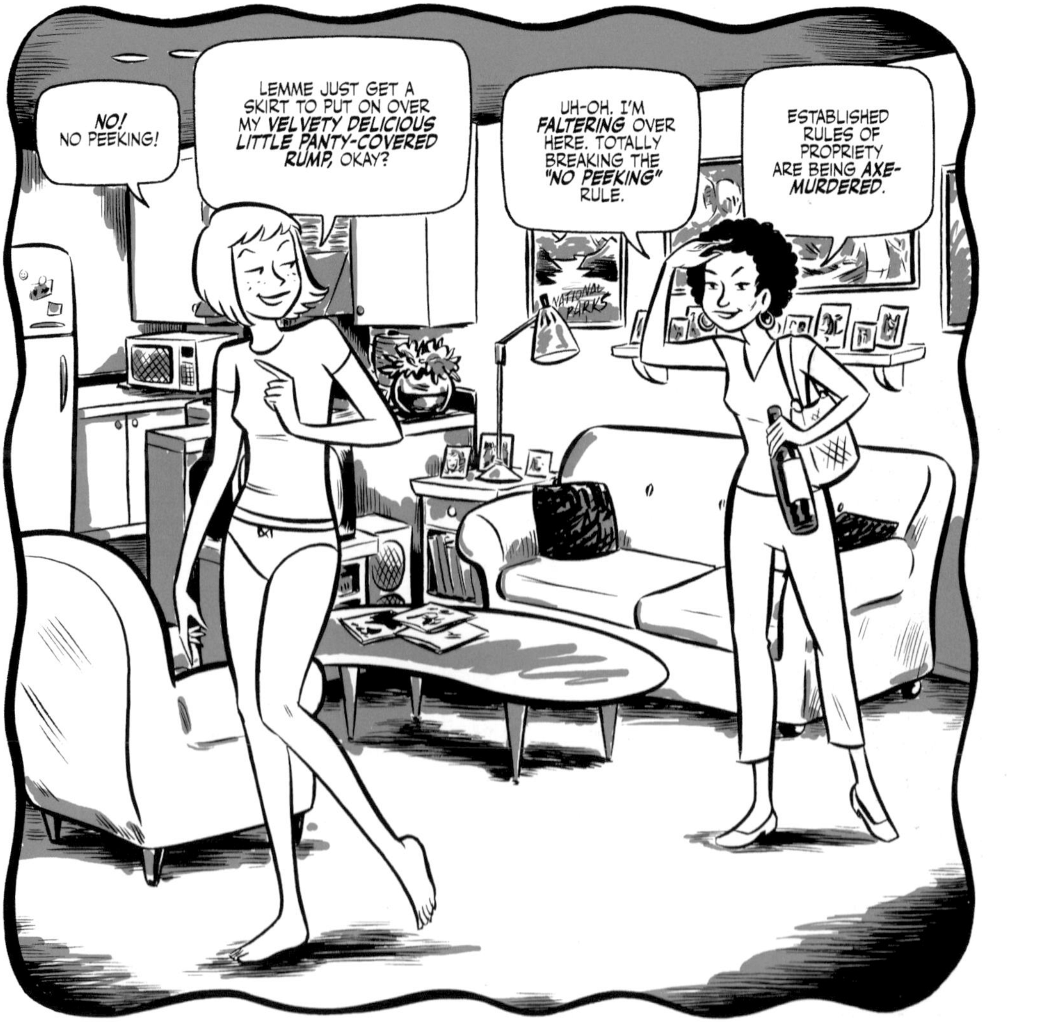
NO! NO PEEKING!
LEMME JUST GET A SKIRT TO PUT ON OVER MY VELVETY DELICIOUS LITTLE PANTY-COVERED RUMP, OKAY?
UH-OH. I'M FALTERING OVER HERE. TOTALLY BREAKING THE "NO PEEKING" RULE.
ESTABLISHED RULES OF PROPRIETY ARE BEING AXE-MURDERED.
NATIONAL PARKS

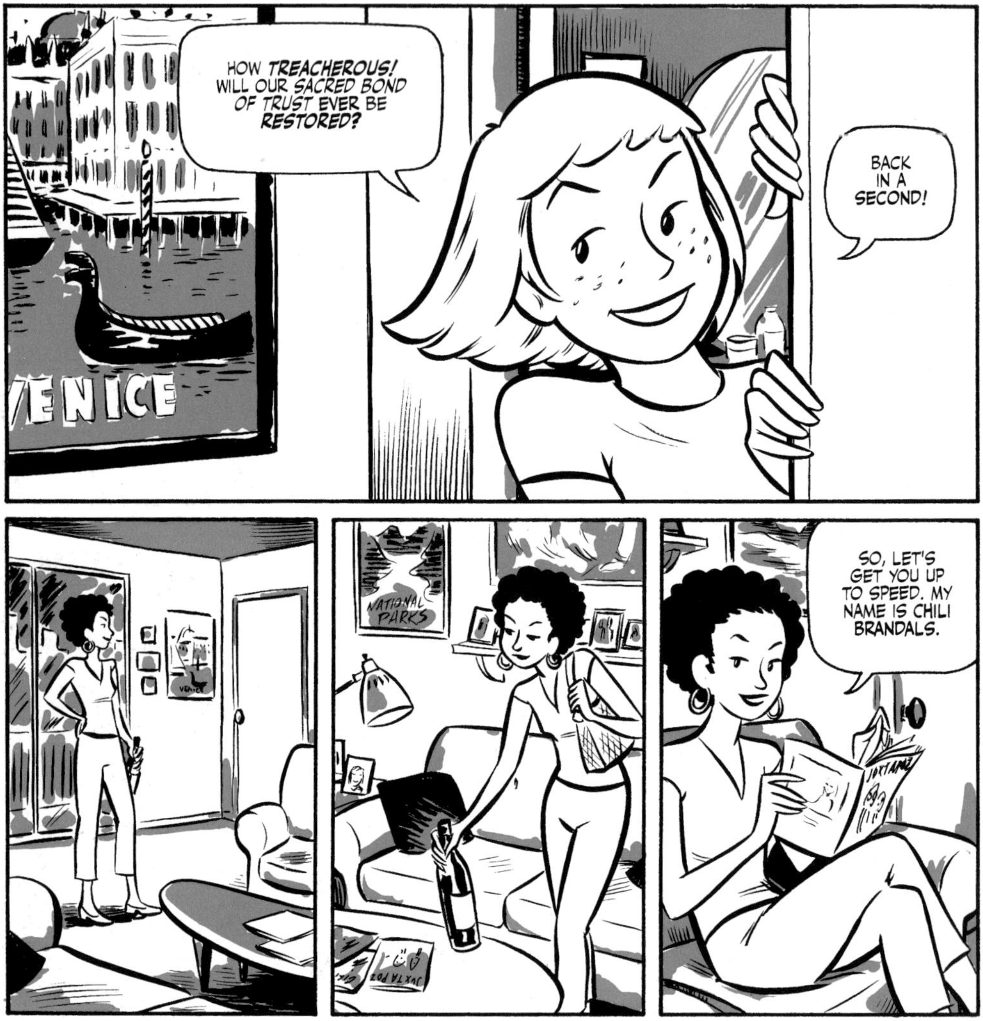
HOW TREACHEROUS! WILL OUR SACRED BOND OF TRUST EVER BE RESTORED?
VENICE
BACK IN A SECOND!
NATIONAL PARKS
SO, LET'S GET YOU UP TO SPEED. MY NAME IS CHILI BRANDALS.

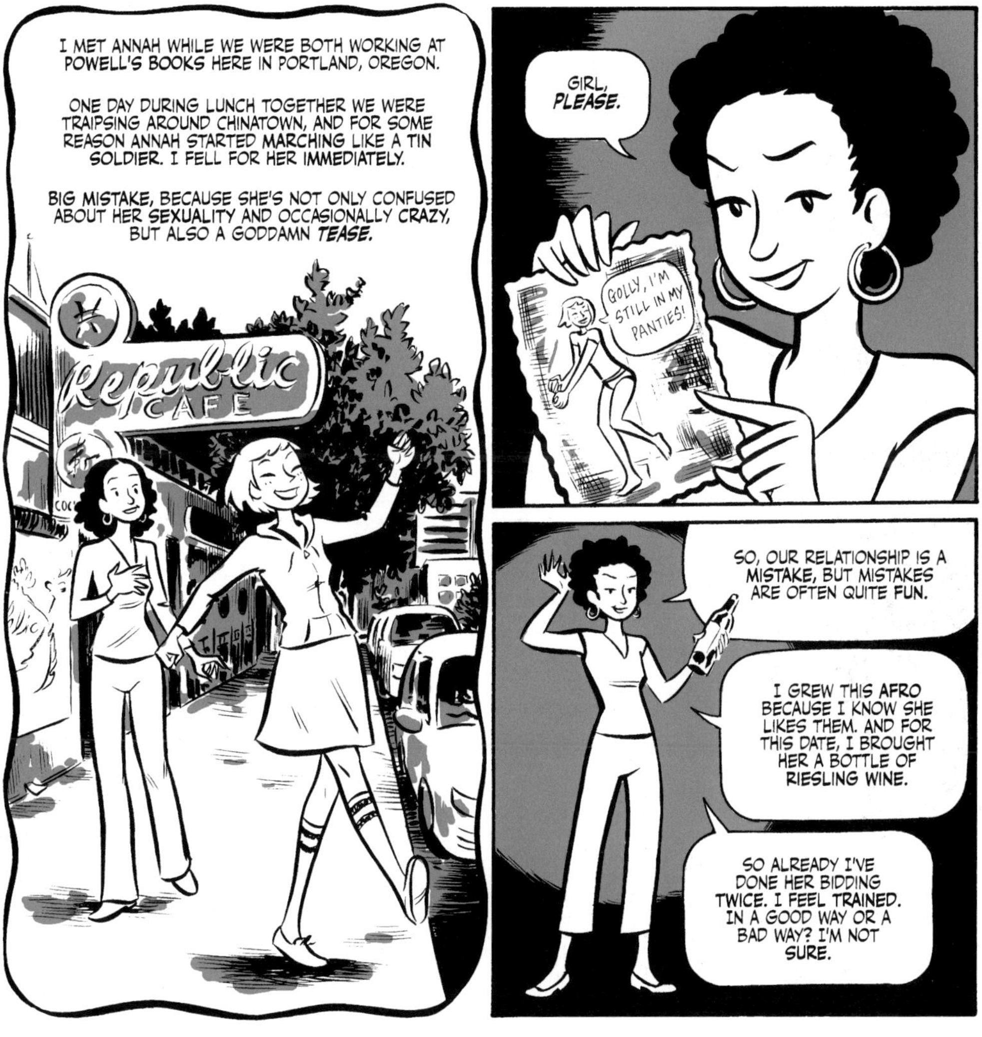
I MET ANNAH WHILE WE WERE BOTH WORKING AT POWELL'S BOOKS HERE IN PORTLAND, OREGON.
ONE DAY DURING LUNCH TOGETHER WE WERE TRAIPSING AROUND CHINATOWN, AND FOR SOME REASON ANNAH STARTED MARCHING LIKE A TIN SOLDIER. I FELL FOR HER IMMEDIATELY.
BIG MISTAKE, BECAUSE SHE'S NOT ONLY CONFUSED ABOUT HER SEXUALITY AND OCCASIONALLY CRAZY, BUT ALSO A GODDAMN *TEASE.*
Republic CAFE
GIRL, *PLEASE.*
GOLLY, I'M STILL IN MY PANTIES!
SO, OUR RELATIONSHIP IS A MISTAKE, BUT MISTAKES ARE OFTEN QUITE FUN.
I GREW THIS AFRO BECAUSE I KNOW SHE LIKES THEM. AND FOR THIS DATE, I BROUGHT HER A BOTTLE OF RIESLING WINE.
SO ALREADY I'VE DONE HER BIDDING TWICE. I FEEL TRAINED. IN A GOOD WAY OR A BAD WAY? I'M NOT SURE.

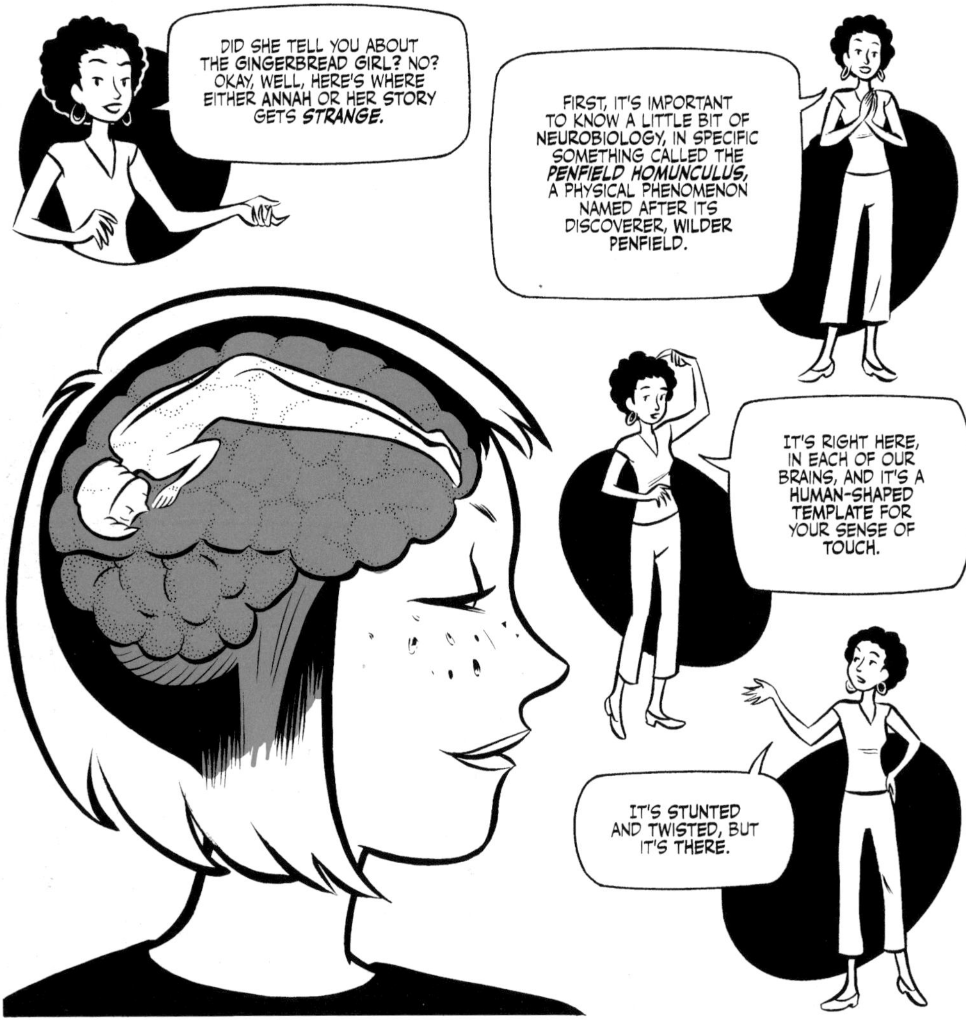
DID SHE TELL YOU ABOUT THE GINGERBREAD GIRL? NO? OKAY, WELL, HERE'S WHERE EITHER ANNAH OR HER STORY GETS *STRANGE.*
FIRST, IT'S IMPORTANT TO KNOW A LITTLE BIT OF NEUROBIOLOGY, IN SPECIFIC SOMETHING CALLED THE ***PENFIELD HOMUNCULUS,*** A PHYSICAL PHENOMENON NAMED AFTER ITS DISCOVERER, WILDER PENFIELD.
IT'S RIGHT HERE, IN EACH OF OUR BRAINS, AND IT'S A HUMAN-SHAPED TEMPLATE FOR YOUR SENSE OF TOUCH.
IT'S STUNTED AND TWISTED, BUT IT'S THERE.

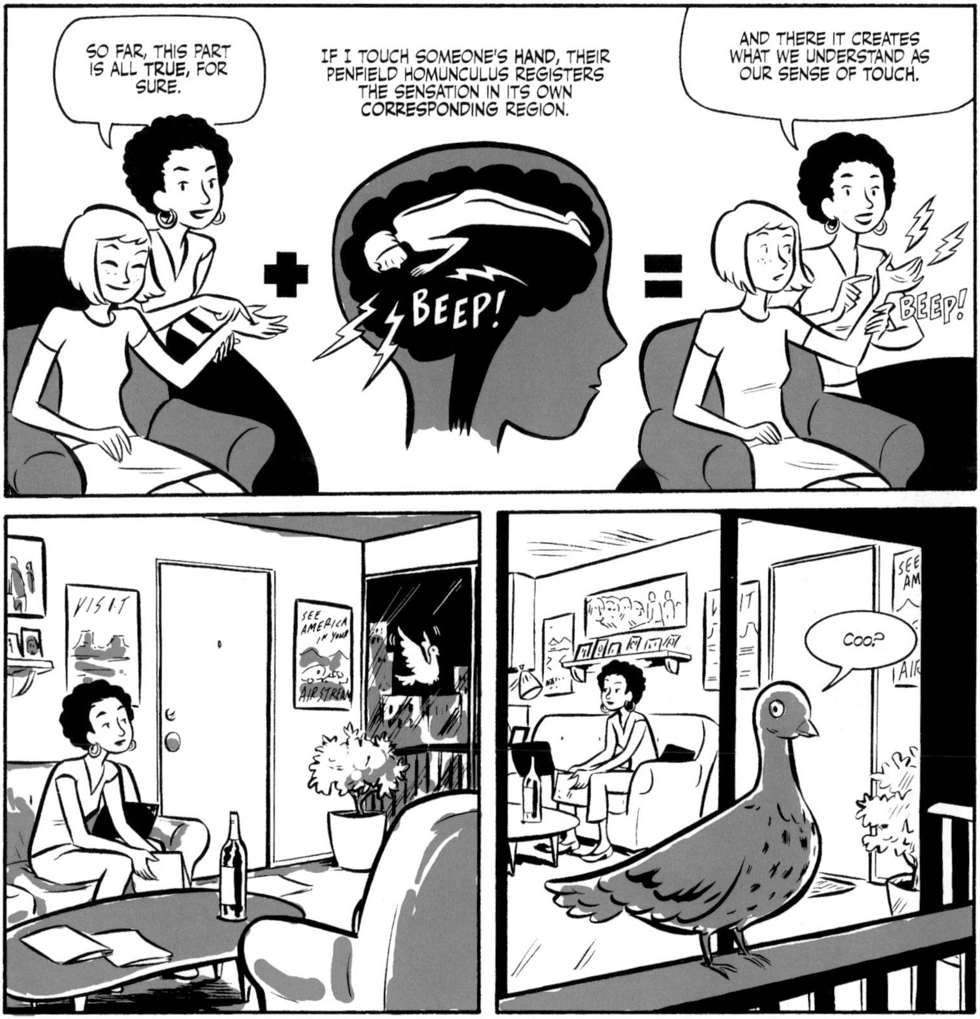
SO FAR, THIS PART IS ALL TRUE, FOR SURE.
IF I TOUCH SOMEONE'S HAND, THEIR PENFIELD HOMUNCULUS REGISTERS THE SENSATION IN ITS OWN CORRESPONDING REGION.
BEEP!
AND THERE IT CREATES WHAT WE UNDERSTAND AS OUR SENSE OF TOUCH.
BEEP!
VISIT
SEE AMERICA IN YOUR AIRSTREAM
COO?

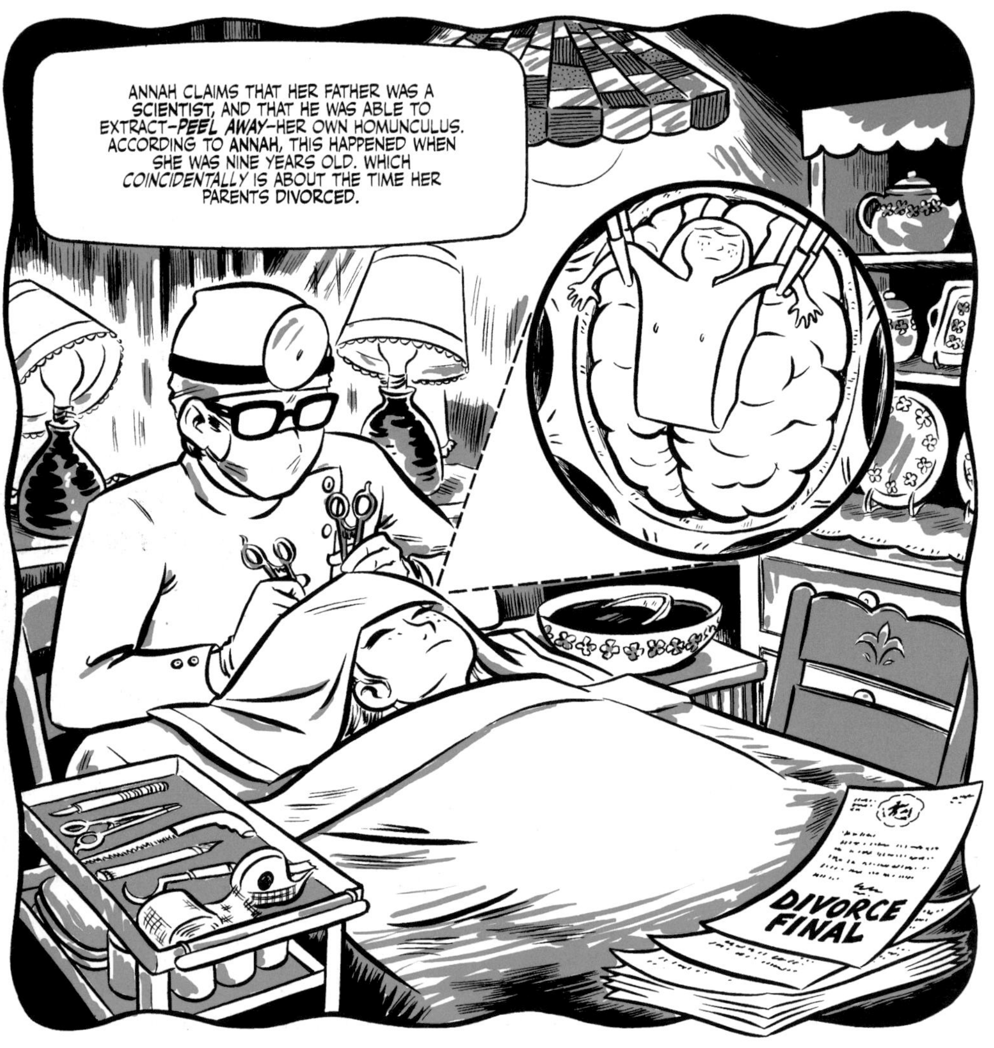
ANNAH CLAIMS THAT HER FATHER WAS A SCIENTIST, AND THAT HE WAS ABLE TO EXTRACT–*PEEL AWAY*–HER OWN HOMUNCULUS. ACCORDING TO ANNAH, THIS HAPPENED WHEN SHE WAS NINE YEARS OLD. WHICH *COINCIDENTALLY* IS ABOUT THE TIME HER PARENTS DIVORCED.
DIVORCE FINAL

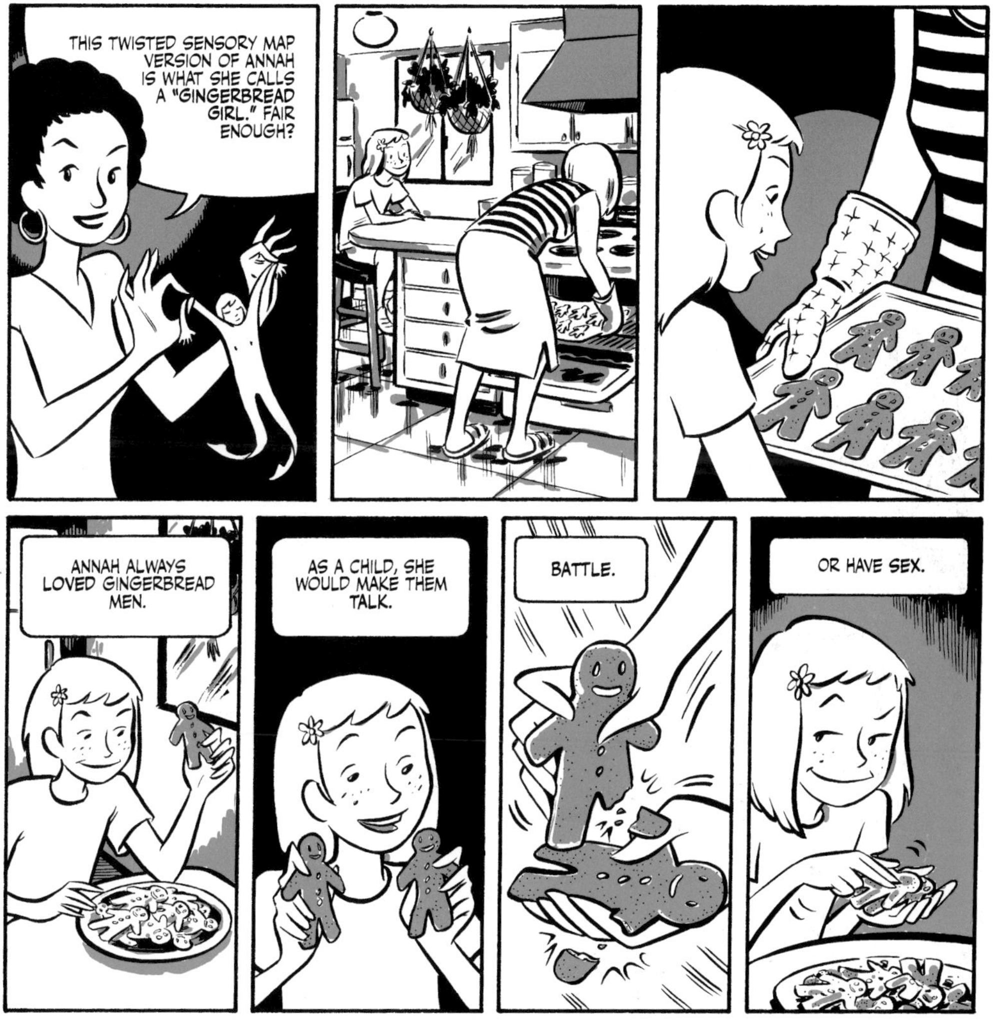
THIS TWISTED SENSORY MAP VERSION OF ANNAH IS WHAT SHE CALLS A "GINGERBREAD GIRL." FAIR ENOUGH?
ANNAH ALWAYS LOVED GINGERBREAD MEN.
AS A CHILD, SHE WOULD MAKE THEM TALK.
BATTLE.
OR HAVE SEX.

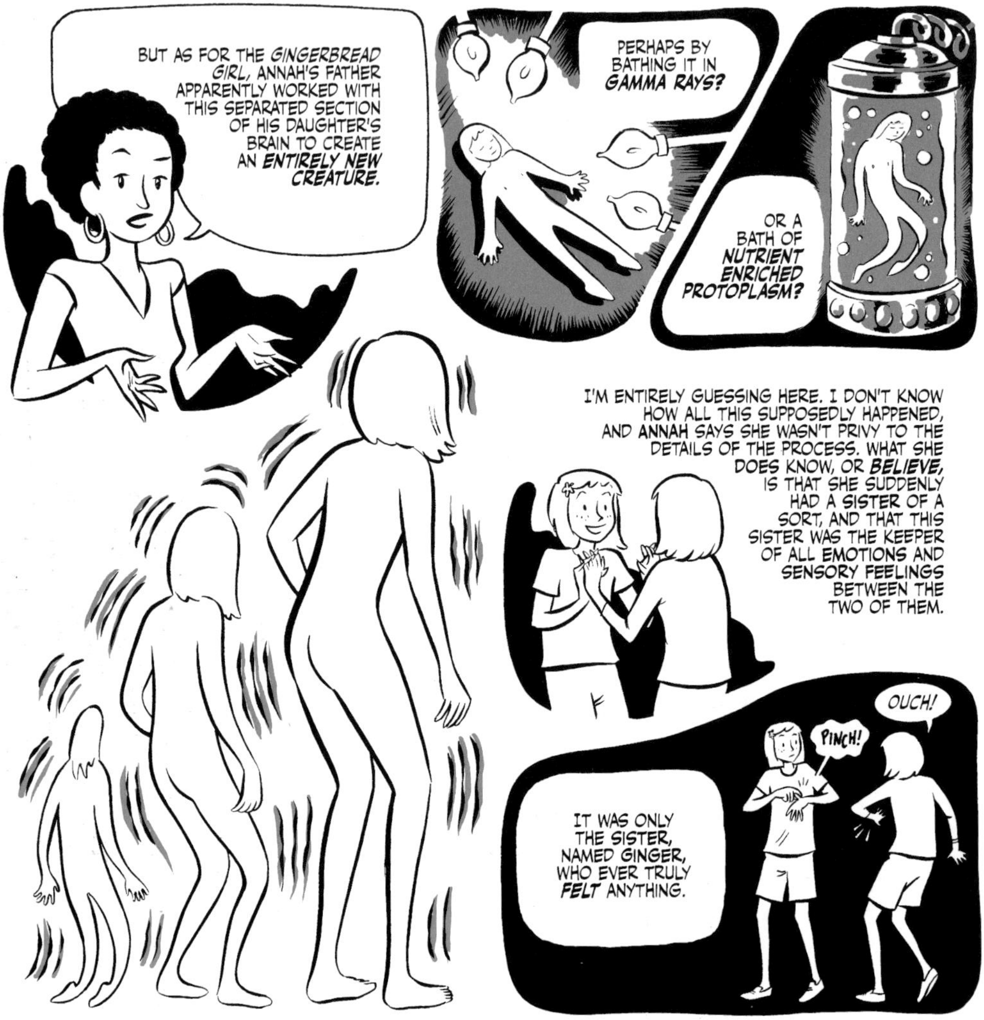

BUT AS FOR THE GINGERBREAD GIRL, ANNAH'S FATHER APPARENTLY WORKED WITH THIS SEPARATED SECTION OF HIS DAUGHTER'S BRAIN TO CREATE AN ENTIRELY NEW CREATURE.
PERHAPS BY BATHING IT IN GAMMA RAYS?
OR A BATH OF NUTRIENT ENRICHED PROTOPLASM?
I'M ENTIRELY GUESSING HERE. I DON'T KNOW HOW ALL THIS SUPPOSEDLY HAPPENED, AND ANNAH SAYS SHE WASN'T PRIVY TO THE DETAILS OF THE PROCESS. WHAT SHE DOES KNOW, OR BELIEVE, IS THAT SHE SUDDENLY HAD A SISTER OF A SORT, AND THAT THIS SISTER WAS THE KEEPER OF ALL EMOTIONS AND SENSORY FEELINGS BETWEEN THE TWO OF THEM.
IT WAS ONLY THE SISTER, NAMED GINGER, WHO EVER TRULY FELT ANYTHING.
PINCH!
OUCH!

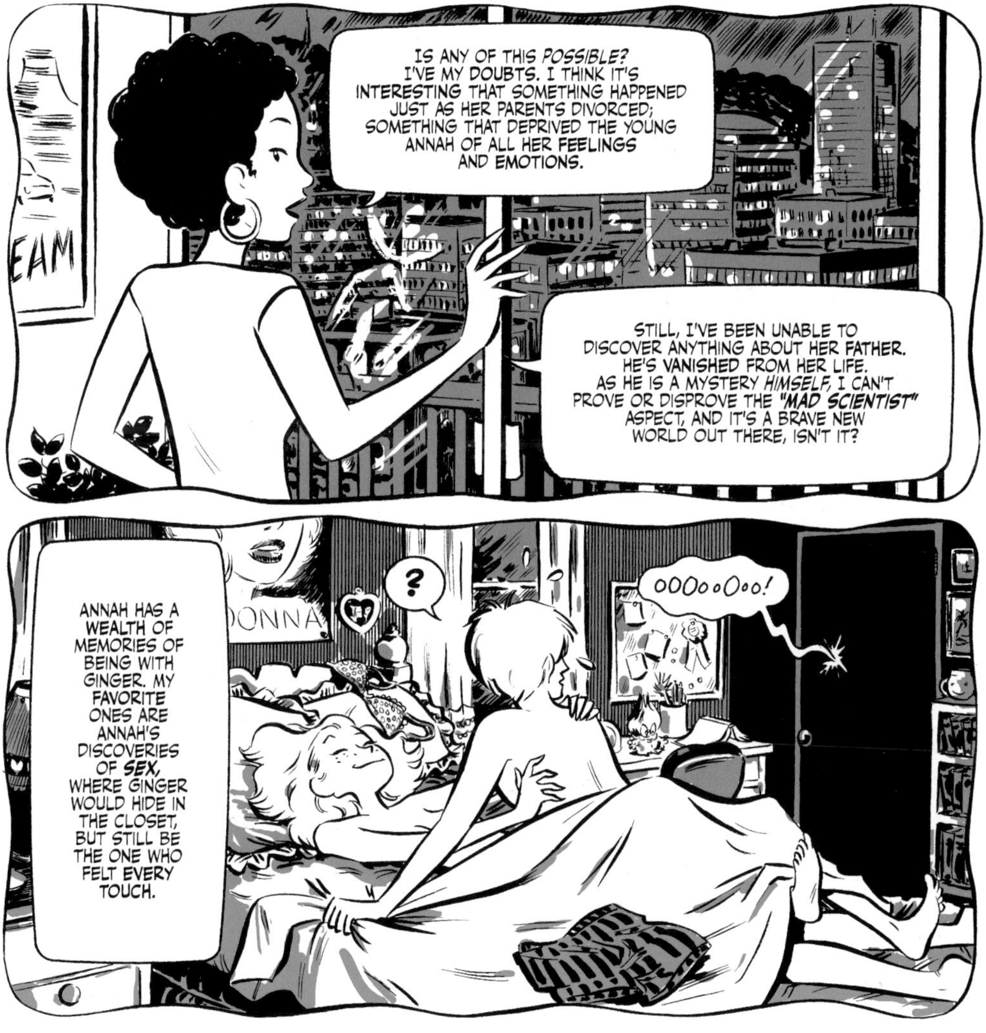
IS ANY OF THIS *POSSIBLE?* I'VE MY **DOUBTS**. I THINK IT'S **INTERESTING** THAT SOMETHING HAPPENED JUST AS HER PARENTS DIVORCED; SOMETHING THAT DEPRIVED THE YOUNG ANNAH OF ALL HER **FEELINGS** AND **EMOTIONS**.
STILL, I'VE BEEN UNABLE TO DISCOVER ANYTHING ABOUT HER **FATHER**. HE'S **VANISHED** FROM HER LIFE. AS HE IS A MYSTERY *HIMSELF*, I CAN'T PROVE OR DISPROVE THE ***"MAD SCIENTIST"*** ASPECT, AND IT'S A BRAVE NEW WORLD OUT THERE, ISN'T IT?
EAM
ANNAH HAS A **WEALTH** OF **MEMORIES** OF BEING WITH GINGER. MY **FAVORITE** ONES ARE ANNAH'S **DISCOVERIES** OF ***SEX,*** WHERE GINGER WOULD HIDE IN THE CLOSET, BUT STILL BE THE ONE WHO FELT **EVERY** TOUCH.
DONNA
?
OOOoOoo!

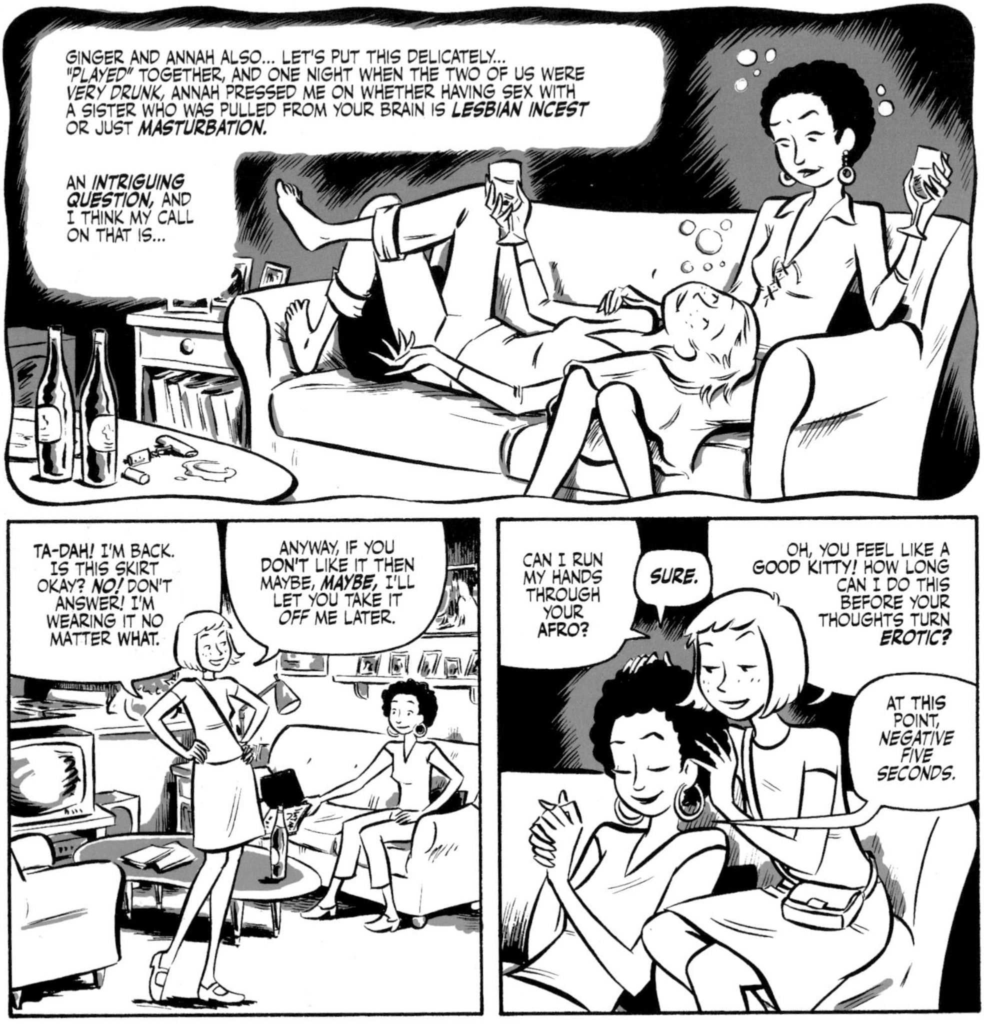
GINGER AND ANNAH ALSO... LET'S PUT THIS DELICATELY... "PLAYED" TOGETHER, AND ONE NIGHT WHEN THE TWO OF US WERE VERY DRUNK, ANNAH PRESSED ME ON WHETHER HAVING SEX WITH A SISTER WHO WAS PULLED FROM YOUR BRAIN IS LESBIAN INCEST OR JUST MASTURBATION.
AN INTRIGUING QUESTION, AND I THINK MY CALL ON THAT IS...
TA-DAH! I'M BACK. IS THIS SKIRT OKAY? NO! DON'T ANSWER! I'M WEARING IT NO MATTER WHAT.
ANYWAY, IF YOU DON'T LIKE IT THEN MAYBE, MAYBE, I'LL LET YOU TAKE IT OFF ME LATER.
CAN I RUN MY HANDS THROUGH YOUR AFRO?
SURE.
OH, YOU FEEL LIKE A GOOD KITTY! HOW LONG CAN I DO THIS BEFORE YOUR THOUGHTS TURN EROTIC?
AT THIS POINT, NEGATIVE FIVE SECONDS.

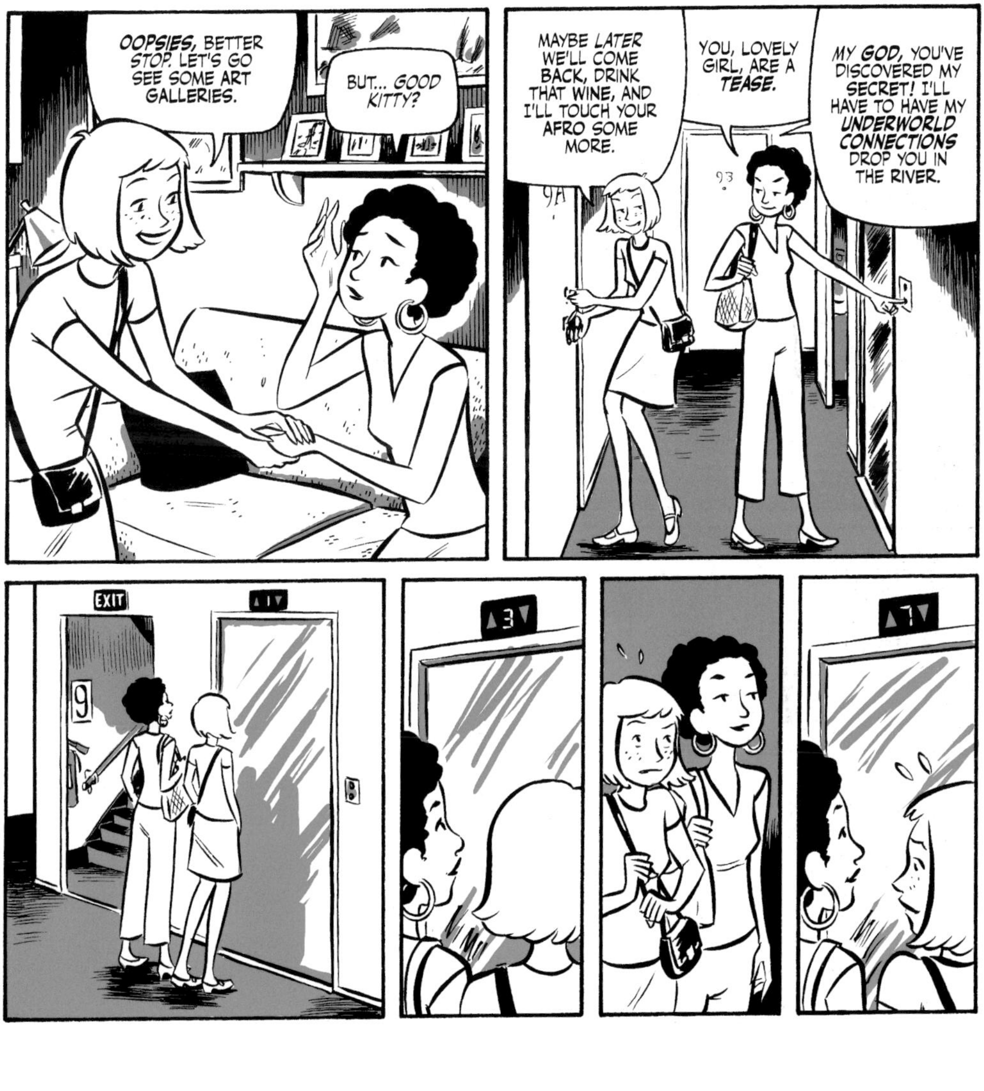
OOPSIES, BETTER STOP. LET'S GO SEE SOME ART GALLERIES.
BUT... GOOD KITTY?
MAYBE LATER WE'LL COME BACK, DRINK THAT WINE, AND I'LL TOUCH YOUR AFRO SOME MORE.
YOU, LOVELY GIRL, ARE A TEASE.
MY GOD, YOU'VE DISCOVERED MY SECRET! I'LL HAVE TO HAVE MY UNDERWORLD CONNECTIONS DROP YOU IN THE RIVER.
EXIT

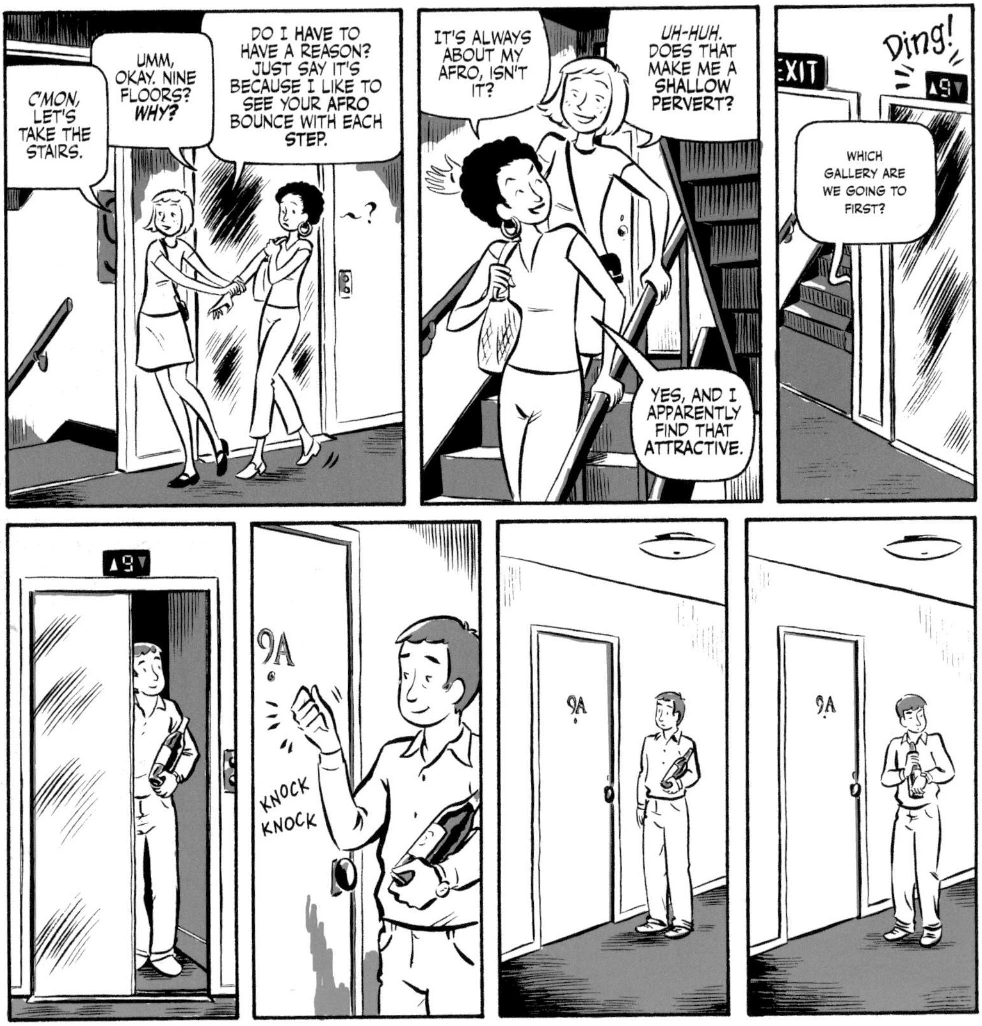
C'MON, LET'S TAKE THE STAIRS.
UMM, OKAY. NINE FLOORS? WHY?
DO I HAVE TO HAVE A REASON? JUST SAY IT'S BECAUSE I LIKE TO SEE YOUR AFRO BOUNCE WITH EACH STEP.
~?
IT'S ALWAYS ABOUT MY AFRO, ISN'T IT?
UH-HUH. DOES THAT MAKE ME A SHALLOW PERVERT?
YES, AND I APPARENTLY FIND THAT ATTRACTIVE.
EXIT
Ding!
9
WHICH GALLERY ARE WE GOING TO FIRST?
9
9A
KNOCK KNOCK
9A
9A

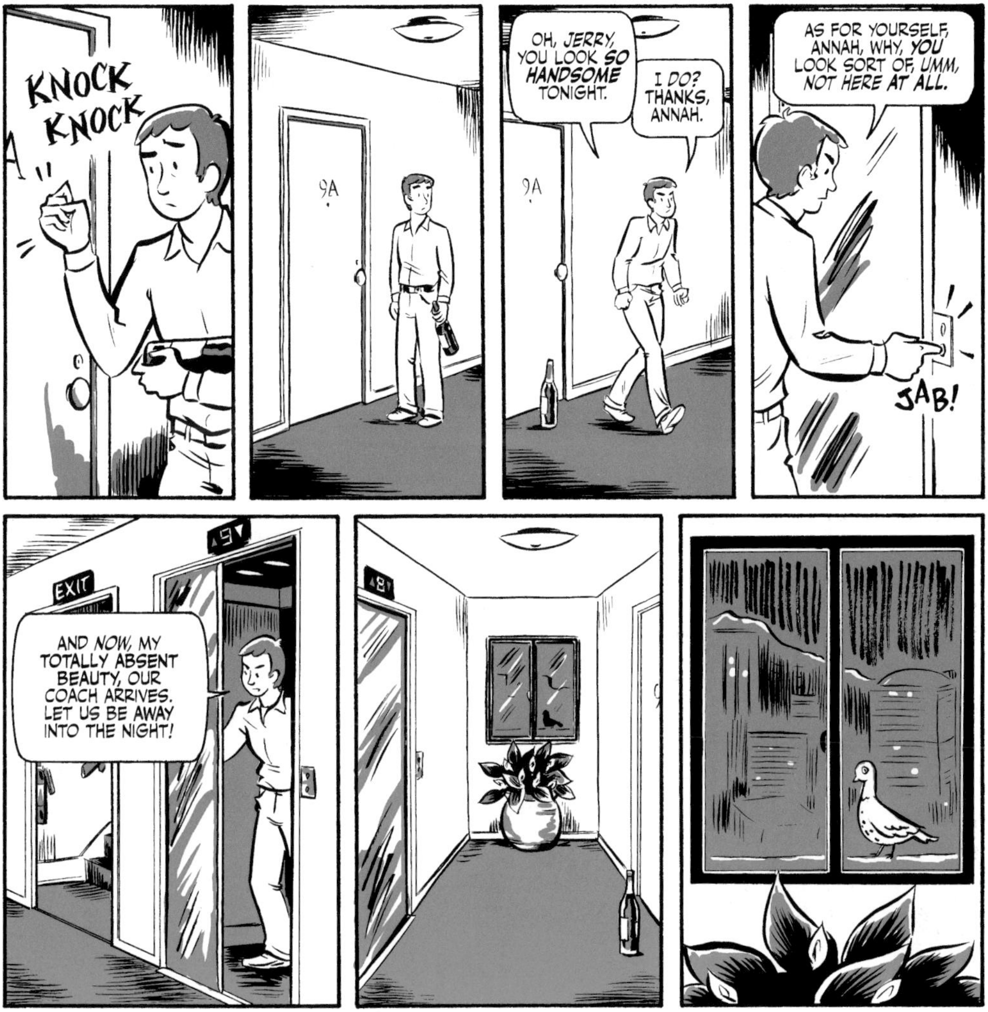
KNOCK KNOCK
OH, JERRY, YOU LOOK SO HANDSOME TONIGHT.
I DO? THANKS, ANNAH.
AS FOR YOURSELF, ANNAH, WHY, YOU LOOK SORT OF, UMM, NOT HERE AT ALL.
JAB!
EXIT
AND NOW, MY TOTALLY ABSENT BEAUTY, OUR COACH ARRIVES. LET US BE AWAY INTO THE NIGHT!

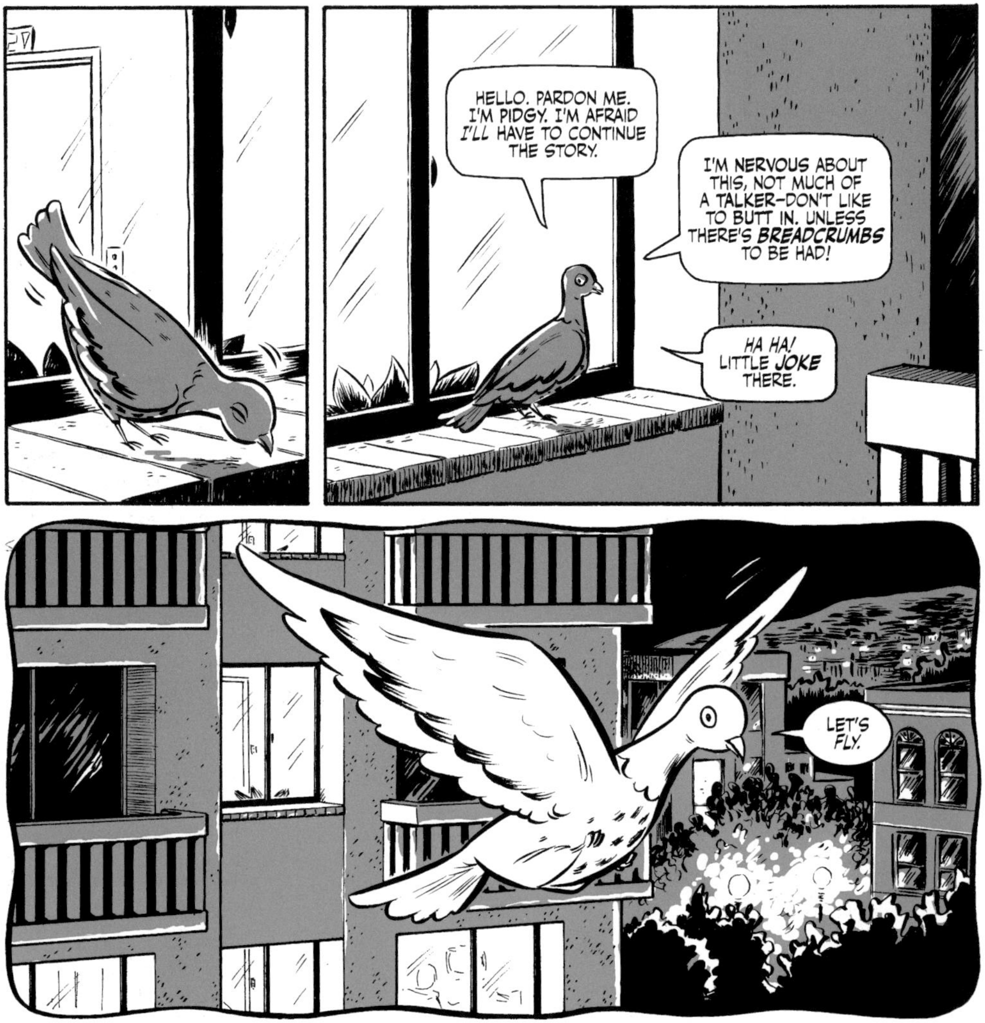
HELLO. PARDON ME. I'M PIDGY. I'M AFRAID *I'LL* HAVE TO CONTINUE THE STORY.
I'M NERVOUS ABOUT THIS, NOT MUCH OF A TALKER—DON'T LIKE TO BUTT IN. UNLESS THERE'S ***BREADCRUMBS*** TO BE HAD!
HA HA! LITTLE ***JOKE*** THERE.
LET'S *FLY.*

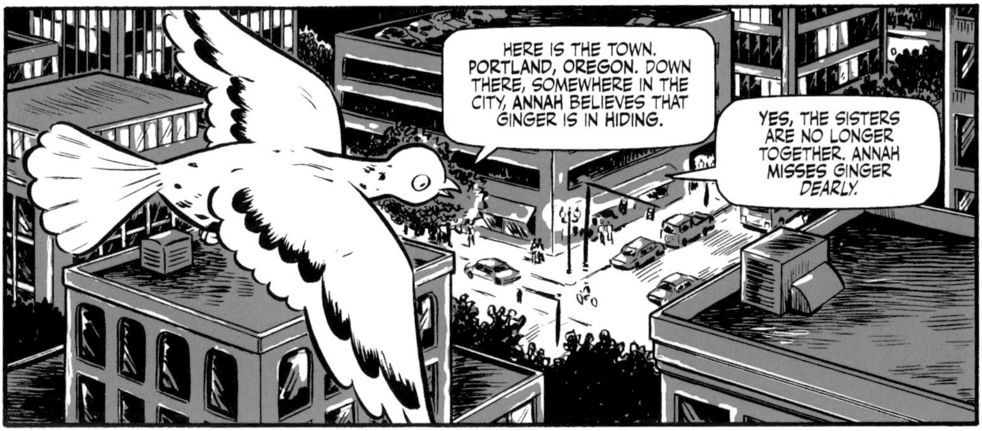
HERE IS THE TOWN. PORTLAND, OREGON. DOWN THERE, SOMEWHERE IN THE CITY, ANNAH BELIEVES THAT GINGER IS IN HIDING.
YES, THE SISTERS ARE NO LONGER TOGETHER. ANNAH MISSES GINGER DEARLY.

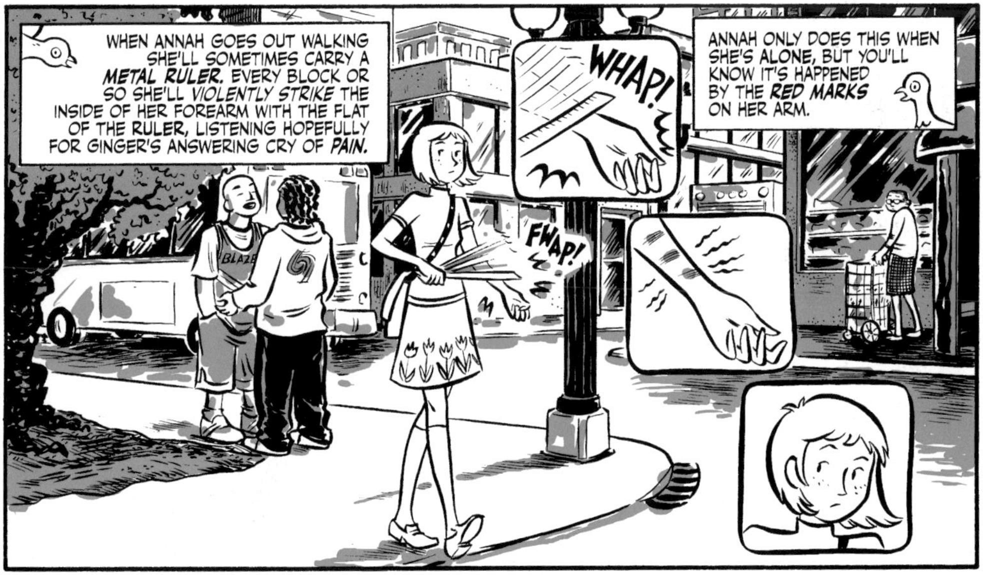
WHEN ANNAH GOES OUT WALKING SHE'LL SOMETIMES CARRY A METAL RULER. EVERY BLOCK OR SO SHE'LL VIOLENTLY STRIKE THE INSIDE OF HER FOREARM WITH THE FLAT OF THE RULER, LISTENING HOPEFULLY FOR GINGER'S ANSWERING CRY OF PAIN.
WHAP!
FWAP!
BLAZE
ANNAH ONLY DOES THIS WHEN SHE'S ALONE, BUT YOU'LL KNOW IT'S HAPPENED BY THE RED MARKS ON HER ARM.

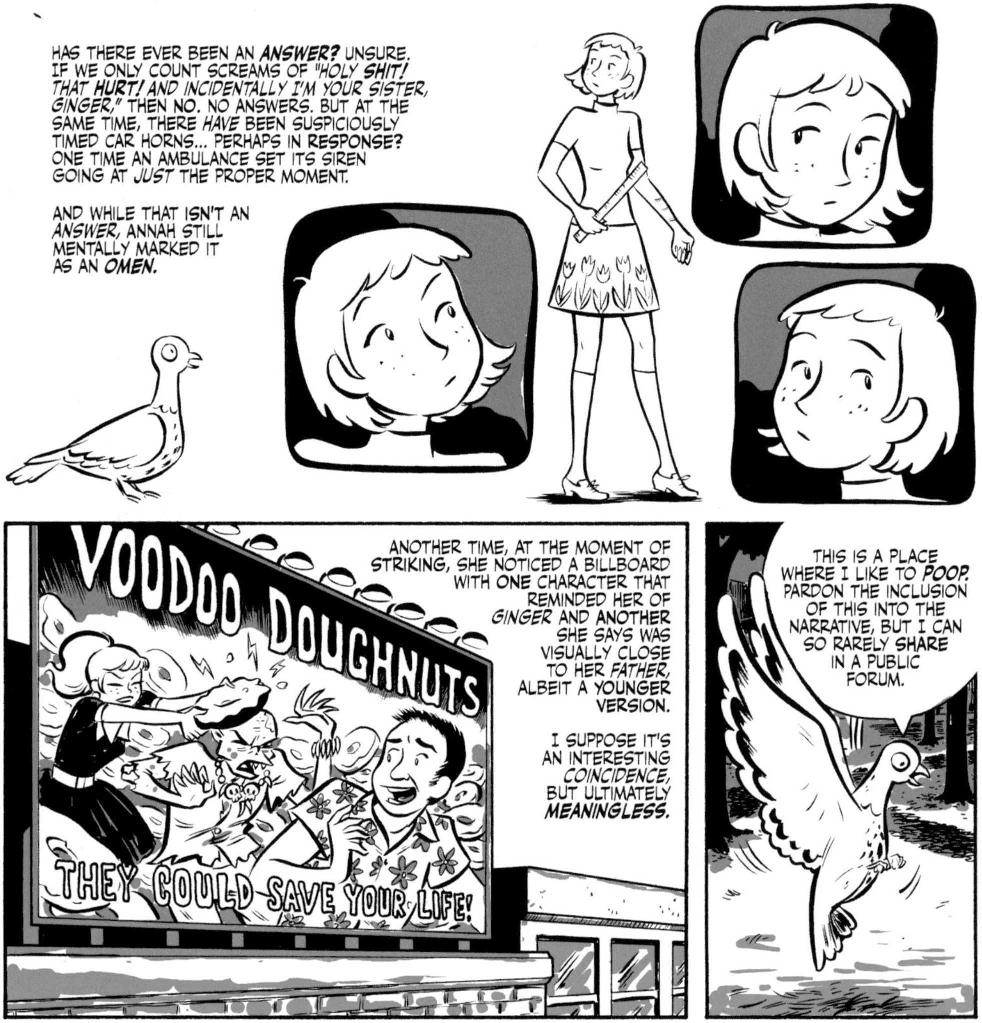
HAS THERE EVER BEEN AN *ANSWER?* UNSURE. IF WE ONLY COUNT SCREAMS OF *"HOLY SHIT! THAT HURT! AND INCIDENTALLY I'M YOUR SISTER, GINGER,"* THEN NO. NO ANSWERS. BUT AT THE SAME TIME, THERE *HAVE* BEEN SUSPICIOUSLY TIMED CAR HORNS... PERHAPS IN **RESPONSE?** ONE TIME AN AMBULANCE SET ITS SIREN GOING AT *JUST* THE PROPER MOMENT.
AND WHILE THAT **ISN'T** AN *ANSWER,* ANNAH STILL MENTALLY MARKED IT AS AN ***OMEN.***
VOODOO DOUGHNUTS
THEY COULD SAVE YOUR LIFE!
ANOTHER TIME, AT THE MOMENT OF **STRIKING,** SHE NOTICED A BILLBOARD WITH **ONE** CHARACTER THAT REMINDED HER OF *GINGER* AND **ANOTHER** SHE SAYS WAS VISUALLY CLOSE TO HER *FATHER,* ALBEIT A **YOUNGER VERSION.**
I SUPPOSE IT'S AN INTERESTING *COINCIDENCE,* BUT ULTIMATELY ***MEANINGLESS.***
THIS IS A PLACE WHERE I LIKE TO ***POOP.*** PARDON THE INCLUSION OF THIS INTO THE NARRATIVE, BUT I CAN SO RARELY **SHARE** IN A PUBLIC FORUM.

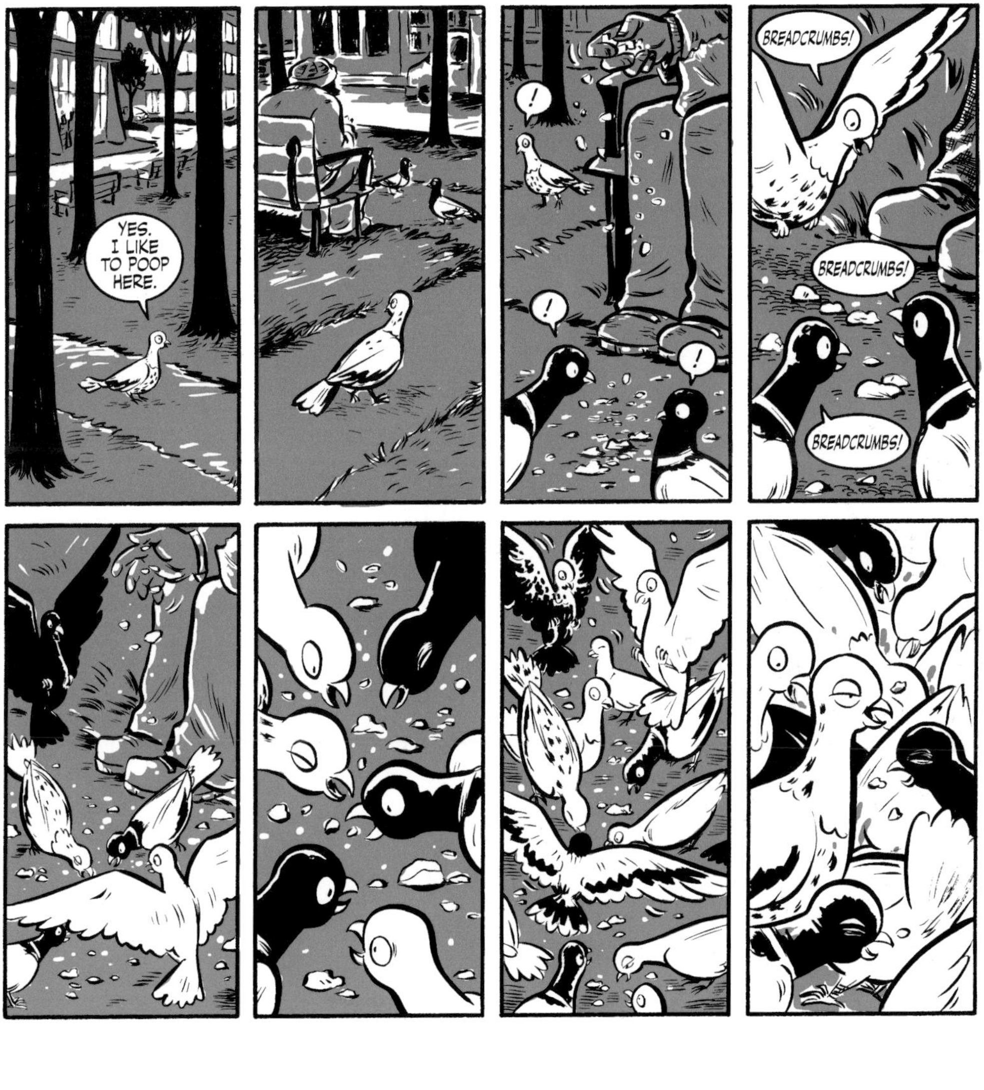
YES. I LIKE TO POOP HERE.
!
!
!
BREADCRUMBS!
BREADCRUMBS!
BREADCRUMBS!

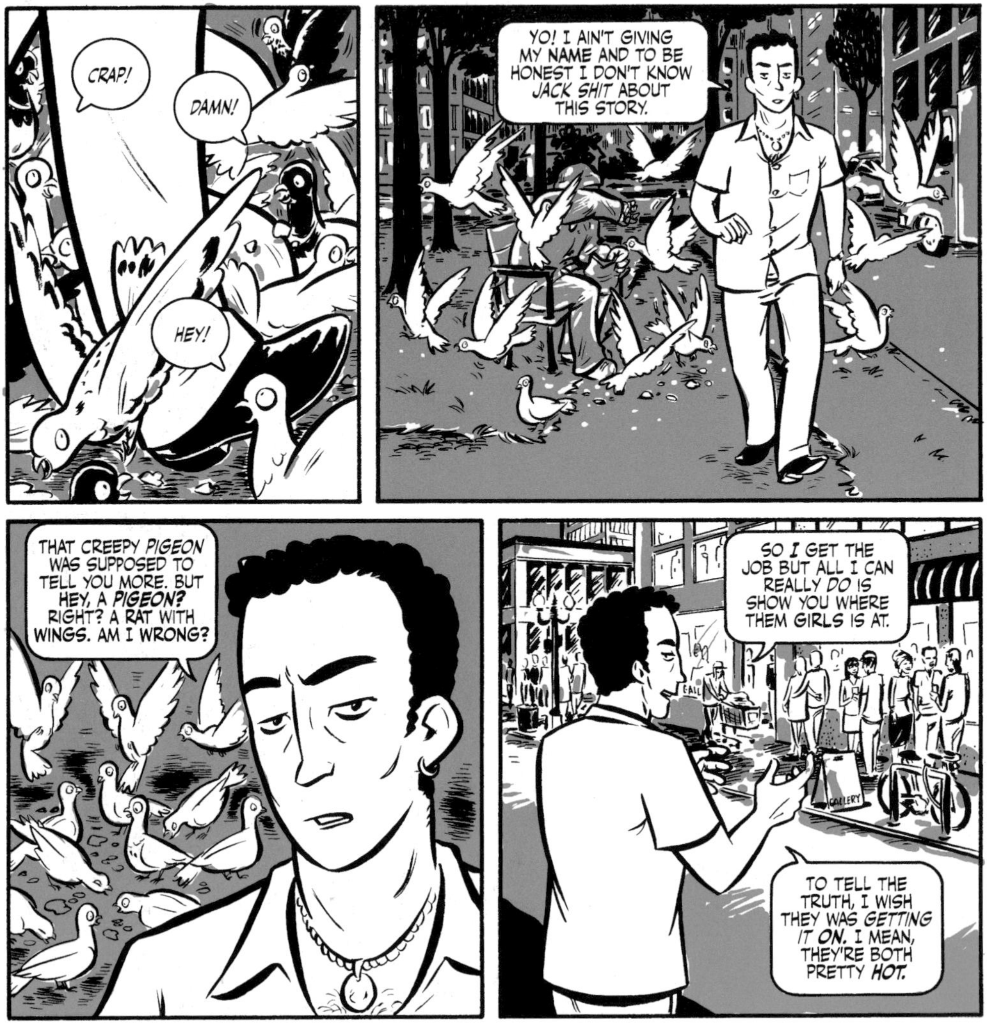
CRAP!
DAMN!
HEY!
YO! I AIN'T GIVING MY NAME AND TO BE HONEST I DON'T KNOW JACK SHIT ABOUT THIS STORY.
THAT CREEPY PIGEON WAS SUPPOSED TO TELL YOU MORE. BUT HEY, A PIGEON? RIGHT? A RAT WITH WINGS. AM I WRONG?
SO I GET THE JOB BUT ALL I CAN REALLY DO IS SHOW YOU WHERE THEM GIRLS IS AT.
TO TELL THE TRUTH, I WISH THEY WAS GETTING IT ON. I MEAN, THEY'RE BOTH PRETTY HOT.

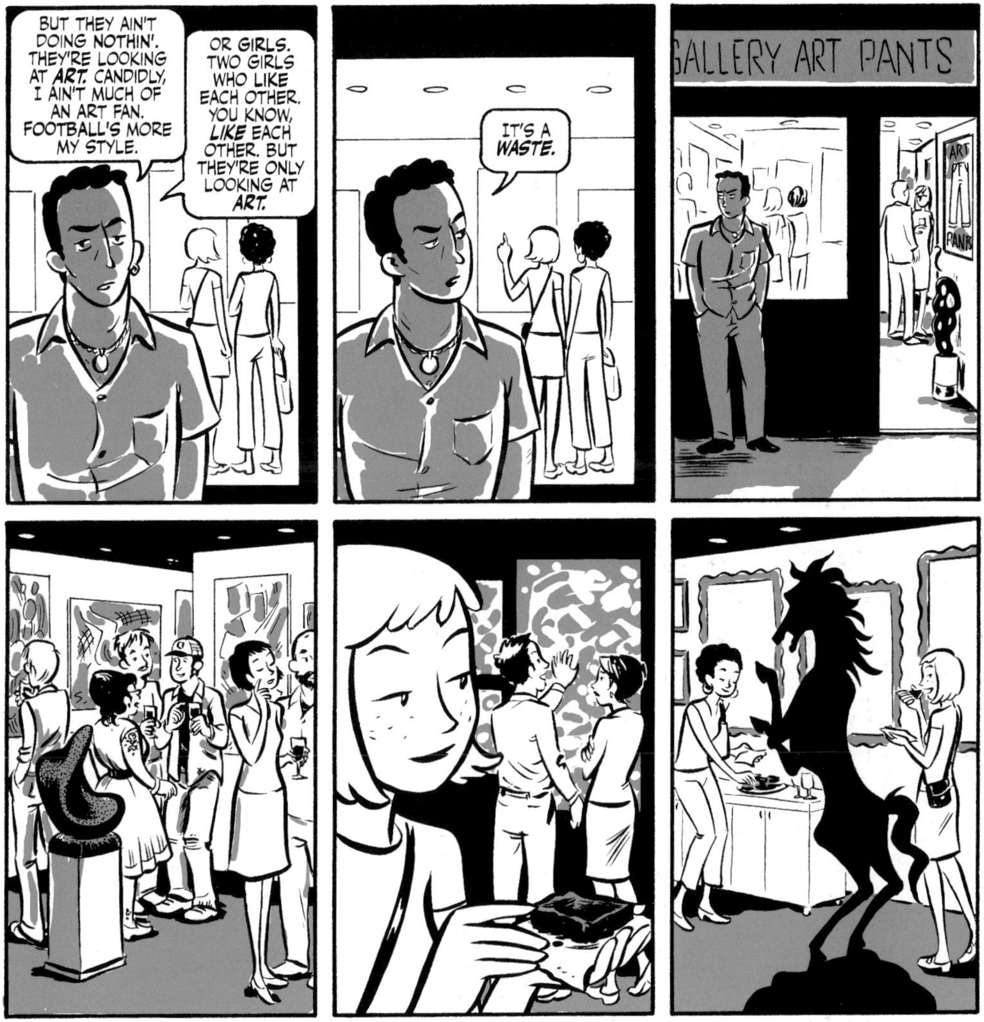
BUT THEY AIN'T DOING NOTHIN'. THEY'RE LOOKING AT ART. CANDIDLY, I AIN'T MUCH OF AN ART FAN. FOOTBALL'S MORE MY STYLE.
OR GIRLS. TWO GIRLS WHO LIKE EACH OTHER. YOU KNOW, LIKE EACH OTHER. BUT THEY'RE ONLY LOOKING AT ART.
IT'S A WASTE.
GALLERY ART PANTS

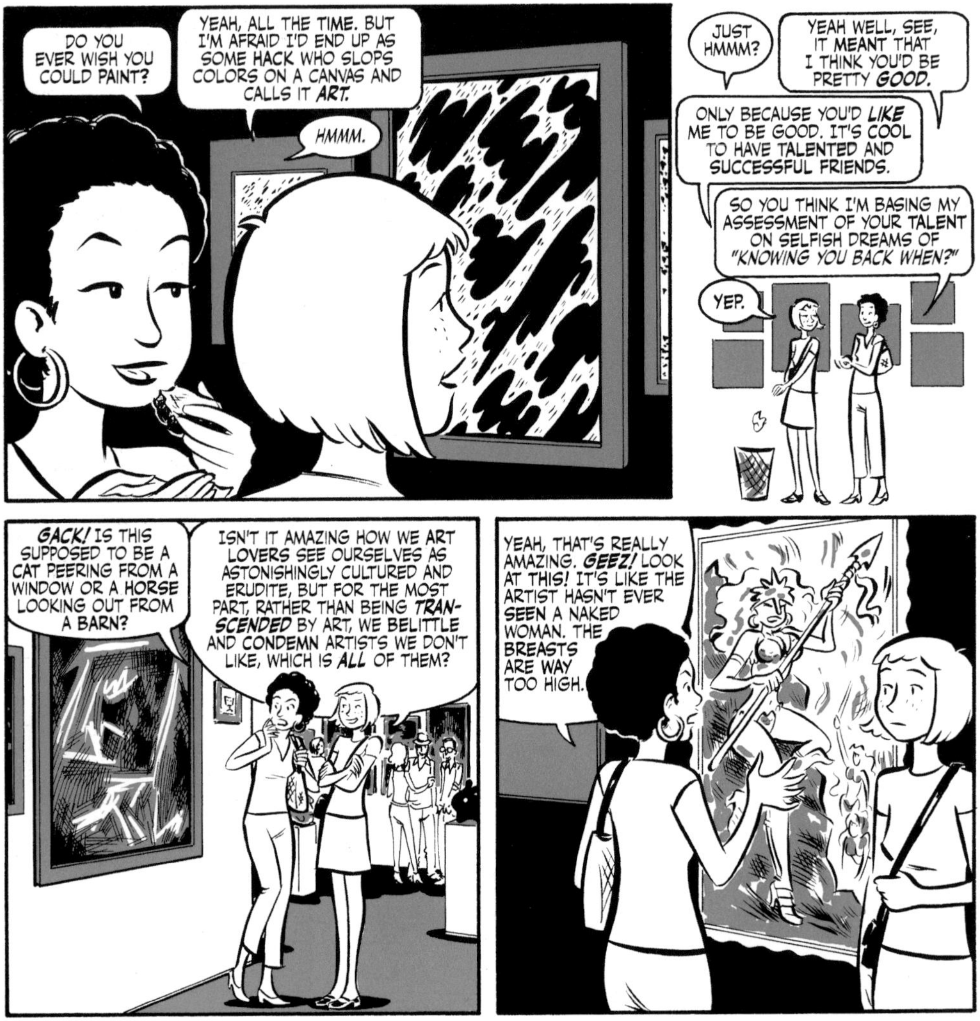
DO YOU EVER WISH YOU COULD PAINT?
YEAH, ALL THE TIME. BUT I'M AFRAID I'D END UP AS SOME HACK WHO SLOPS COLORS ON A CANVAS AND CALLS IT ART.
HMMM.
JUST HMMM?
YEAH WELL, SEE, IT MEANT THAT I THINK YOU'D BE PRETTY GOOD.
ONLY BECAUSE YOU'D LIKE ME TO BE GOOD. IT'S COOL TO HAVE TALENTED AND SUCCESSFUL FRIENDS.
SO YOU THINK I'M BASING MY ASSESSMENT OF YOUR TALENT ON SELFISH DREAMS OF "KNOWING YOU BACK WHEN?"
YEP.
GACK! IS THIS SUPPOSED TO BE A CAT PEERING FROM A WINDOW OR A HORSE LOOKING OUT FROM A BARN?
ISN'T IT AMAZING HOW WE ART LOVERS SEE OURSELVES AS ASTONISHINGLY CULTURED AND ERUDITE, BUT FOR THE MOST PART, RATHER THAN BEING TRAN-SCENDED BY ART, WE BELITTLE AND CONDEMN ARTISTS WE DON'T LIKE, WHICH IS ALL OF THEM?
YEAH, THAT'S REALLY AMAZING. GEEZ! LOOK AT THIS! IT'S LIKE THE ARTIST HASN'T EVER SEEN A NAKED WOMAN. THE BREASTS ARE WAY TOO HIGH.

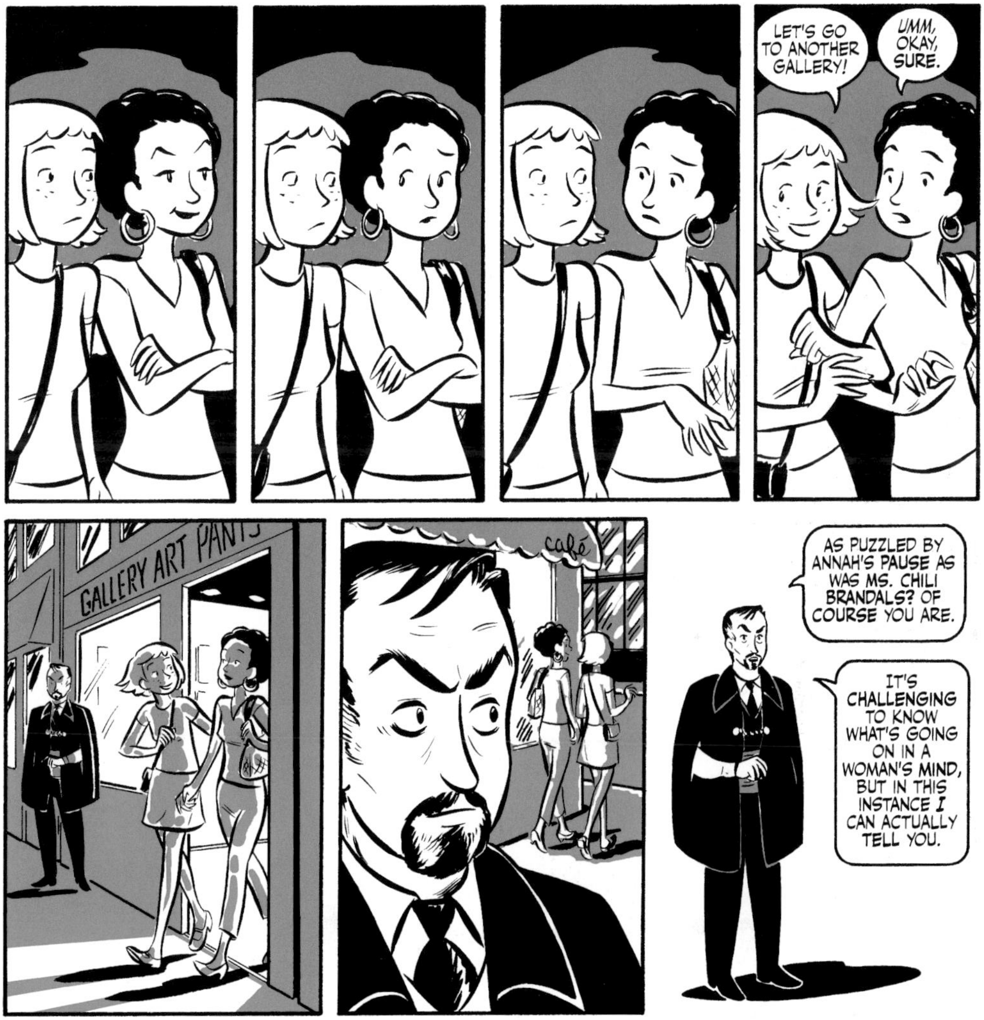
LET'S GO TO ANOTHER GALLERY!
UMM, OKAY, SURE.
GALLERY ART PANT
GALLERY ART
café
AS PUZZLED BY ANNAH'S PAUSE AS WAS MS. CHILI BRANDALS? OF COURSE YOU ARE.
IT'S CHALLENGING TO KNOW WHAT'S GOING ON IN A WOMAN'S MIND, BUT IN THIS INSTANCE I CAN ACTUALLY TELL YOU.

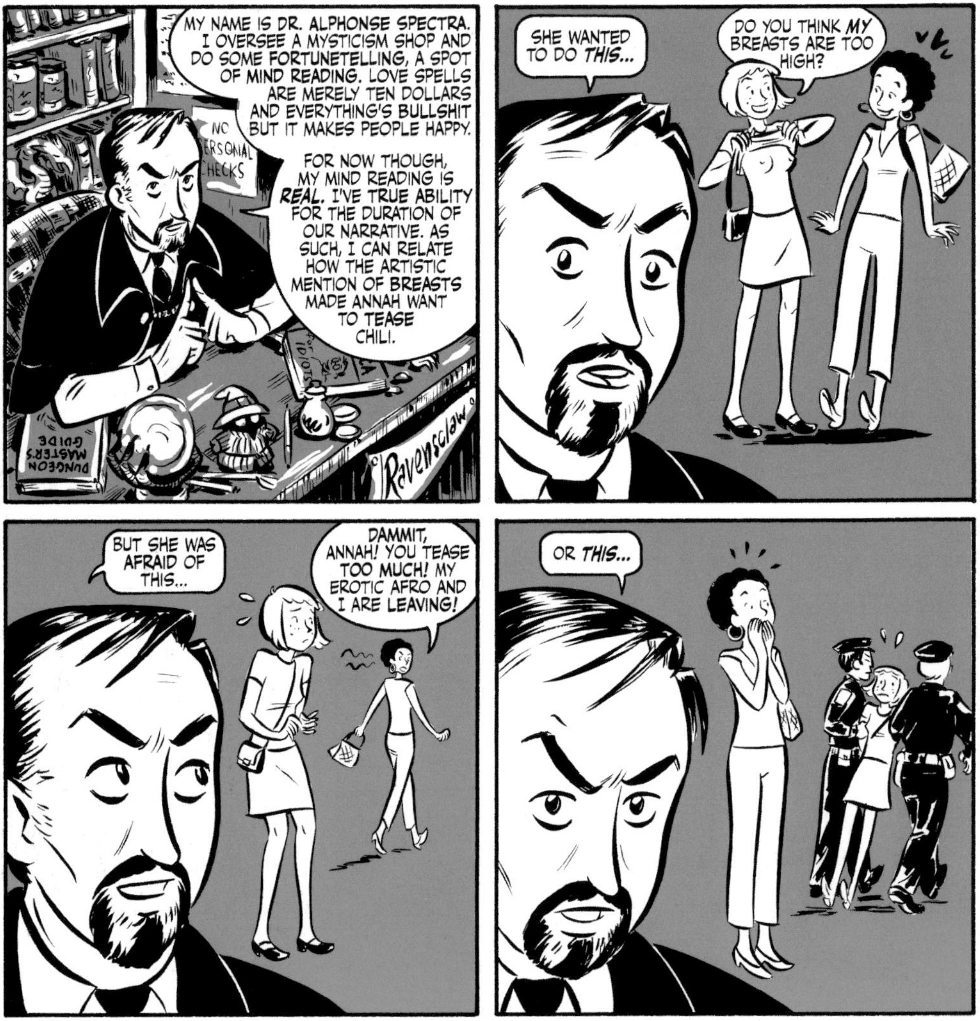
MY NAME IS DR. ALPHONSE SPECTRA. I OVERSEE A MYSTICISM SHOP AND DO SOME FORTUNETELLING, A SPOT OF MIND READING. LOVE SPELLS ARE MERELY TEN DOLLARS AND EVERYTHING'S BULLSHIT BUT IT MAKES PEOPLE HAPPY.
FOR NOW THOUGH, MY MIND READING IS REAL. I'VE TRUE ABILITY FOR THE DURATION OF OUR NARRATIVE. AS SUCH, I CAN RELATE HOW THE ARTISTIC MENTION OF BREASTS MADE ANNAH WANT TO TEASE CHILI.
Ravensclaw
SHE WANTED TO DO THIS...
DO YOU THINK MY BREASTS ARE TOO HIGH?
BUT SHE WAS AFRAID OF THIS...
DAMMIT, ANNAH! YOU TEASE TOO MUCH! MY EROTIC AFRO AND I ARE LEAVING!
OR THIS...

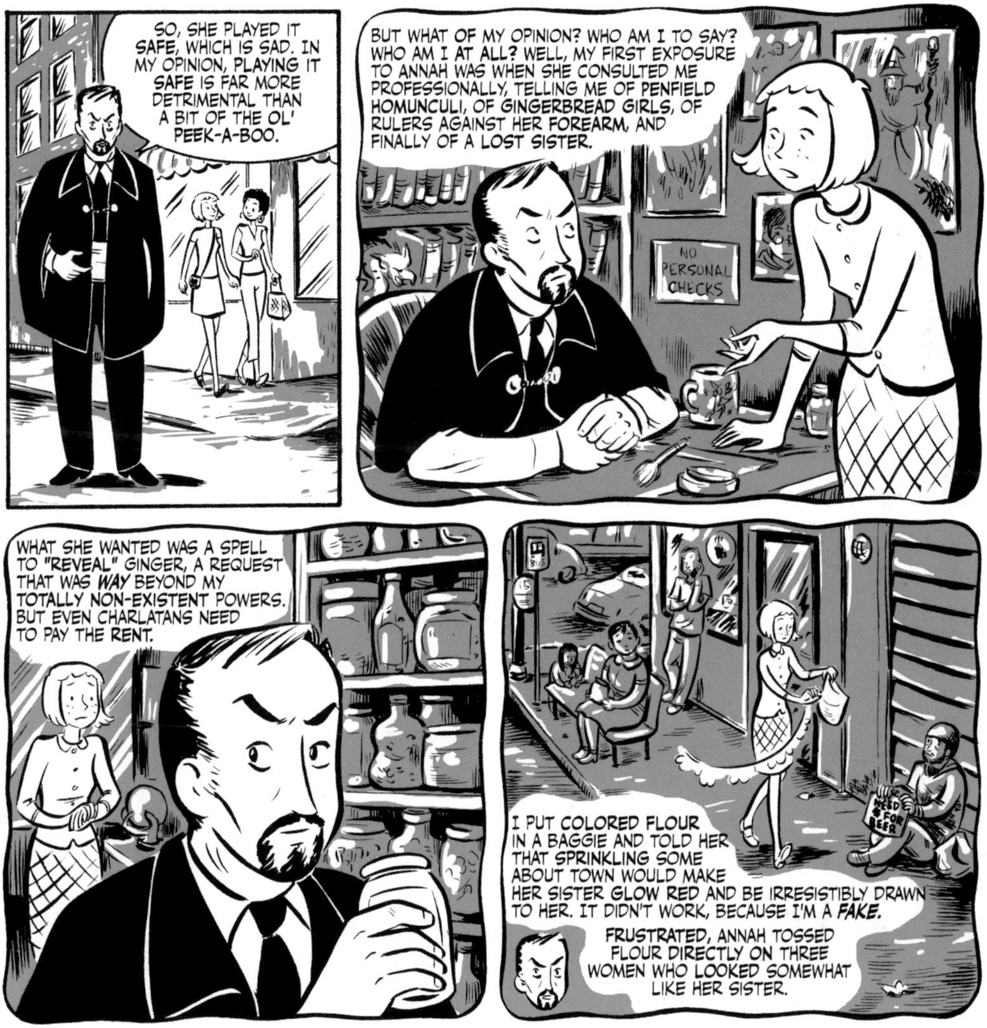
SO, SHE PLAYED IT SAFE, WHICH IS SAD. IN MY OPINION, PLAYING IT SAFE IS FAR MORE DETRIMENTAL THAN A BIT OF THE OL' PEEK-A-BOO.
BUT WHAT OF MY OPINION? WHO AM I TO SAY? WHO AM I AT ALL? WELL, MY FIRST EXPOSURE TO ANNAH WAS WHEN SHE CONSULTED ME PROFESSIONALLY, TELLING ME OF PENFIELD HOMUNCULI, OF GINGERBREAD GIRLS, OF RULERS AGAINST HER FOREARM, AND FINALLY OF A LOST SISTER.
NO PERSONAL CHECKS
WHAT SHE WANTED WAS A SPELL TO "REVEAL" GINGER, A REQUEST THAT WAS WAY BEYOND MY TOTALLY NON-EXISTENT POWERS. BUT EVEN CHARLATANS NEED TO PAY THE RENT.
I PUT COLORED FLOUR IN A BAGGIE AND TOLD HER THAT SPRINKLING SOME ABOUT TOWN WOULD MAKE HER SISTER GLOW RED AND BE IRRESISTIBLY DRAWN TO HER. IT DIDN'T WORK, BECAUSE I'M A FAKE.
NEED $ FOR BEER
FRUSTRATED, ANNAH TOSSED FLOUR DIRECTLY ON THREE WOMEN WHO LOOKED SOMEWHAT LIKE HER SISTER.

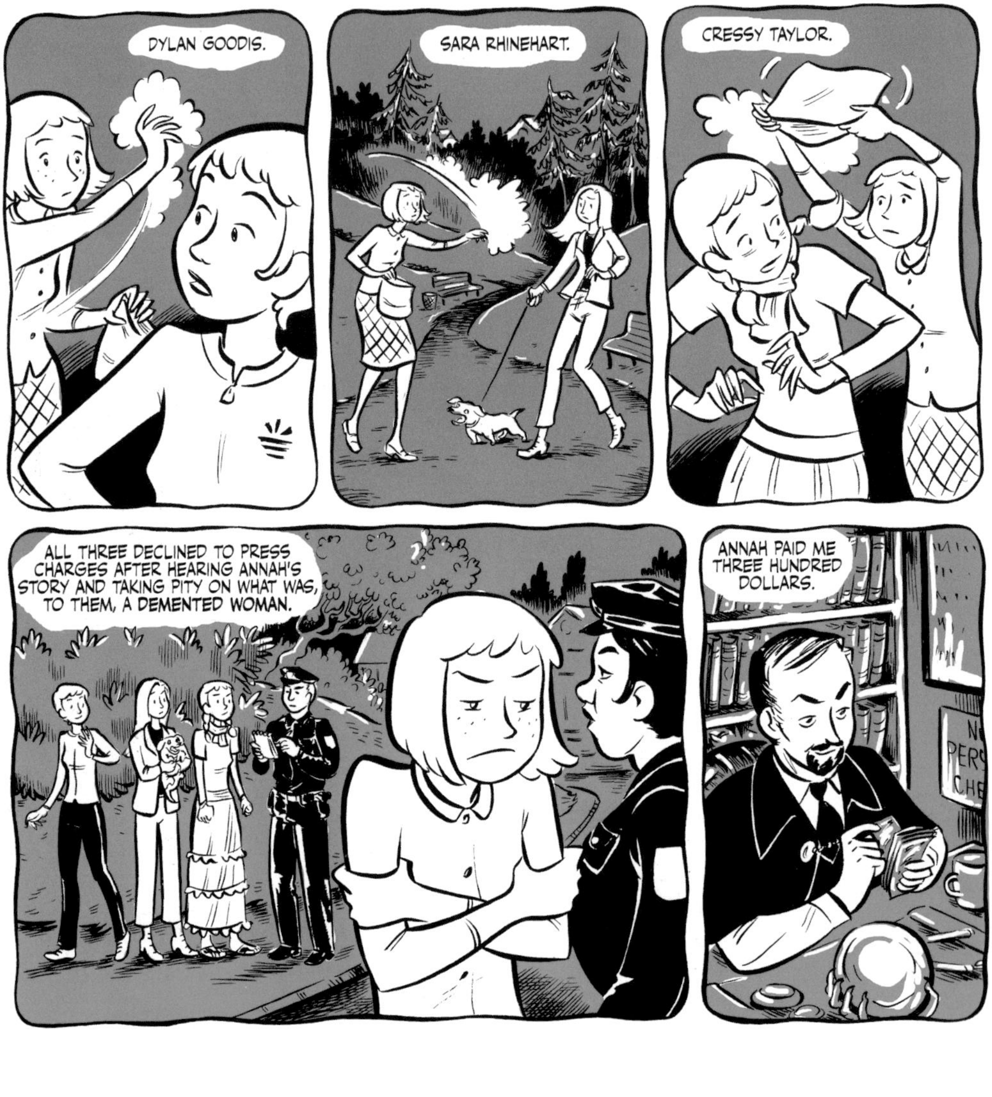
DYLAN GOODIS.
SARA RHINEHART.
CRESSY TAYLOR.
ALL THREE DECLINED TO PRESS CHARGES AFTER HEARING ANNAH'S STORY AND TAKING PITY ON WHAT WAS, TO THEM, A DEMENTED WOMAN.
ANNAH PAID ME THREE HUNDRED DOLLARS.

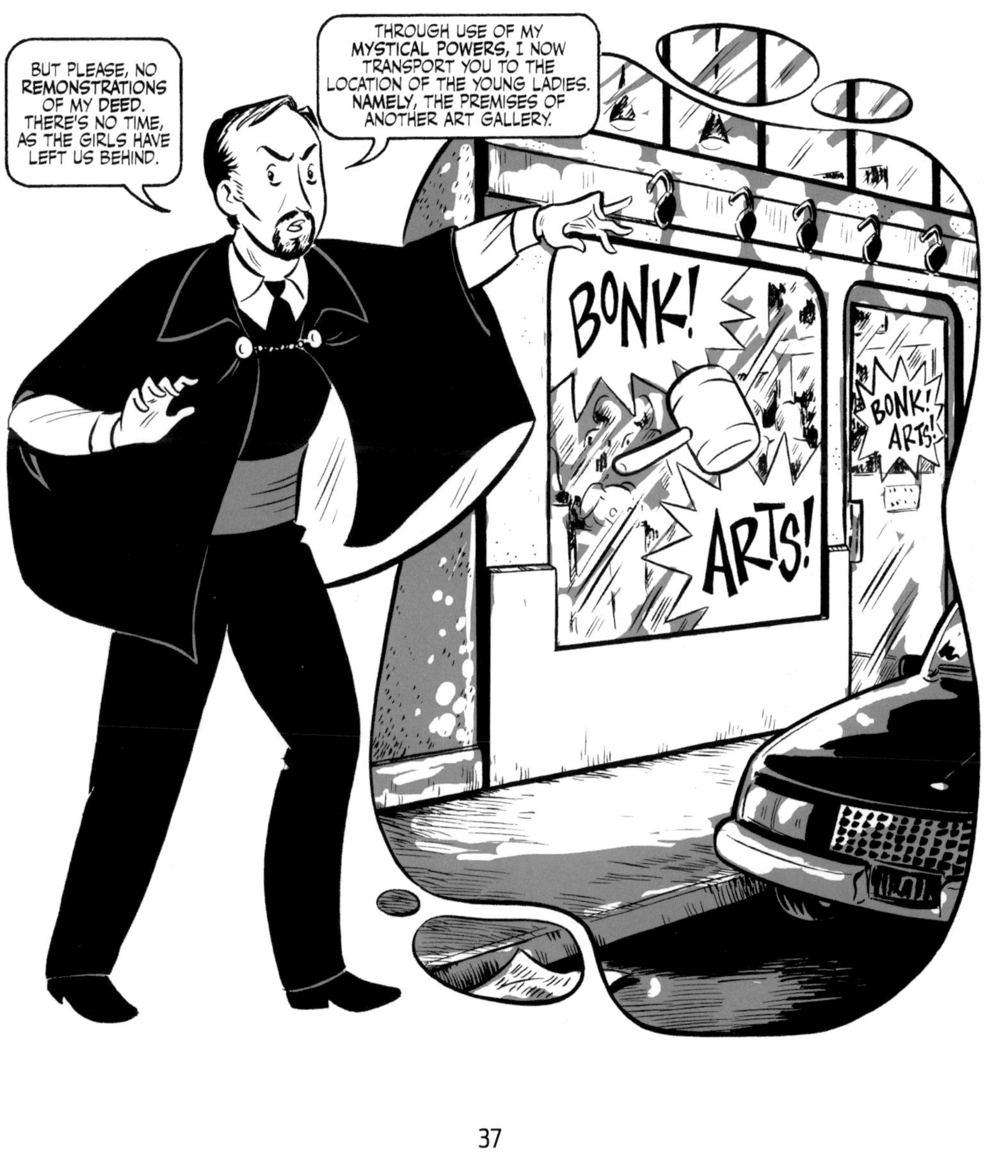
BUT PLEASE, NO REMONSTRATIONS OF MY DEED. THERE'S NO TIME, AS THE GIRLS HAVE LEFT US BEHIND.
THROUGH USE OF MY MYSTICAL POWERS, I NOW TRANSPORT YOU TO THE LOCATION OF THE YOUNG LADIES. NAMELY, THE PREMISES OF ANOTHER ART GALLERY.
BONK! ARTS!
BONK! ARTS!

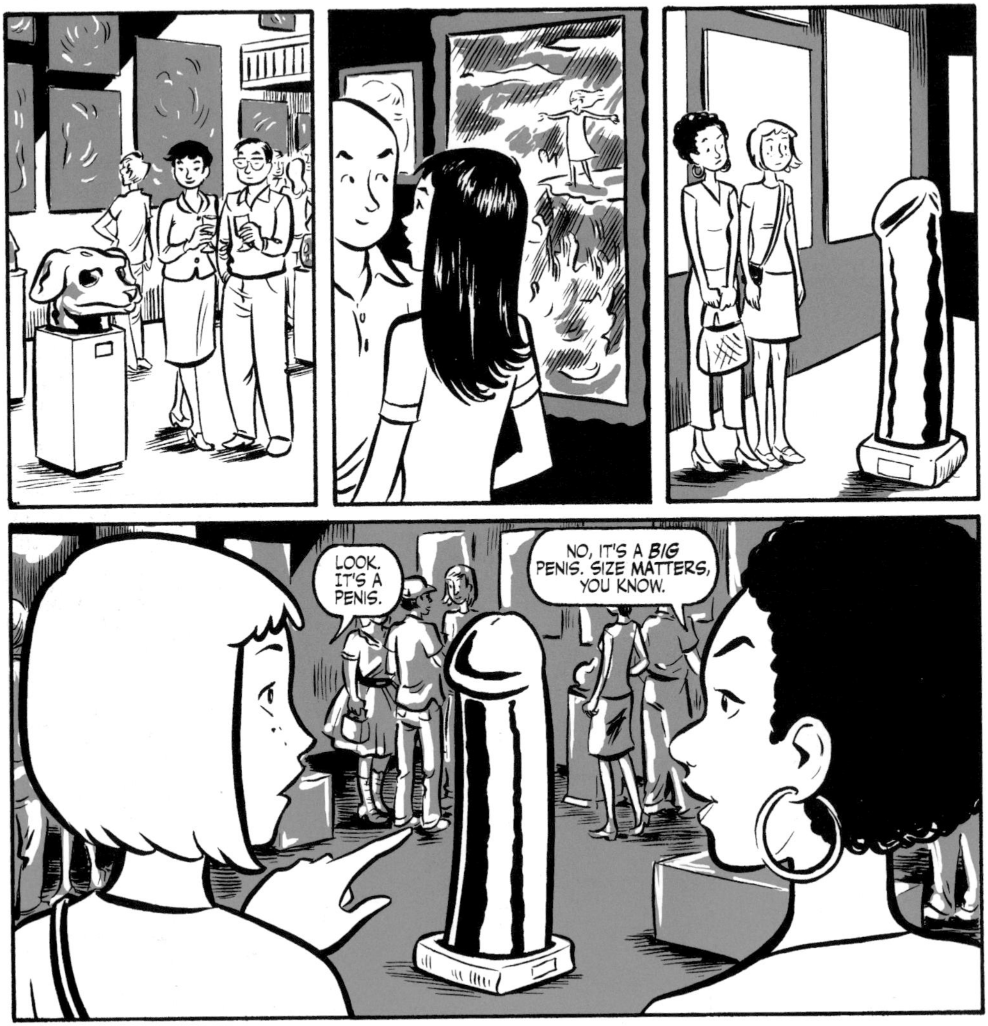
LOOK. IT'S A PENIS.
NO, IT'S A *BIG* PENIS. SIZE MATTERS, YOU KNOW.

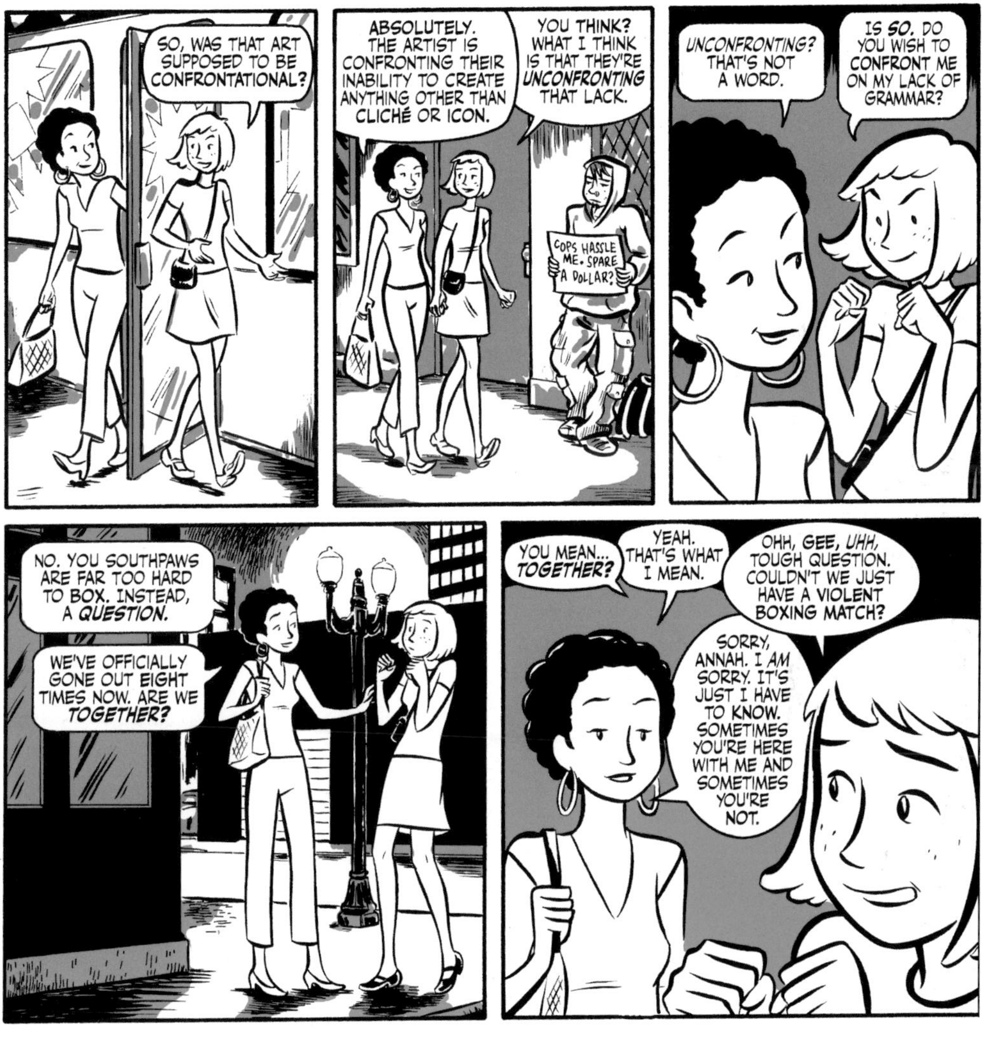

SO, WAS THAT ART SUPPOSED TO BE CONFRONTATIONAL?
ABSOLUTELY. THE ARTIST IS CONFRONTING THEIR INABILITY TO CREATE ANYTHING OTHER THAN CLICHÉ OR ICON.
YOU THINK? WHAT I THINK IS THAT THEY'RE *UNCONFRONTING* THAT LACK.
COPS HASSLE ME. SPARE A DOLLAR?
UNCONFRONTING? THAT'S NOT A WORD.
IS *SO.* DO YOU WISH TO CONFRONT ME ON MY LACK OF GRAMMAR?
NO. YOU SOUTHPAWS ARE FAR TOO HARD TO BOX. INSTEAD, A *QUESTION.*
WE'VE OFFICIALLY GONE OUT EIGHT TIMES NOW. ARE WE *TOGETHER?*
YOU MEAN... *TOGETHER?*
YEAH. THAT'S WHAT I MEAN.
OHH, GEE, *UHH,* TOUGH QUESTION. COULDN'T WE JUST HAVE A VIOLENT BOXING MATCH?
SORRY, ANNAH. I *AM* SORRY. IT'S JUST I HAVE TO KNOW. SOMETIMES YOU'RE HERE WITH ME AND SOMETIMES YOU'RE NOT.

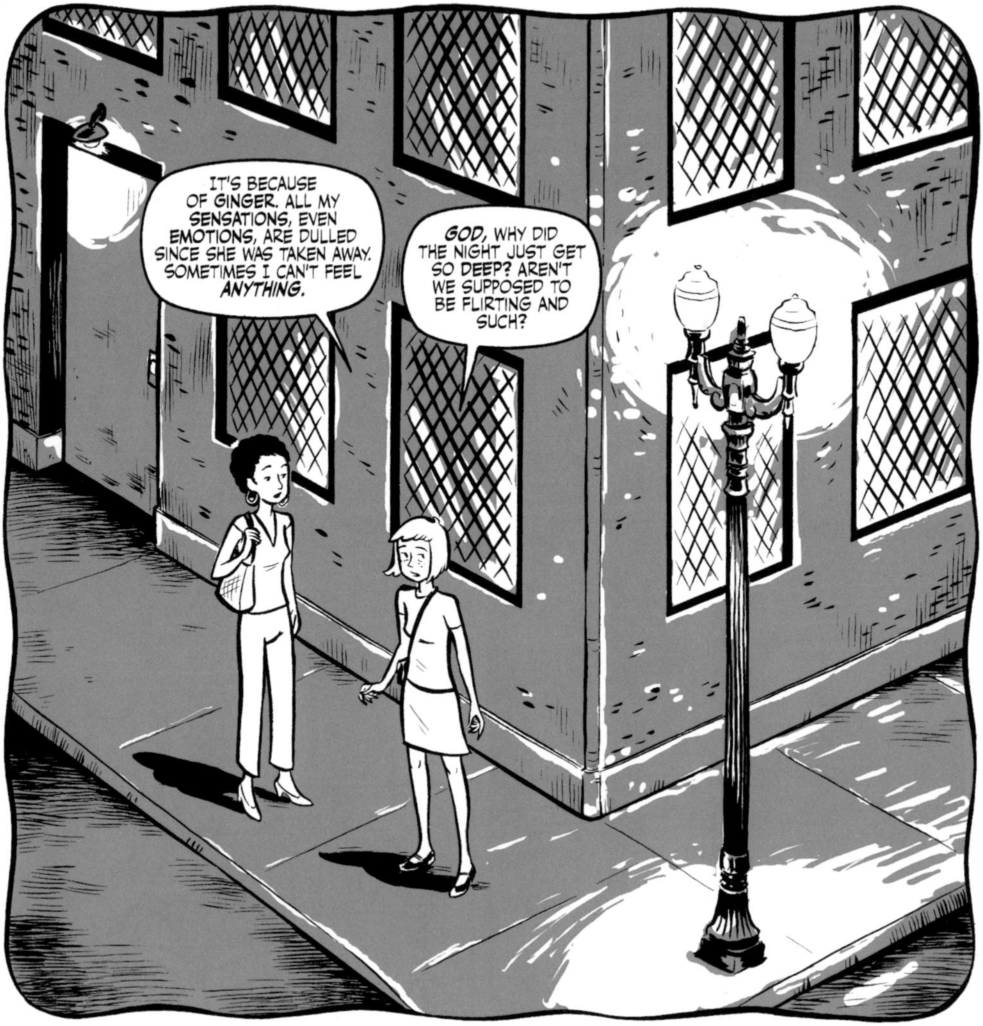
IT'S BECAUSE OF GINGER. ALL MY SENSATIONS, EVEN EMOTIONS, ARE DULLED SINCE SHE WAS TAKEN AWAY. SOMETIMES I CAN'T FEEL *ANYTHING.*
GOD, WHY DID THE NIGHT JUST GET SO DEEP? AREN'T WE SUPPOSED TO BE FLIRTING AND SUCH?

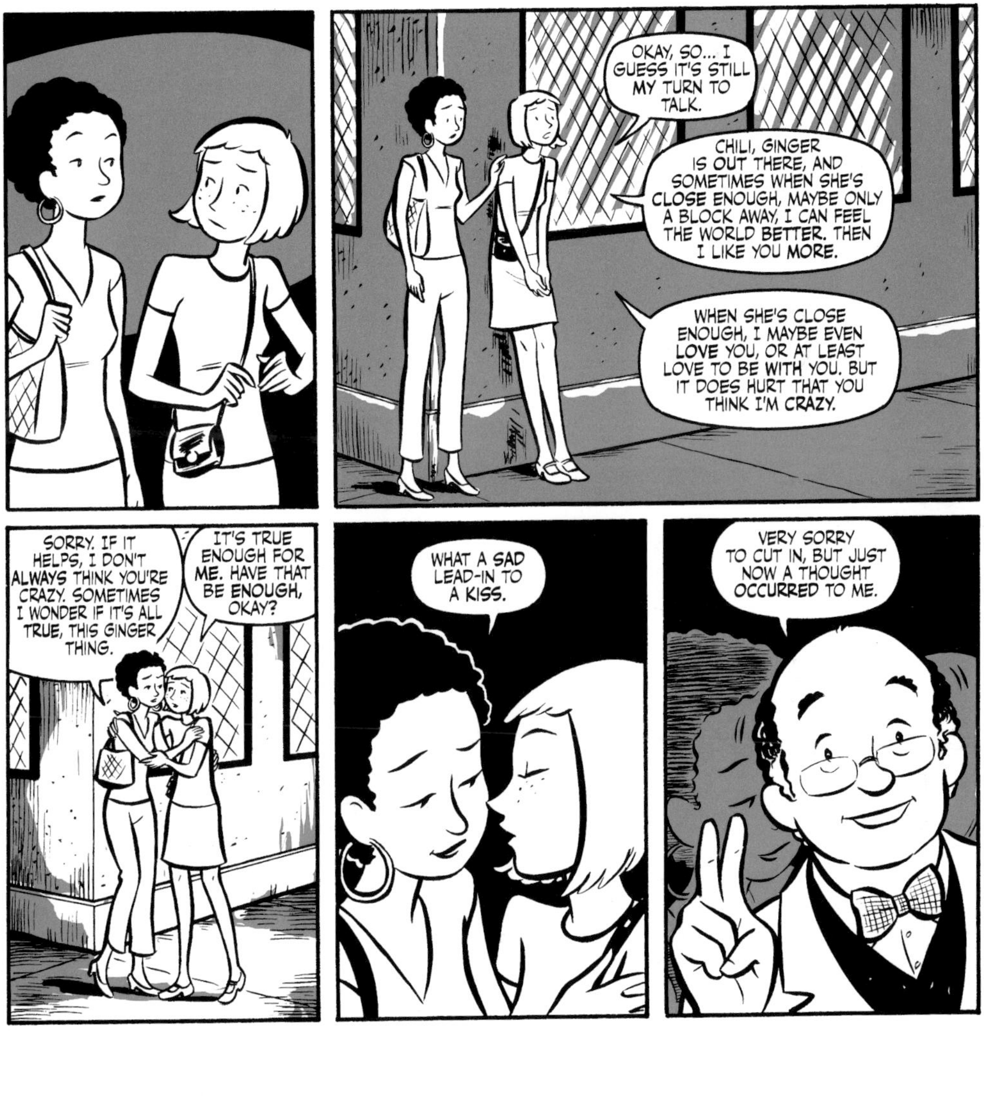
OKAY, SO... I GUESS IT'S STILL MY TURN TO TALK.
CHILI, GINGER IS OUT THERE, AND SOMETIMES WHEN SHE'S CLOSE ENOUGH, MAYBE ONLY A BLOCK AWAY, I CAN FEEL THE WORLD BETTER. THEN I LIKE YOU MORE.
WHEN SHE'S CLOSE ENOUGH, I MAYBE EVEN LOVE YOU, OR AT LEAST LOVE TO BE WITH YOU. BUT IT DOES HURT THAT YOU THINK I'M CRAZY.
SORRY. IF IT HELPS, I DON'T ALWAYS THINK YOU'RE CRAZY. SOMETIMES I WONDER IF IT'S ALL TRUE, THIS GINGER THING.
IT'S TRUE ENOUGH FOR ME. HAVE THAT BE ENOUGH, OKAY?
WHAT A SAD LEAD-IN TO A KISS.
VERY SORRY TO CUT IN, BUT JUST NOW A THOUGHT OCCURRED TO ME.

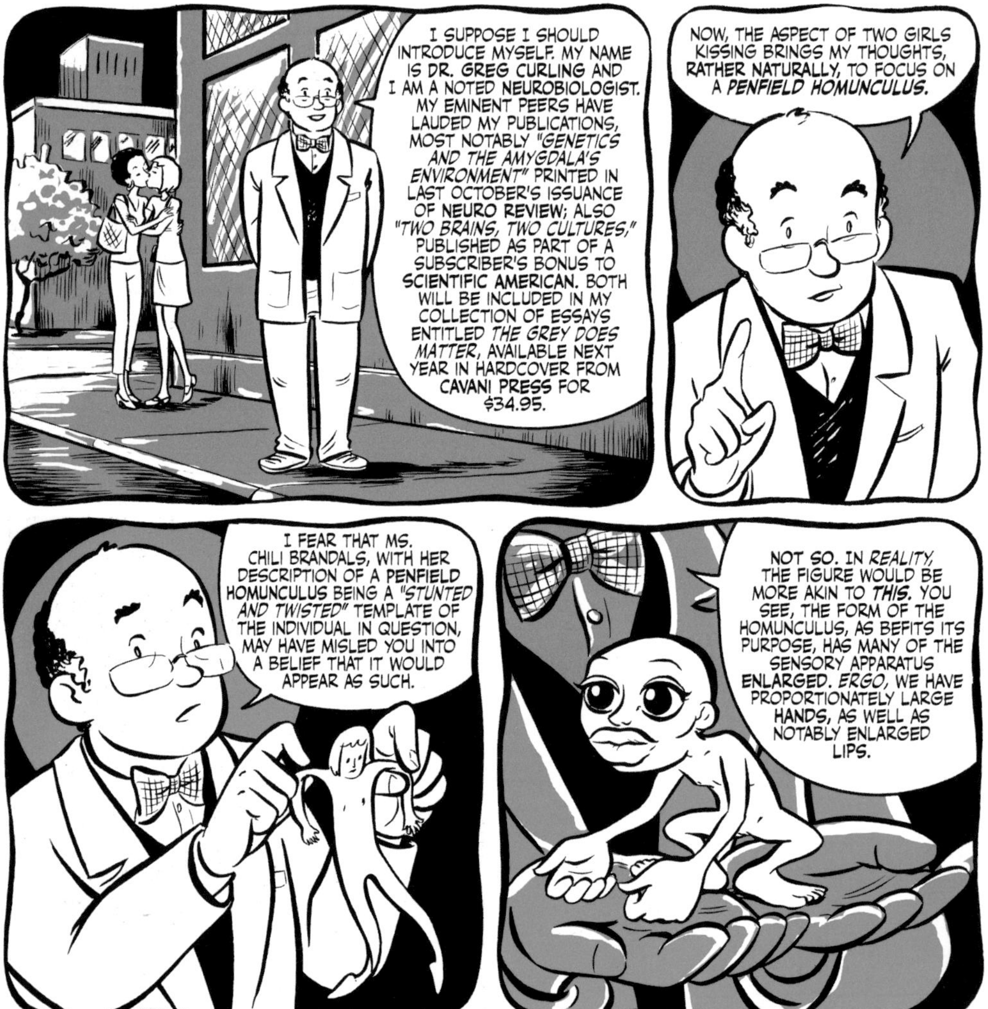
I SUPPOSE I SHOULD INTRODUCE MYSELF. MY NAME IS DR. GREG CURLING AND I AM A NOTED NEUROBIOLOGIST. MY EMINENT PEERS HAVE LAUDED MY PUBLICATIONS, MOST NOTABLY "GENETICS AND THE AMYGDALA'S ENVIRONMENT" PRINTED IN LAST OCTOBER'S ISSUANCE OF NEURO REVIEW; ALSO "TWO BRAINS, TWO CULTURES," PUBLISHED AS PART OF A SUBSCRIBER'S BONUS TO SCIENTIFIC AMERICAN. BOTH WILL BE INCLUDED IN MY COLLECTION OF ESSAYS ENTITLED THE GREY DOES MATTER, AVAILABLE NEXT YEAR IN HARDCOVER FROM CAVANI PRESS FOR $34.95.
NOW, THE ASPECT OF TWO GIRLS KISSING BRINGS MY THOUGHTS, RATHER NATURALLY, TO FOCUS ON A PENFIELD HOMUNCULUS.
I FEAR THAT MS. CHILI BRANDALS, WITH HER DESCRIPTION OF A PENFIELD HOMUNCULUS BEING A "STUNTED AND TWISTED" TEMPLATE OF THE INDIVIDUAL IN QUESTION, MAY HAVE MISLED YOU INTO A BELIEF THAT IT WOULD APPEAR AS SUCH.
NOT SO. IN REALITY, THE FIGURE WOULD BE MORE AKIN TO THIS. YOU SEE, THE FORM OF THE HOMUNCULUS, AS BEFITS ITS PURPOSE, HAS MANY OF THE SENSORY APPARATUS ENLARGED. ERGO, WE HAVE PROPORTIONATELY LARGE HANDS, AS WELL AS NOTABLY ENLARGED LIPS.

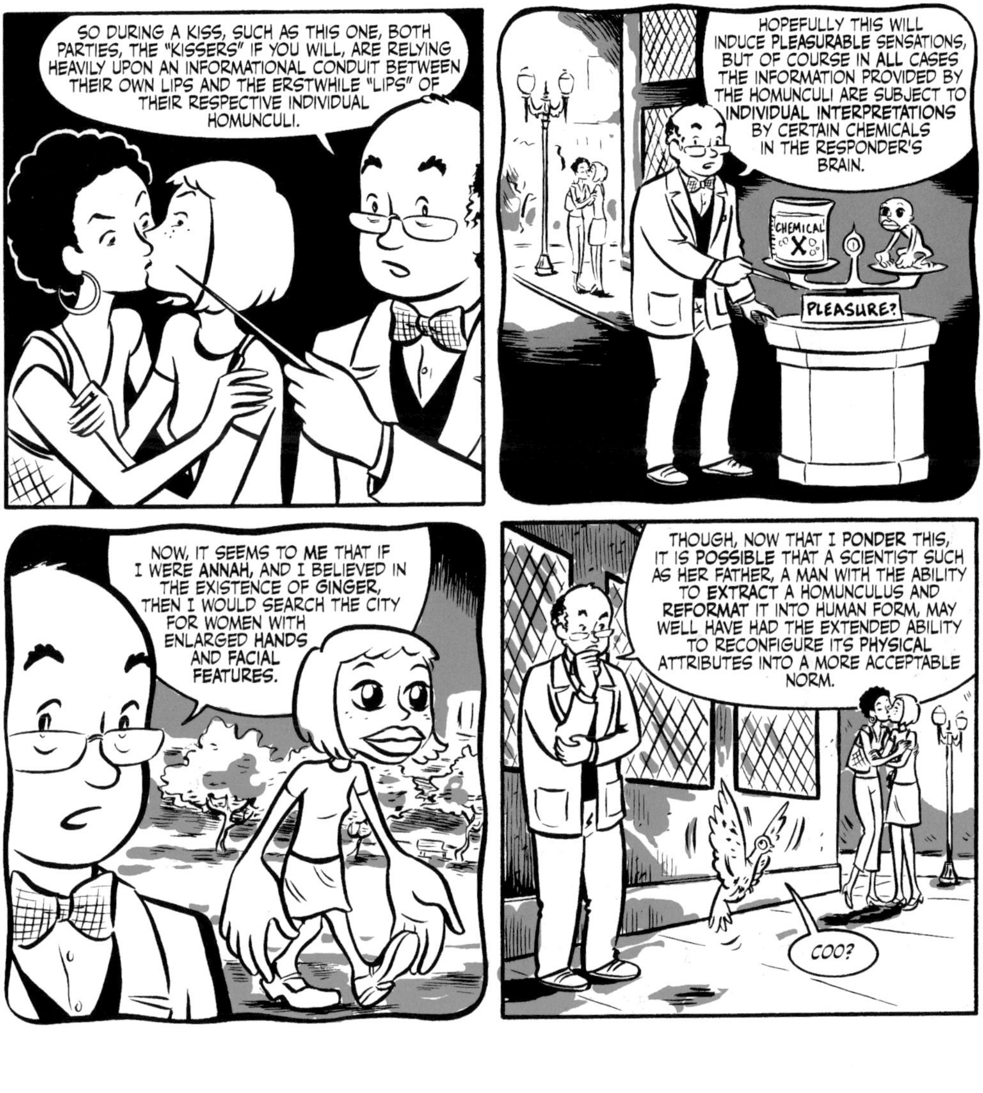
SO DURING A KISS, SUCH AS THIS ONE, BOTH PARTIES, THE "KISSERS" IF YOU WILL, ARE RELYING HEAVILY UPON AN INFORMATIONAL CONDUIT BETWEEN THEIR OWN LIPS AND THE ERSTWHILE "LIPS" OF THEIR RESPECTIVE INDIVIDUAL HOMUNCULI.
HOPEFULLY THIS WILL INDUCE PLEASURABLE SENSATIONS, BUT OF COURSE IN ALL CASES THE INFORMATION PROVIDED BY THE HOMUNCULI ARE SUBJECT TO INDIVIDUAL INTERPRETATIONS BY CERTAIN CHEMICALS IN THE RESPONDER'S BRAIN.
CHEMICAL X
PLEASURE?
NOW, IT SEEMS TO ME THAT IF I WERE ANNAH, AND I BELIEVED IN THE EXISTENCE OF GINGER, THEN I WOULD SEARCH THE CITY FOR WOMEN WITH ENLARGED HANDS AND FACIAL FEATURES.
THOUGH, NOW THAT I PONDER THIS, IT IS POSSIBLE THAT A SCIENTIST SUCH AS HER FATHER, A MAN WITH THE ABILITY TO EXTRACT A HOMUNCULUS AND REFORMAT IT INTO HUMAN FORM, MAY WELL HAVE HAD THE EXTENDED ABILITY TO RECONFIGURE ITS PHYSICAL ATTRIBUTES INTO A MORE ACCEPTABLE NORM.
COO?

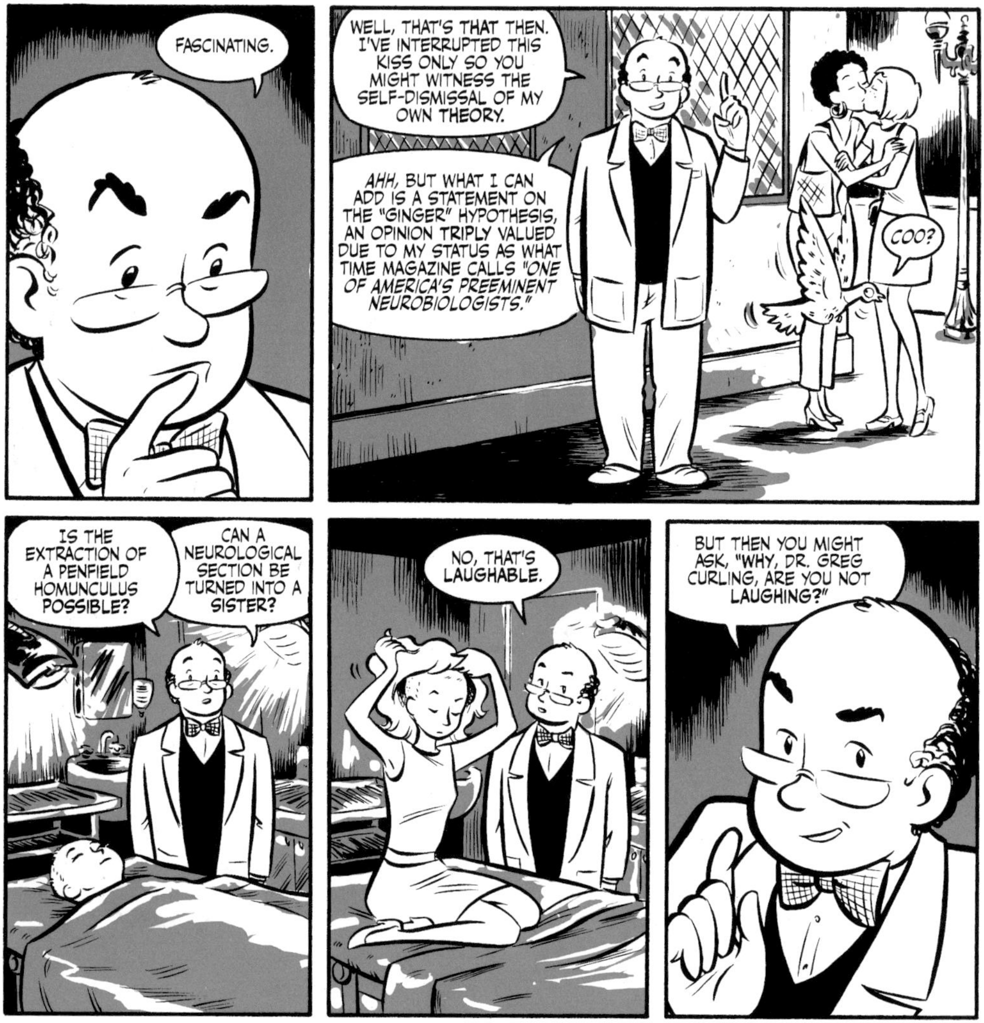
FASCINATING.
WELL, THAT'S THAT THEN. I'VE INTERRUPTED THIS KISS ONLY SO YOU MIGHT WITNESS THE SELF-DISMISSAL OF MY OWN THEORY.
AHH, BUT WHAT I CAN ADD IS A STATEMENT ON THE "GINGER" HYPOTHESIS, AN OPINION TRIPLY VALUED DUE TO MY STATUS AS WHAT TIME MAGAZINE CALLS "ONE OF AMERICA'S PREEMINENT NEUROBIOLOGISTS."
COO?
IS THE EXTRACTION OF A PENFIELD HOMUNCULUS POSSIBLE?
CAN A NEUROLOGICAL SECTION BE TURNED INTO A SISTER?
NO, THAT'S LAUGHABLE.
BUT THEN YOU MIGHT ASK, "WHY, DR. GREG CURLING, ARE YOU NOT LAUGHING?"

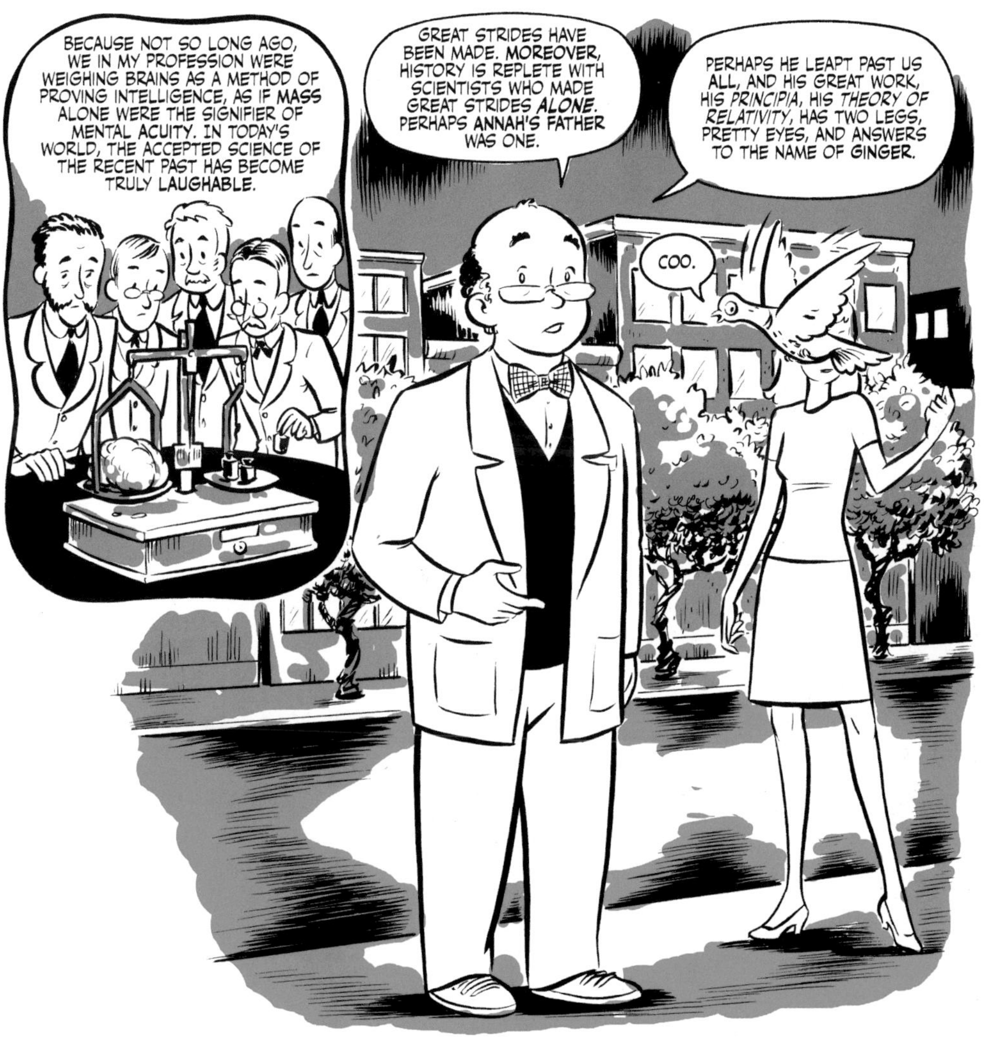
BECAUSE NOT SO LONG AGO, WE IN MY PROFESSION WERE WEIGHING BRAINS AS A METHOD OF PROVING INTELLIGENCE, AS IF **MASS** ALONE WERE THE SIGNIFIER OF MENTAL **ACUITY**. IN TODAY'S WORLD, THE ACCEPTED SCIENCE OF THE RECENT PAST HAS BECOME TRULY **LAUGHABLE**.
GREAT STRIDES HAVE BEEN MADE. **MOREOVER**, HISTORY IS REPLETE WITH SCIENTISTS WHO MADE GREAT STRIDES ***ALONE***. PERHAPS **ANNAH'S FATHER** WAS ONE.
PERHAPS HE LEAPT PAST US **ALL**, AND HIS GREAT WORK, HIS *PRINCIPIA*, HIS *THEORY OF RELATIVITY*, HAS TWO LEGS, PRETTY EYES, AND ANSWERS TO THE NAME OF **GINGER**.
COO.

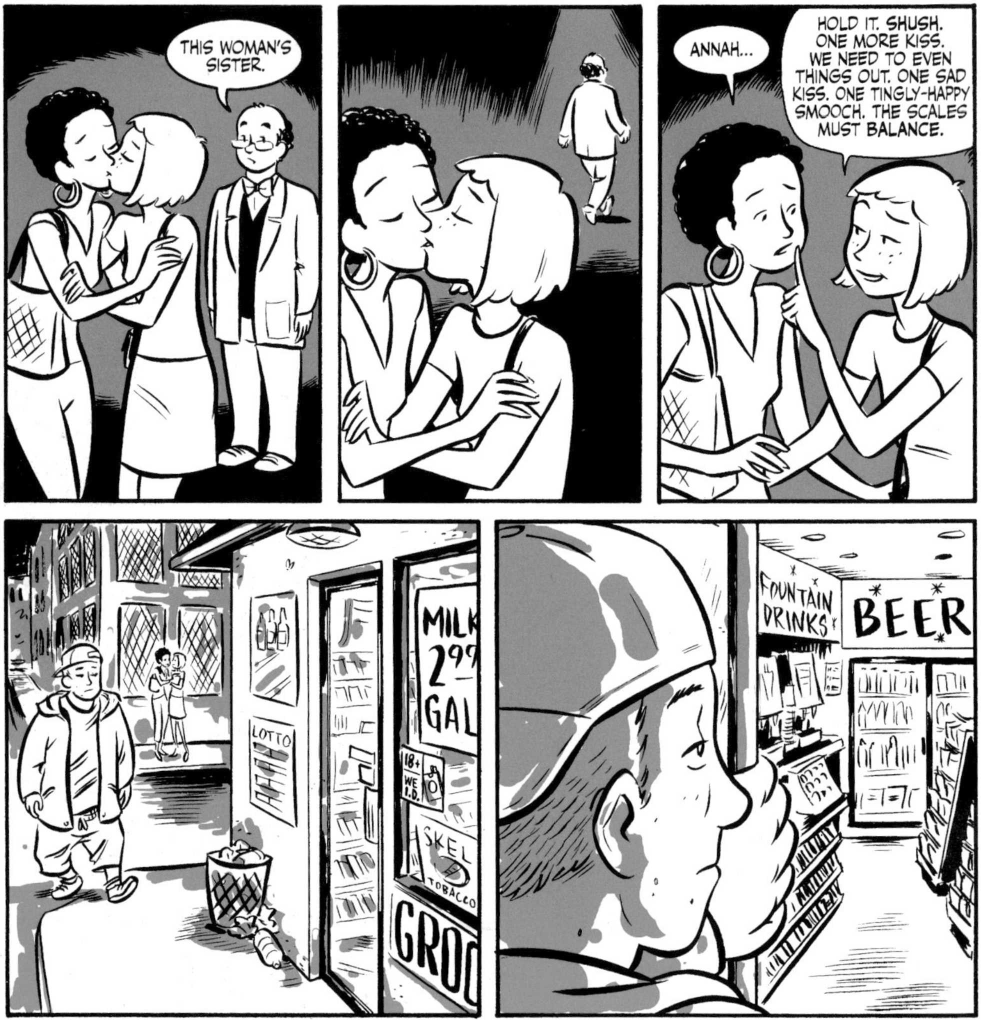
THIS WOMAN'S SISTER.
ANNAH...
HOLD IT. SHUSH. ONE MORE KISS. WE NEED TO EVEN THINGS OUT. ONE SAD KISS. ONE TINGLY-HAPPY SMOOCH. THE SCALES MUST BALANCE.
LOTTO
18+ WE I.D.
TOBACCO
FOUNTAIN DRINKS
BEER

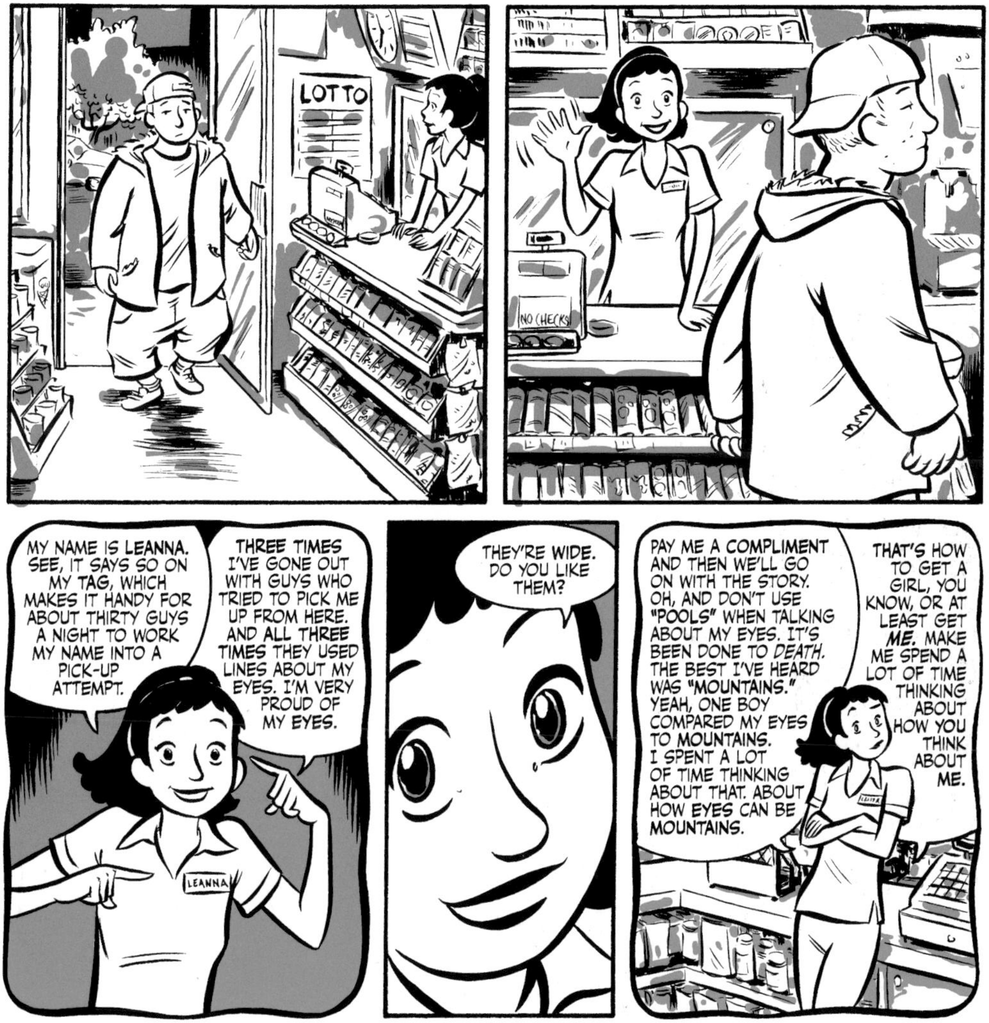

LOTTO
NO CHECKS
MY NAME IS LEANNA. SEE, IT SAYS SO ON MY TAG, WHICH MAKES IT HANDY FOR ABOUT THIRTY GUYS A NIGHT TO WORK MY NAME INTO A PICK-UP ATTEMPT.
THREE TIMES I'VE GONE OUT WITH GUYS WHO TRIED TO PICK ME UP FROM HERE. AND ALL THREE TIMES THEY USED LINES ABOUT MY EYES. I'M VERY PROUD OF MY EYES.
LEANNA
THEY'RE WIDE. DO YOU LIKE THEM?
PAY ME A COMPLIMENT AND THEN WE'LL GO ON WITH THE STORY. OH, AND DON'T USE "POOLS" WHEN TALKING ABOUT MY EYES. IT'S BEEN DONE TO *DEATH*. THE BEST I'VE HEARD WAS "MOUNTAINS." YEAH, ONE BOY COMPARED MY EYES TO MOUNTAINS. I SPENT A LOT OF TIME THINKING ABOUT THAT. ABOUT HOW EYES CAN BE MOUNTAINS.
THAT'S HOW TO GET A GIRL, YOU KNOW, OR AT LEAST GET *ME*. MAKE ME SPEND A LOT OF TIME THINKING ABOUT HOW YOU THINK ABOUT ME.

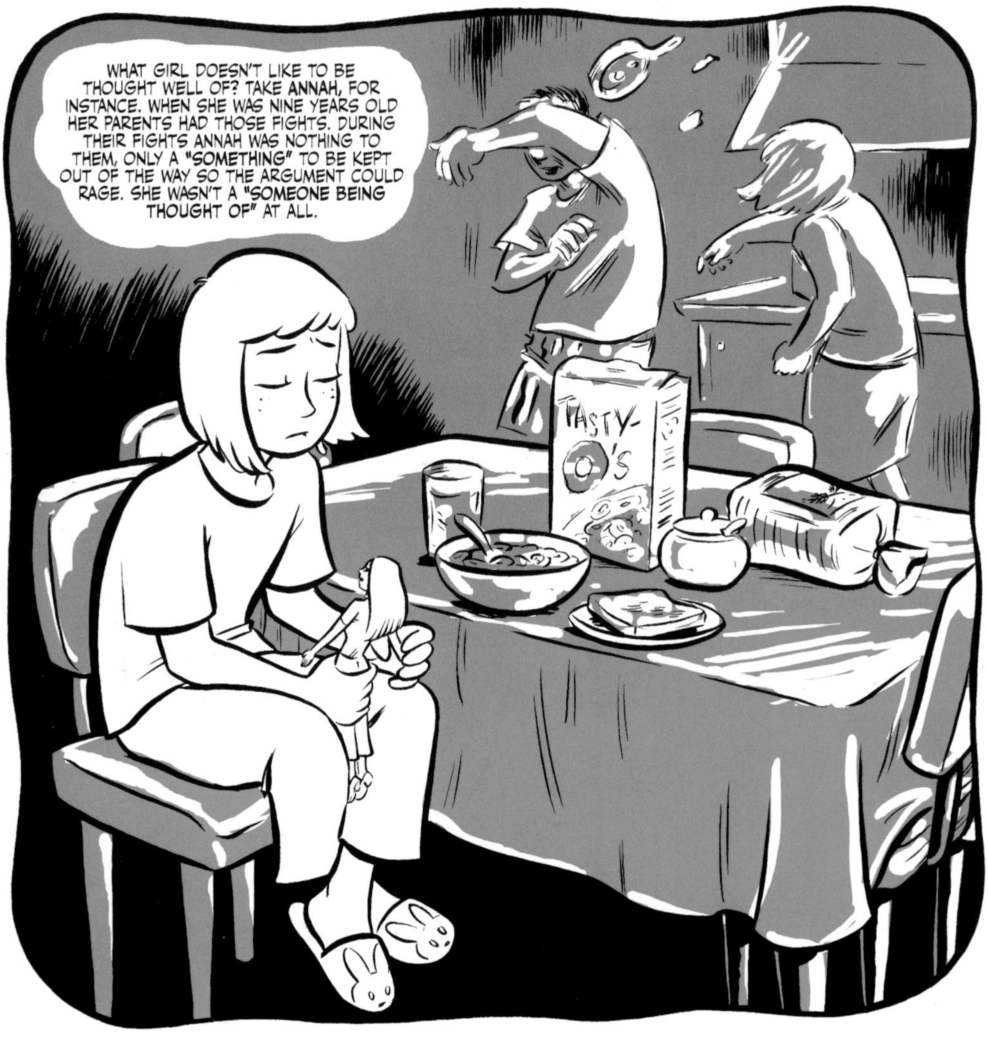
WHAT GIRL DOESN'T LIKE TO BE THOUGHT WELL OF? TAKE ANNAH, FOR INSTANCE. WHEN SHE WAS NINE YEARS OLD HER PARENTS HAD THOSE FIGHTS. DURING THEIR FIGHTS ANNAH WAS NOTHING TO THEM, ONLY A "SOMETHING" TO BE KEPT OUT OF THE WAY SO THE ARGUMENT COULD RAGE. SHE WASN'T A "SOMEONE BEING THOUGHT OF" AT ALL.
TASTY-O'S

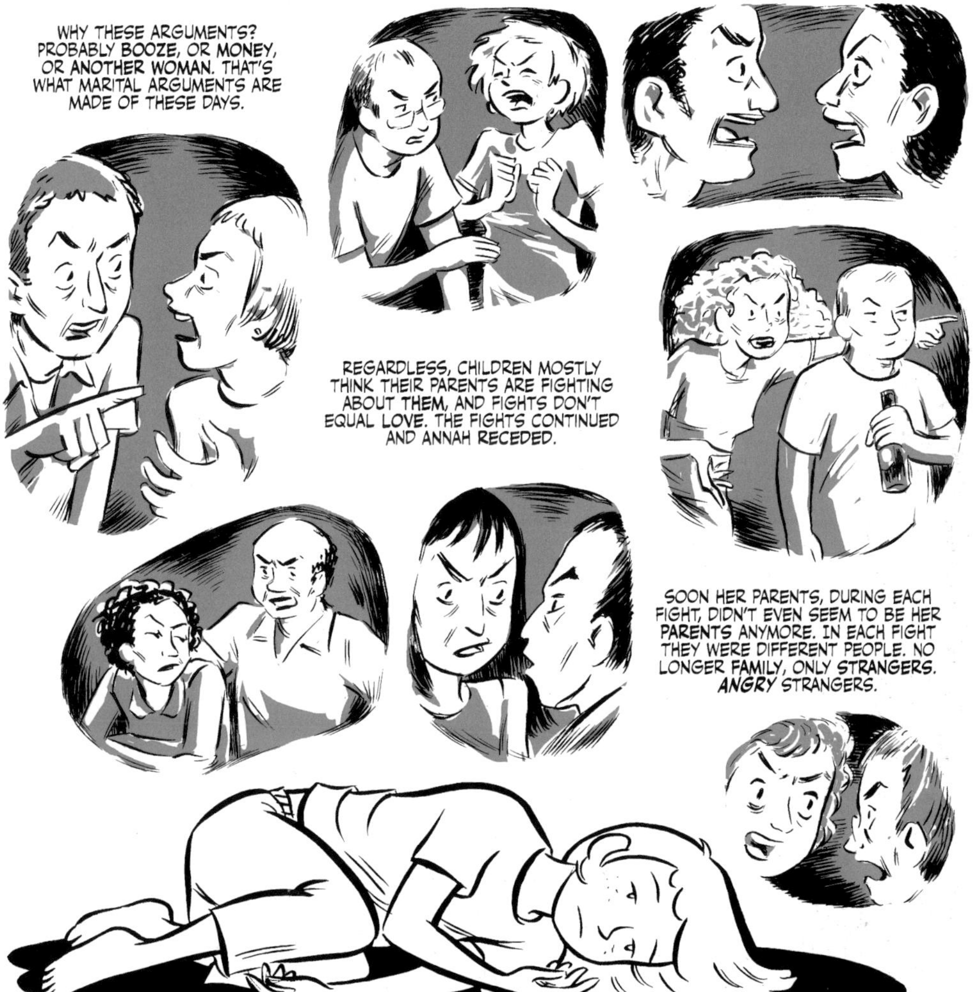
WHY THESE ARGUMENTS? PROBABLY BOOZE, OR MONEY, OR ANOTHER WOMAN. THAT'S WHAT MARITAL ARGUMENTS ARE MADE OF THESE DAYS.
REGARDLESS, CHILDREN MOSTLY THINK THEIR PARENTS ARE FIGHTING ABOUT THEM, AND FIGHTS DON'T EQUAL LOVE. THE FIGHTS CONTINUED AND ANNAH RECEDED.
SOON HER PARENTS, DURING EACH FIGHT, DIDN'T EVEN SEEM TO BE HER PARENTS ANYMORE. IN EACH FIGHT THEY WERE DIFFERENT PEOPLE. NO LONGER FAMILY, ONLY STRANGERS. ANGRY STRANGERS.

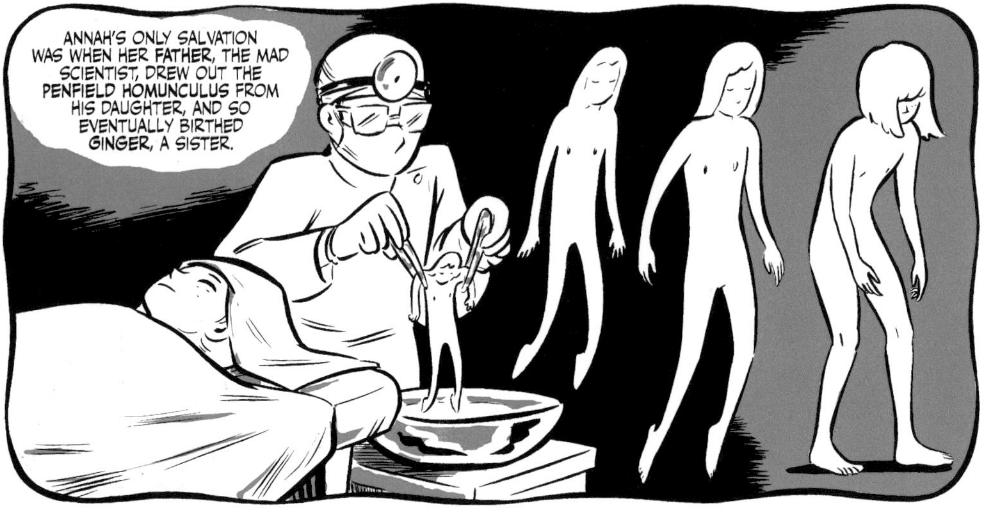
ANNAH'S ONLY SALVATION WAS WHEN HER FATHER, THE MAD SCIENTIST, DREW OUT THE PENFIELD HOMUNCULUS FROM HIS DAUGHTER, AND SO EVENTUALLY BIRTHED GINGER, A SISTER.

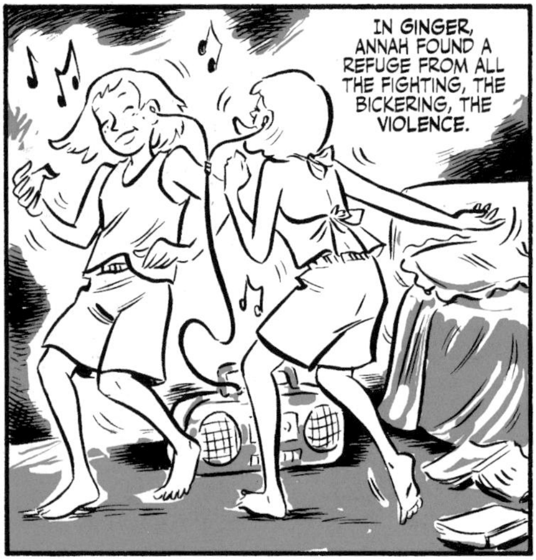
IN GINGER, ANNAH FOUND A REFUGE FROM ALL THE FIGHTING, THE BICKERING, THE VIOLENCE.

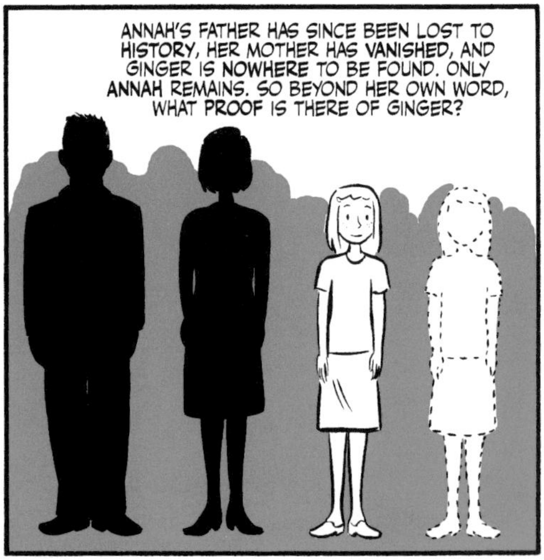
ANNAH'S FATHER HAS SINCE BEEN LOST TO HISTORY, HER MOTHER HAS VANISHED, AND GINGER IS NOWHERE TO BE FOUND. ONLY ANNAH REMAINS. SO BEYOND HER OWN WORD, WHAT PROOF IS THERE OF GINGER?

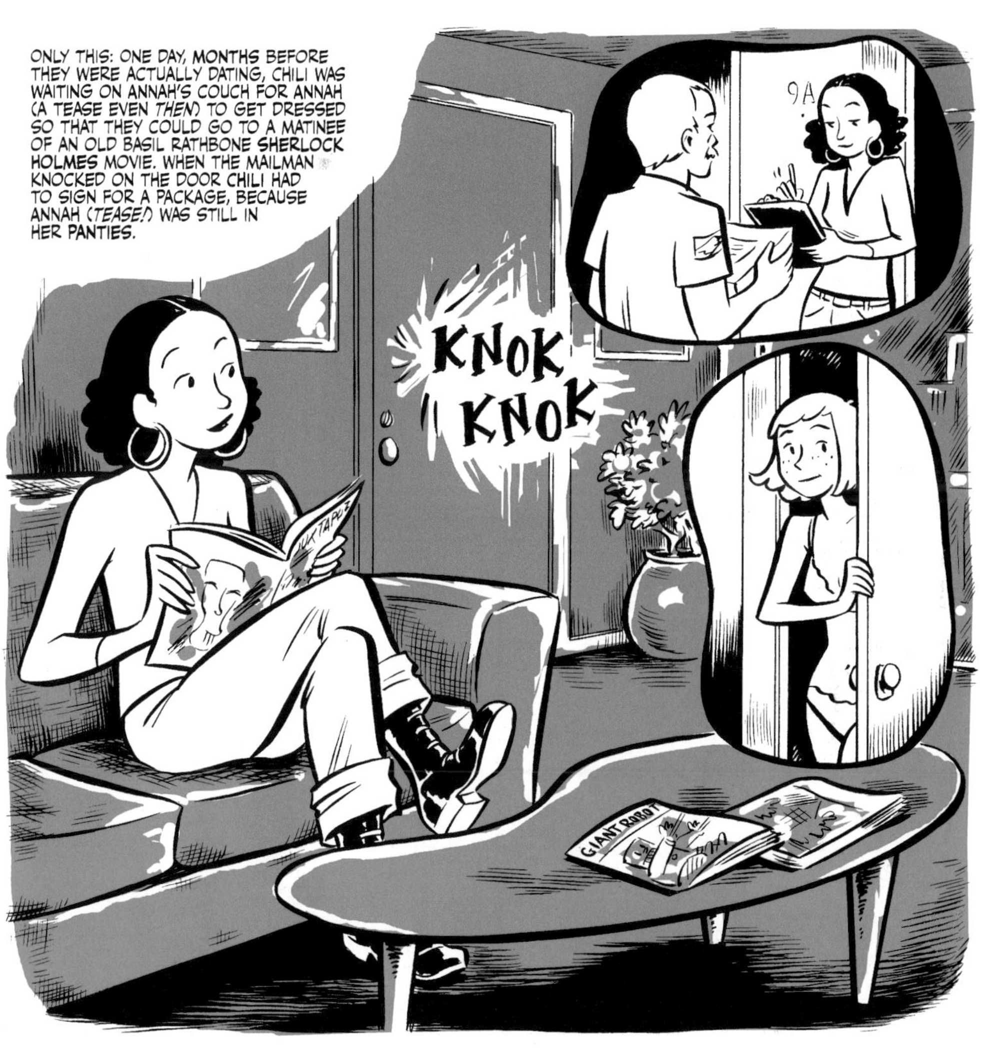
ONLY THIS: ONE DAY, MONTHS BEFORE THEY WERE ACTUALLY DATING, CHILI WAS WAITING ON ANNAH'S COUCH FOR ANNAH (A TEASE EVEN *THEN*) TO GET DRESSED SO THAT THEY COULD GO TO A MATINEE OF AN OLD BASIL RATHBONE **SHERLOCK HOLMES** MOVIE. WHEN THE MAILMAN KNOCKED ON THE DOOR CHILI HAD TO SIGN FOR A PACKAGE, BECAUSE ANNAH (*TEASE!*) WAS STILL IN HER **PANTIES**.
9A
KNOK KNOK
GIANT ROBOT

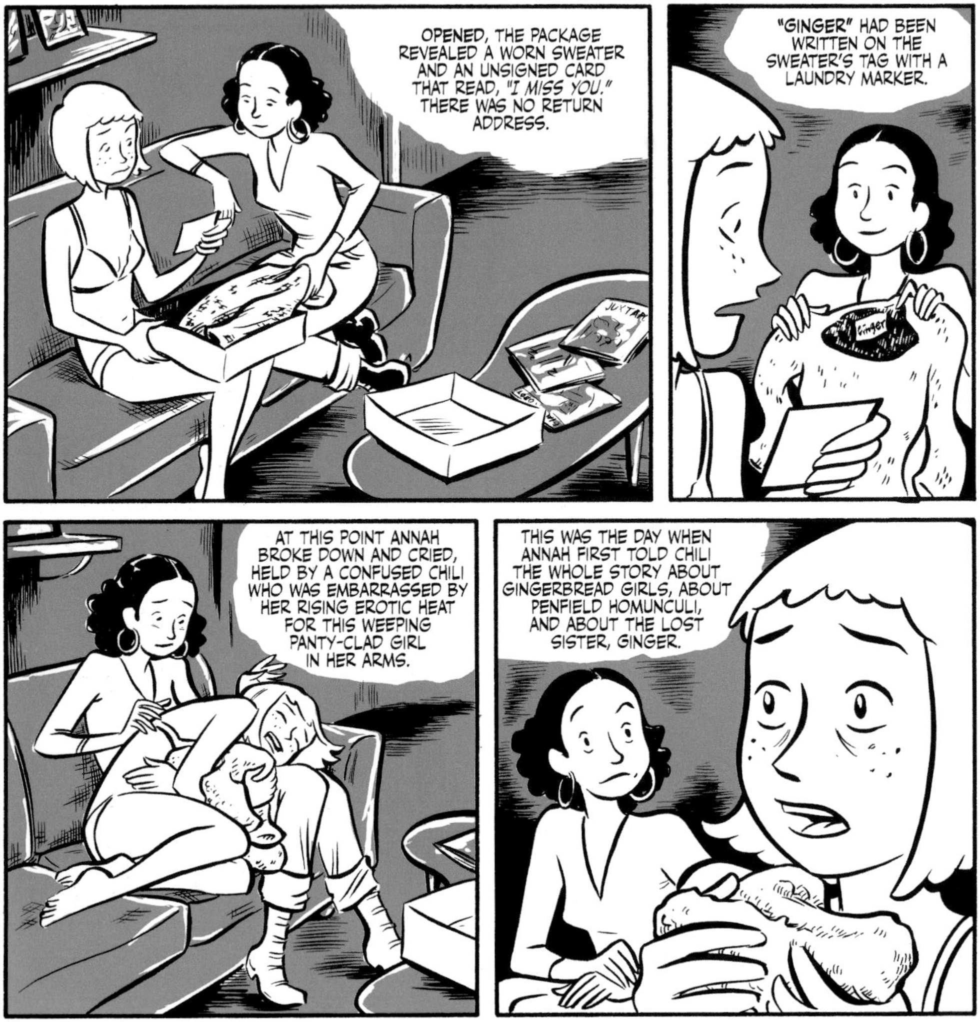
OPENED, THE PACKAGE REVEALED A WORN SWEATER AND AN UNSIGNED CARD THAT READ, "I MISS YOU." THERE WAS NO RETURN ADDRESS.
"GINGER" HAD BEEN WRITTEN ON THE SWEATER'S TAG WITH A LAUNDRY MARKER.
Ginger
AT THIS POINT ANNAH BROKE DOWN AND CRIED, HELD BY A CONFUSED CHILI WHO WAS EMBARRASSED BY HER RISING EROTIC HEAT FOR THIS WEEPING PANTY-CLAD GIRL IN HER ARMS.
THIS WAS THE DAY WHEN ANNAH FIRST TOLD CHILI THE WHOLE STORY ABOUT GINGERBREAD GIRLS, ABOUT PENFIELD HOMUNCULI, AND ABOUT THE LOST SISTER, GINGER.

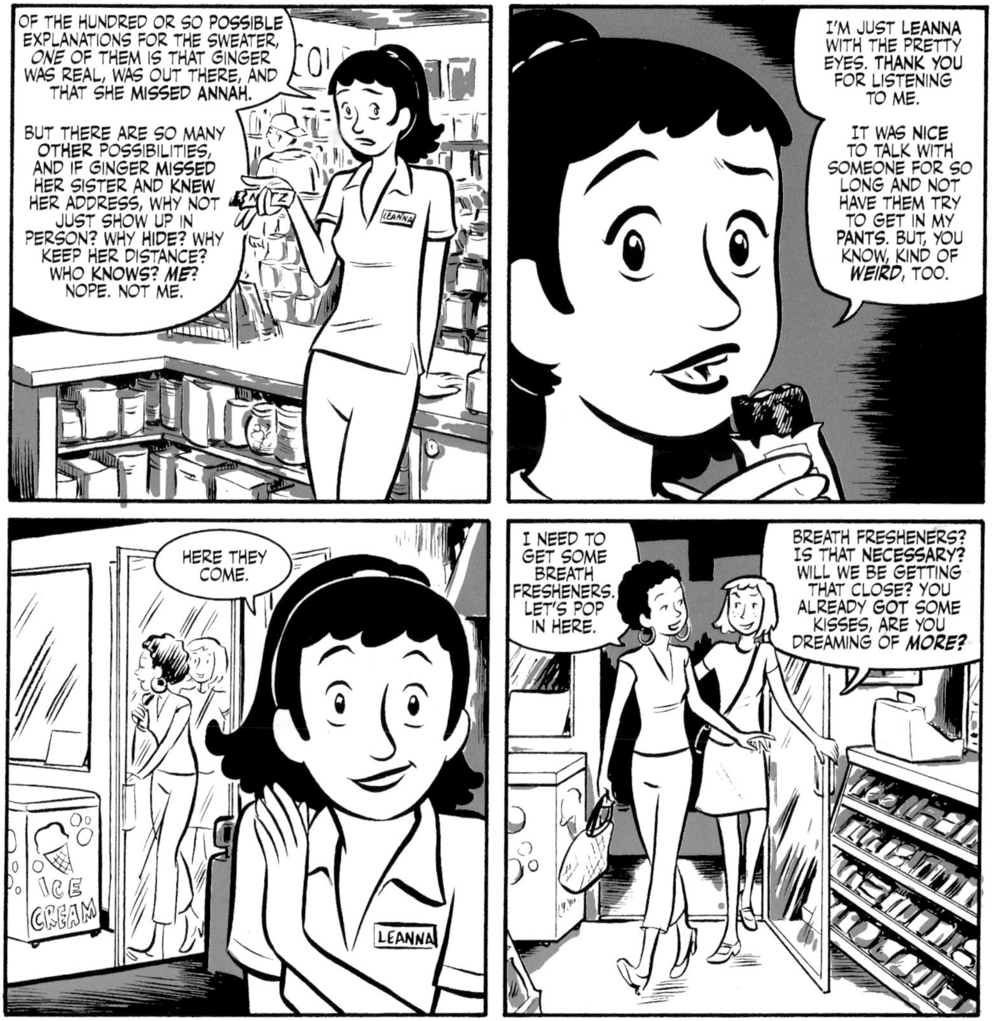
OF THE HUNDRED OR SO POSSIBLE EXPLANATIONS FOR THE SWEATER, *ONE* OF THEM IS THAT GINGER WAS REAL, WAS OUT THERE, AND THAT SHE MISSED ANNAH.
BUT THERE ARE SO MANY OTHER POSSIBILITIES, AND IF GINGER MISSED HER SISTER AND KNEW HER ADDRESS, WHY NOT JUST SHOW UP IN PERSON? WHY HIDE? WHY KEEP HER DISTANCE? WHO KNOWS? *ME?* NOPE. NOT ME.
LEANNA
I'M JUST LEANNA WITH THE PRETTY EYES. THANK YOU FOR LISTENING TO ME.
IT WAS NICE TO TALK WITH SOMEONE FOR SO LONG AND NOT HAVE THEM TRY TO GET IN MY PANTS. BUT, YOU KNOW, KIND OF *WEIRD*, TOO.
HERE THEY COME.
ICE CREAM
LEANNA
I NEED TO GET SOME BREATH FRESHENERS. LET'S POP IN HERE.
BREATH FRESHENERS? IS THAT NECESSARY? WILL WE BE GETTING THAT CLOSE? YOU ALREADY GOT SOME KISSES, ARE YOU DREAMING OF *MORE?*

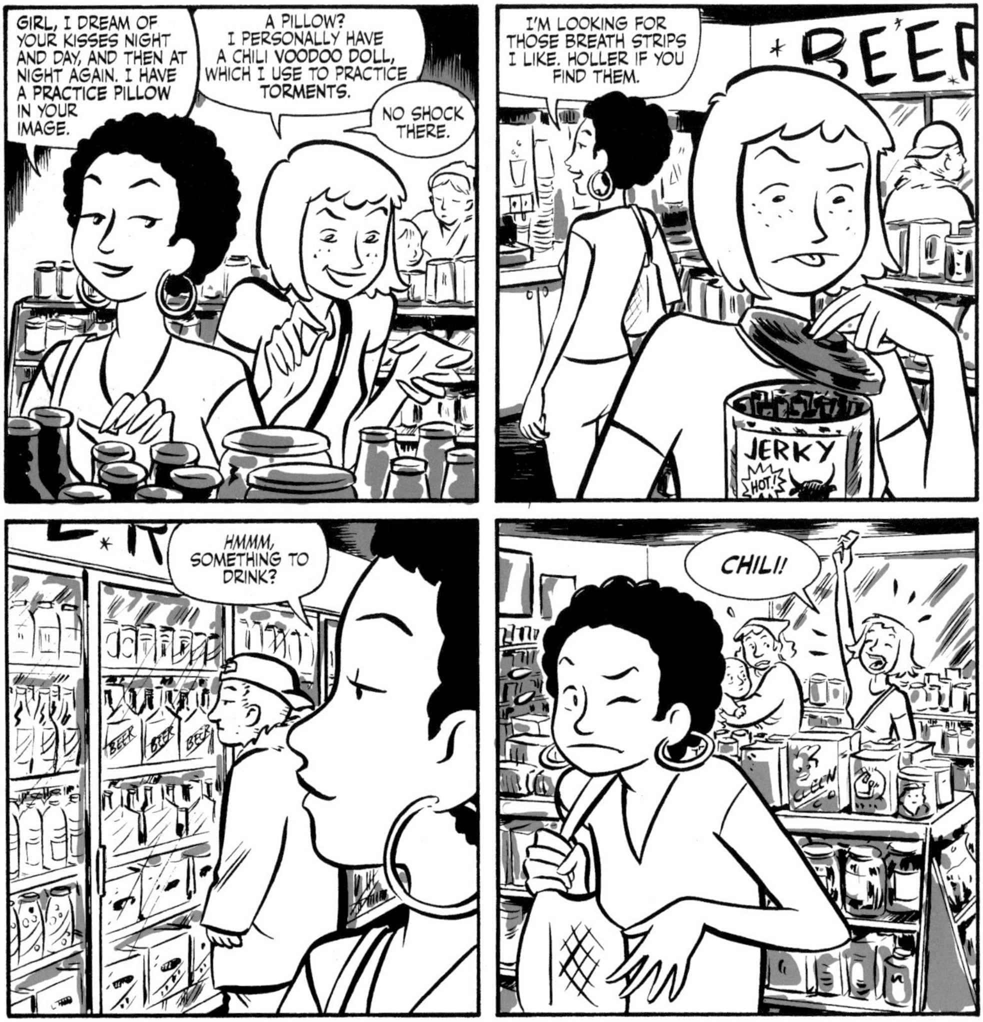
GIRL, I DREAM OF YOUR KISSES NIGHT AND DAY, AND THEN AT NIGHT AGAIN. I HAVE A PRACTICE PILLOW IN YOUR IMAGE.
A PILLOW? I PERSONALLY HAVE A CHILI VOODOO DOLL, WHICH I USE TO PRACTICE TORMENTS.
NO SHOCK THERE.
I'M LOOKING FOR THOSE BREATH STRIPS I LIKE. HOLLER IF YOU FIND THEM.
BEER
JERKY
HOT!
HMMM, SOMETHING TO DRINK?
BEER
BEER
BEER
CHILI!

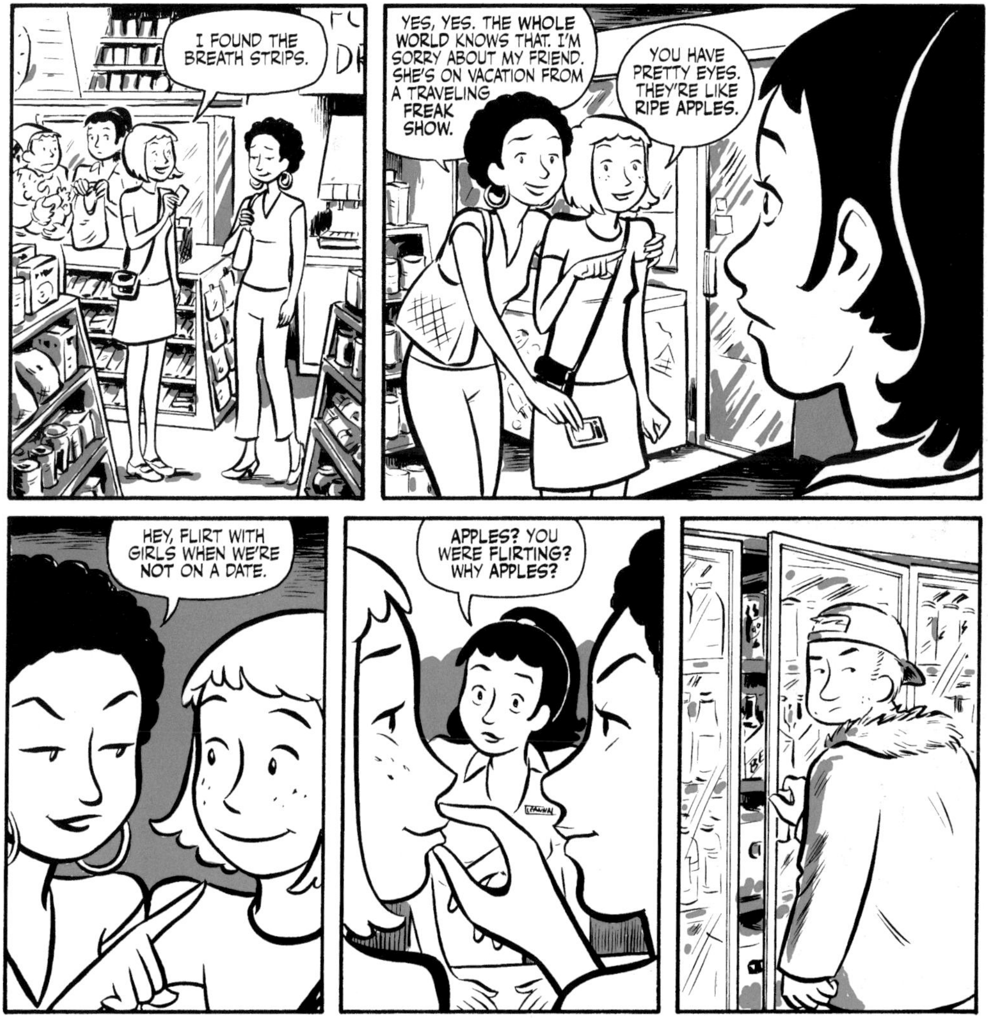
I FOUND THE BREATH STRIPS.
YES, YES. THE WHOLE WORLD KNOWS THAT. I'M SORRY ABOUT MY FRIEND. SHE'S ON VACATION FROM A TRAVELING FREAK SHOW.
YOU HAVE PRETTY EYES. THEY'RE LIKE RIPE APPLES.
HEY, FLIRT WITH GIRLS WHEN WE'RE NOT ON A DATE.
APPLES? YOU WERE FLIRTING? WHY APPLES?

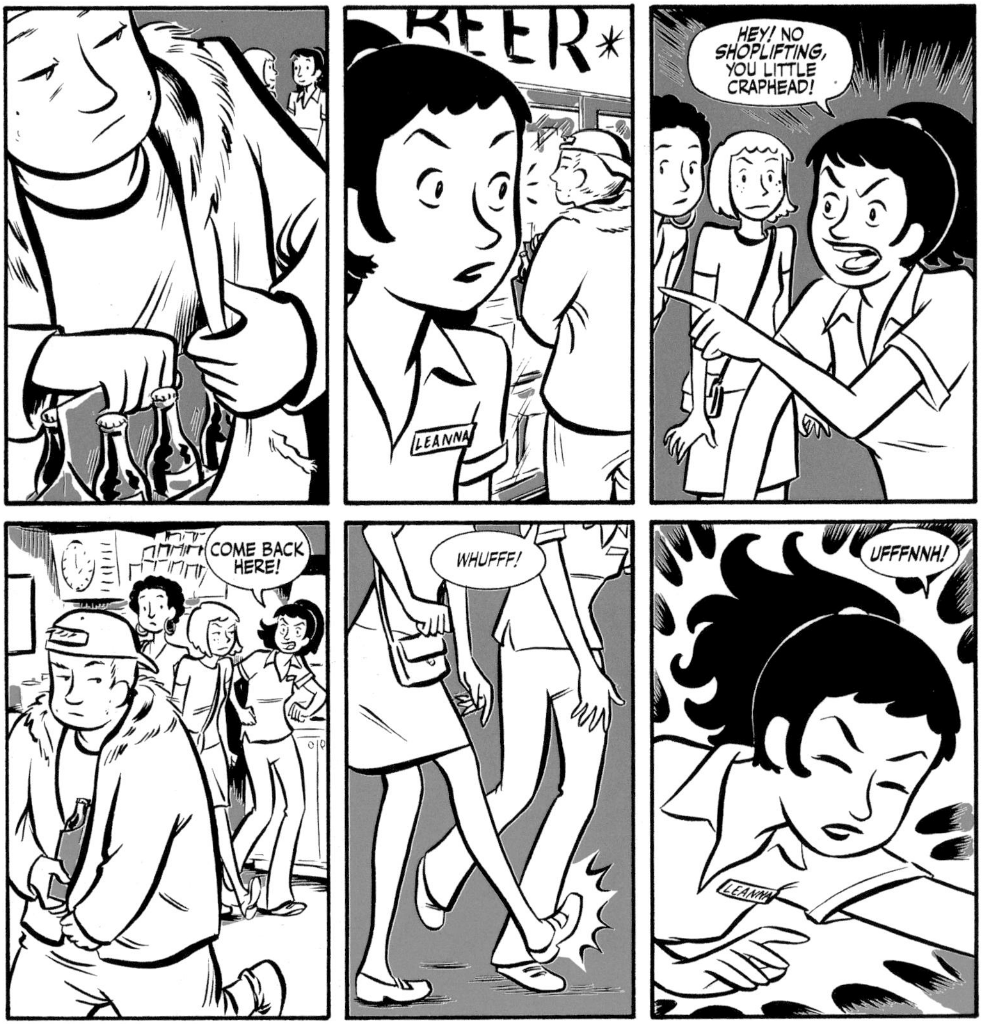
BEER*
LEANNA
HEY! NO SHOPLIFTING, YOU LITTLE CRAPHEAD!
COME BACK HERE!
WHUFFF!
UFFFNNH!
LEANNA

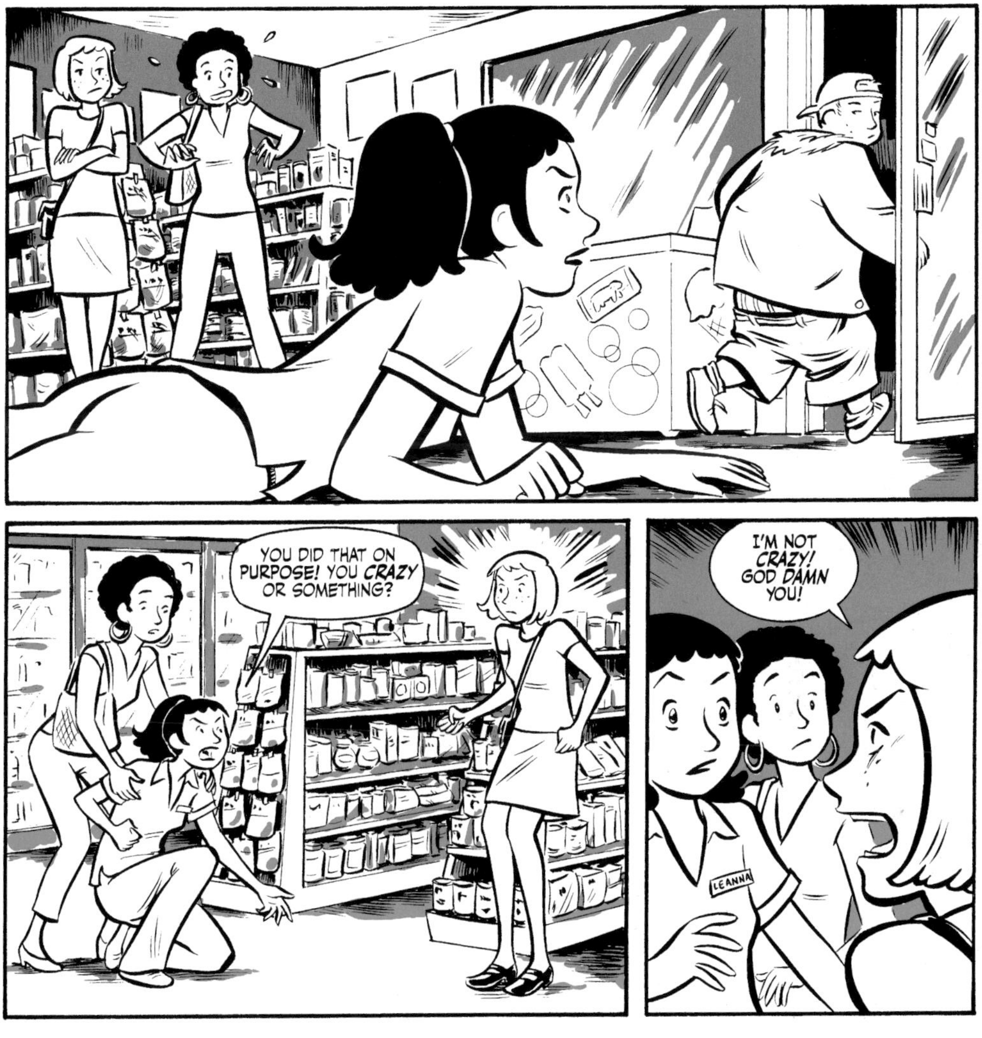
YOU DID THAT ON PURPOSE! YOU *CRAZY* OR SOMETHING?
I'M NOT *CRAZY!* GOD *DAMN* YOU!
LEANNA

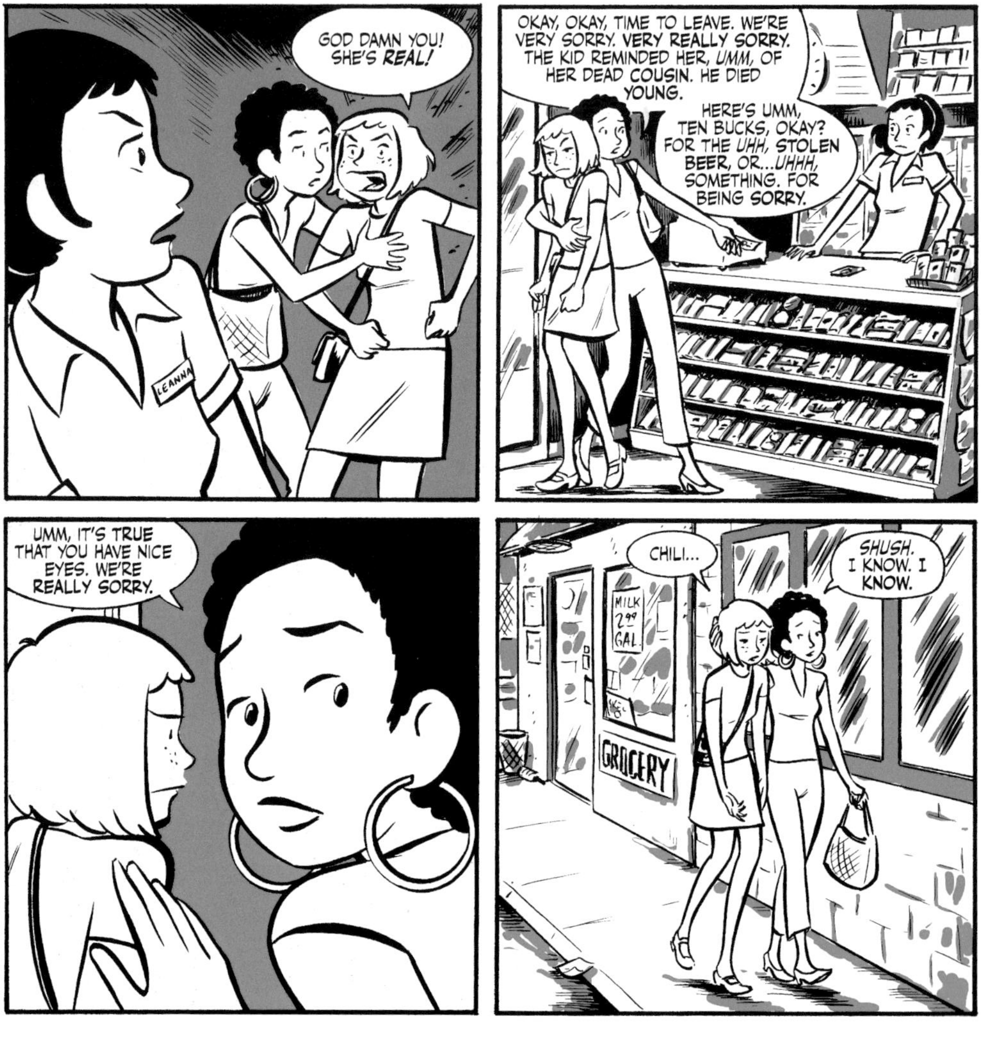
GOD DAMN YOU! SHE'S REAL!
LEANNA
OKAY, OKAY, TIME TO LEAVE. WE'RE VERY SORRY. VERY REALLY SORRY. THE KID REMINDED HER, UMM, OF HER DEAD COUSIN. HE DIED YOUNG.
HERE'S UMM, TEN BUCKS, OKAY? FOR THE UHH, STOLEN BEER, OR...UHHH, SOMETHING. FOR BEING SORRY.
UMM, IT'S TRUE THAT YOU HAVE NICE EYES. WE'RE REALLY SORRY.
CHILI...
SHUSH. I KNOW. I KNOW.
MILK 2.99 GAL.
GROCERY

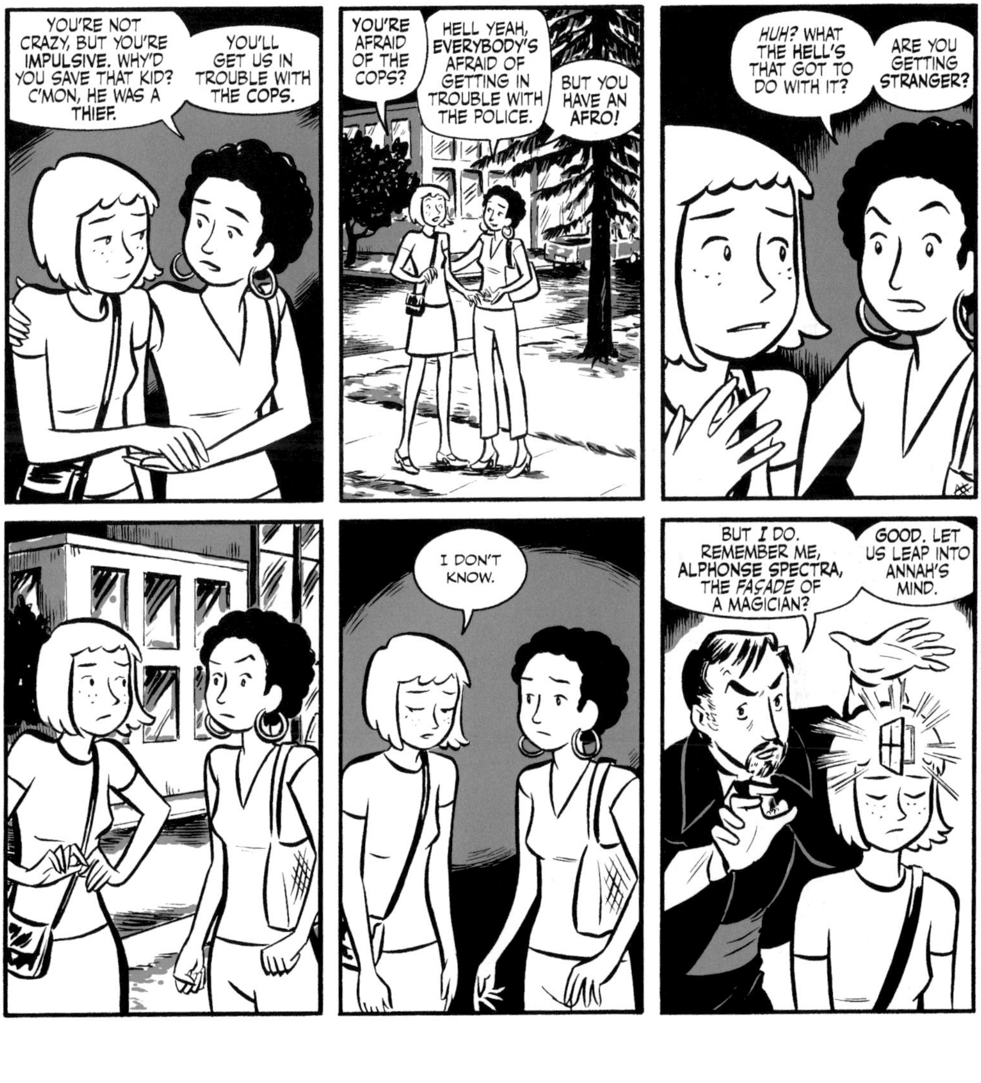
YOU'RE NOT CRAZY, BUT YOU'RE IMPULSIVE. WHY'D YOU SAVE THAT KID? C'MON, HE WAS A THIEF.
YOU'LL GET US IN TROUBLE WITH THE COPS.
YOU'RE AFRAID OF THE COPS?
HELL YEAH, EVERYBODY'S AFRAID OF GETTING IN TROUBLE WITH THE POLICE.
BUT YOU HAVE AN AFRO!
HUH? WHAT THE HELL'S THAT GOT TO DO WITH IT?
ARE YOU GETTING STRANGER?
I DON'T KNOW.
BUT I DO. REMEMBER ME, ALPHONSE SPECTRA, THE FAÇADE OF A MAGICIAN?
GOOD. LET US LEAP INTO ANNAH'S MIND.

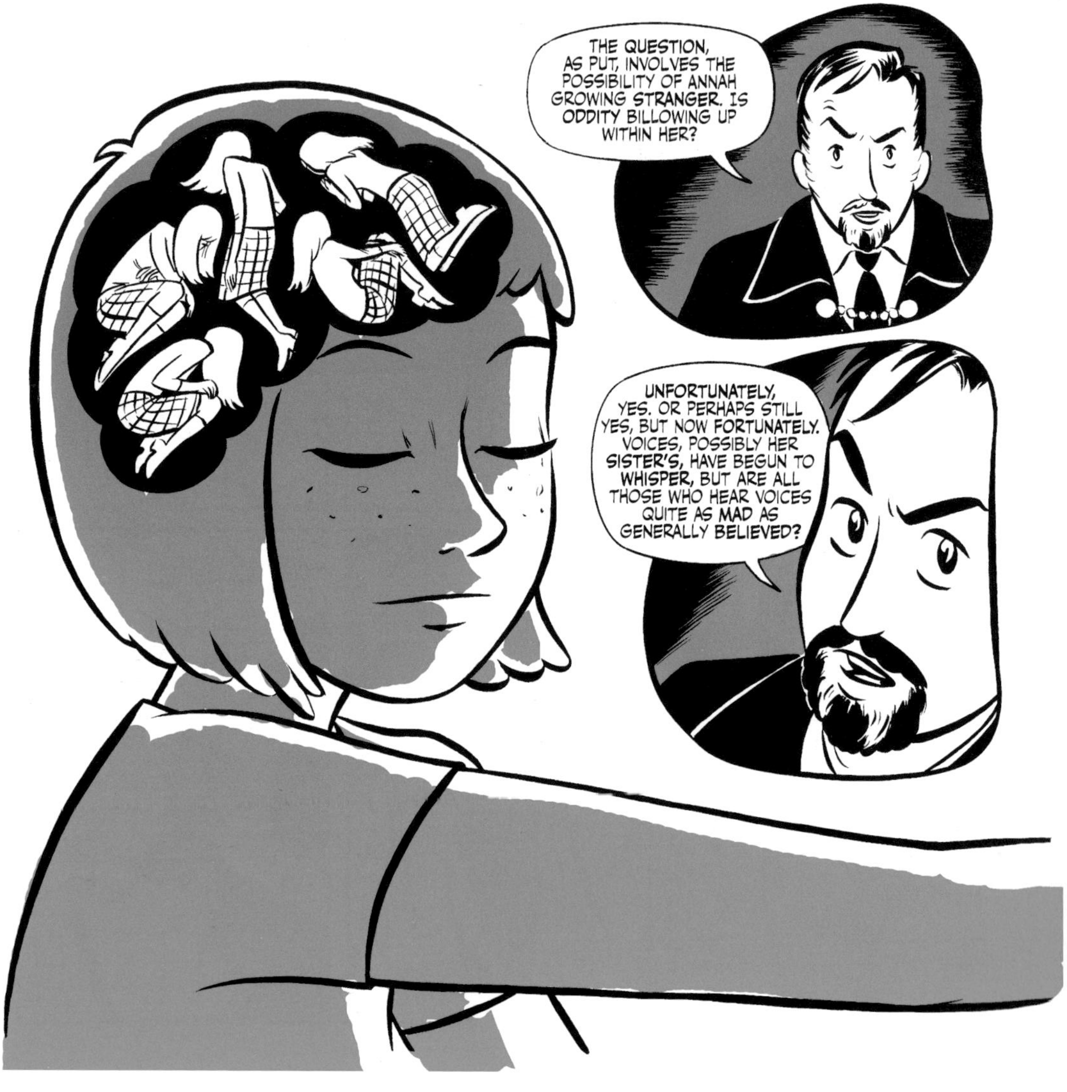
THE QUESTION, AS PUT, INVOLVES THE POSSIBILITY OF ANNAH GROWING STRANGER. IS ODDITY BILLOWING UP WITHIN HER?
UNFORTUNATELY, YES. OR PERHAPS STILL YES, BUT NOW FORTUNATELY. VOICES, POSSIBLY HER SISTER'S, HAVE BEGUN TO WHISPER, BUT ARE ALL THOSE WHO HEAR VOICES QUITE AS MAD AS GENERALLY BELIEVED?

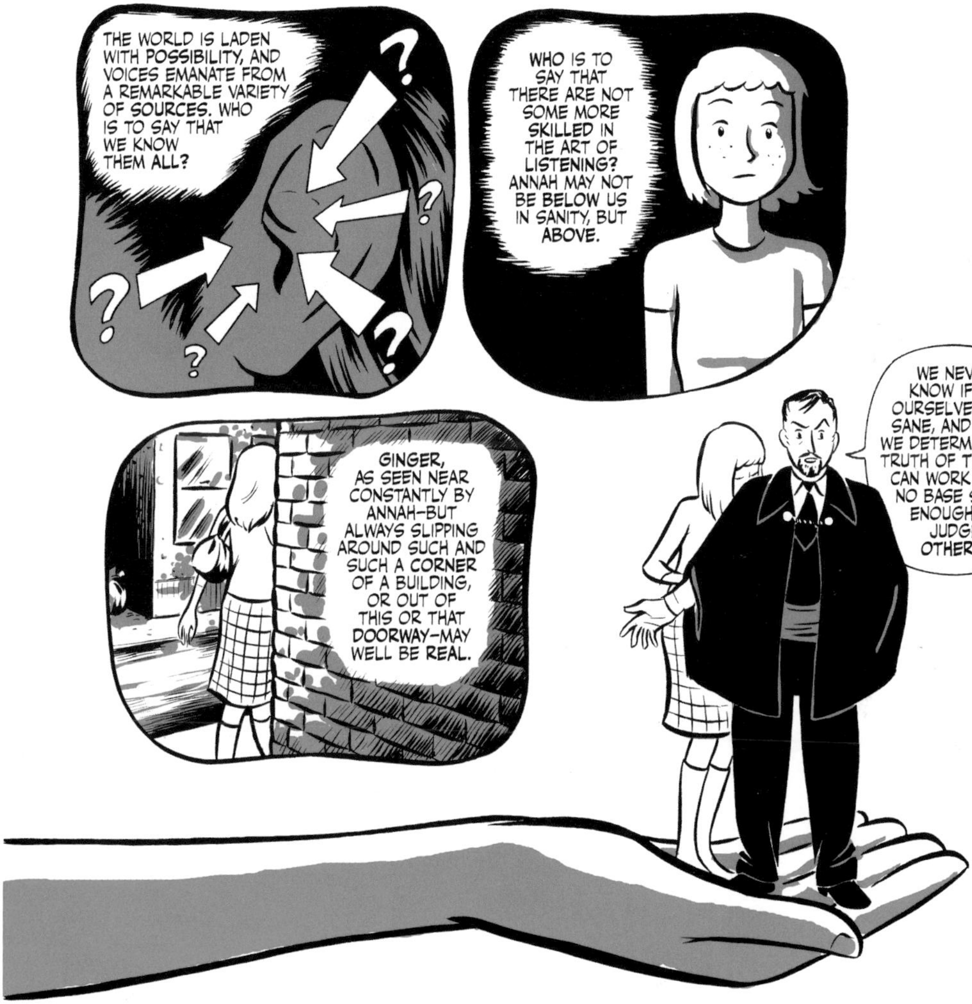
THE WORLD IS LADEN WITH POSSIBILITY, AND VOICES EMANATE FROM A REMARKABLE VARIETY OF SOURCES. WHO IS TO SAY THAT WE KNOW THEM ALL?
WHO IS TO SAY THAT THERE ARE NOT SOME MORE SKILLED IN THE ART OF LISTENING? ANNAH MAY NOT BE BELOW US IN SANITY, BUT ABOVE.
GINGER, AS SEEN NEAR CONSTANTLY BY ANNAH—BUT ALWAYS SLIPPING AROUND SUCH AND SUCH A CORNER OF A BUILDING, OR OUT OF THIS OR THAT DOORWAY—MAY WELL BE REAL.
WE NEVER KNOW IF WE OURSELVES ARE SANE, AND UNTIL WE DETERMINE THE TRUTH OF THAT, WE CAN WORK FROM NO BASE SOLID ENOUGH TO JUDGE OTHERS.

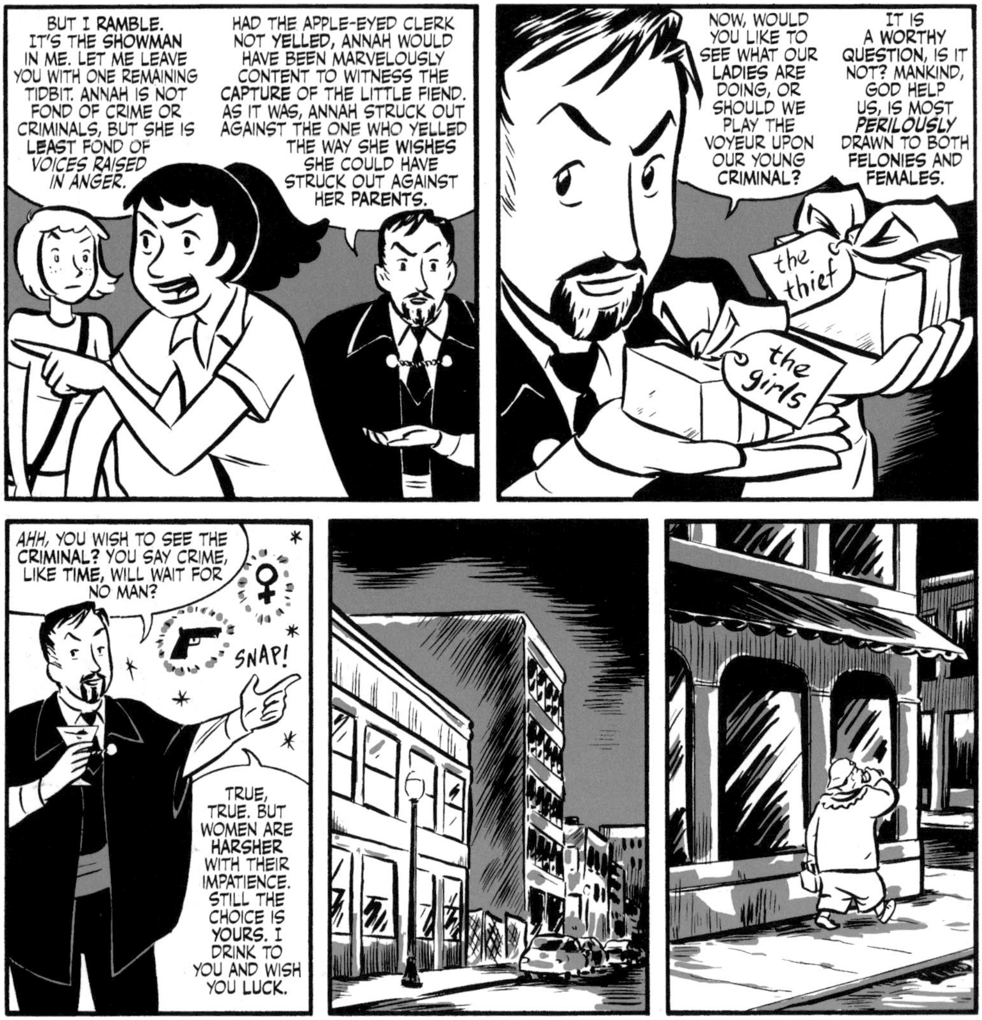
BUT I RAMBLE. IT'S THE SHOWMAN IN ME. LET ME LEAVE YOU WITH ONE REMAINING TIDBIT. ANNAH IS NOT FOND OF CRIME OR CRIMINALS, BUT SHE IS LEAST FOND OF VOICES RAISED IN ANGER.
HAD THE APPLE-EYED CLERK NOT YELLED, ANNAH WOULD HAVE BEEN MARVELOUSLY CONTENT TO WITNESS THE CAPTURE OF THE LITTLE FIEND. AS IT WAS, ANNAH STRUCK OUT AGAINST THE ONE WHO YELLED THE WAY SHE WISHES SHE COULD HAVE STRUCK OUT AGAINST HER PARENTS.
NOW, WOULD YOU LIKE TO SEE WHAT OUR LADIES ARE DOING, OR SHOULD WE PLAY THE VOYEUR UPON OUR YOUNG CRIMINAL?
IT IS A WORTHY QUESTION, IS IT NOT? MANKIND, GOD HELP US, IS MOST PERILOUSLY DRAWN TO BOTH FELONIES AND FEMALES.
the thief
the girls
AHH, YOU WISH TO SEE THE CRIMINAL? YOU SAY CRIME, LIKE TIME, WILL WAIT FOR NO MAN?
SNAP!
TRUE, TRUE. BUT WOMEN ARE HARSHER WITH THEIR IMPATIENCE. STILL THE CHOICE IS YOURS. I DRINK TO YOU AND WISH YOU LUCK.

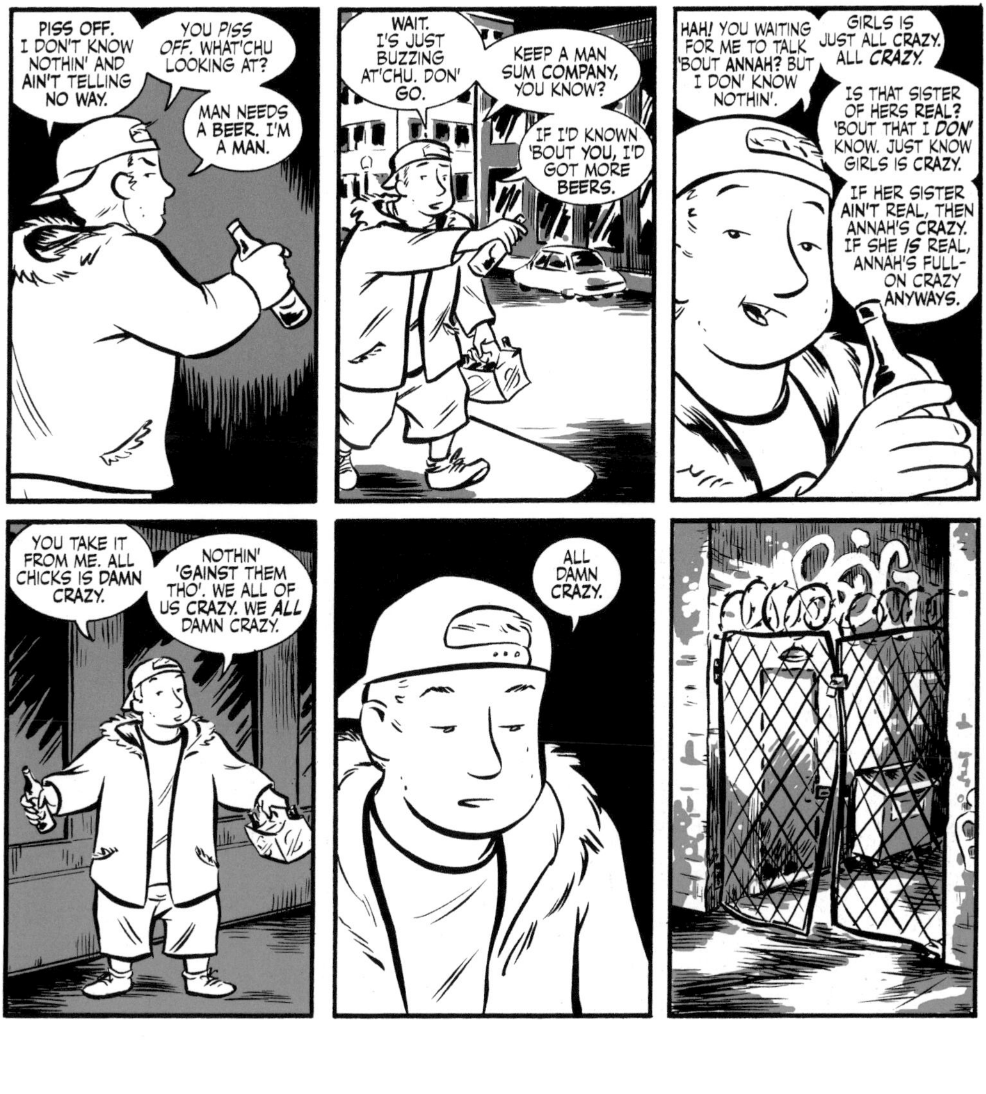
PISS OFF. I DON'T KNOW NOTHIN' AND AIN'T TELLING NO WAY.
YOU PISS OFF. WHAT'CHU LOOKING AT?
MAN NEEDS A BEER. I'M A MAN.
WAIT. I'S JUST BUZZING AT'CHU. DON' GO.
KEEP A MAN SUM COMPANY, YOU KNOW?
IF I'D KNOWN 'BOUT YOU, I'D GOT MORE BEERS.
HAH! YOU WAITING FOR ME TO TALK 'BOUT ANNAH? BUT I DON' KNOW NOTHIN'.
GIRLS IS JUST ALL CRAZY. ALL CRAZY.
IS THAT SISTER OF HERS REAL? 'BOUT THAT I DON' KNOW. JUST KNOW GIRLS IS CRAZY.
IF HER SISTER AIN'T REAL, THEN ANNAH'S CRAZY. IF SHE IS REAL, ANNAH'S FULL-ON CRAZY ANYWAYS.
YOU TAKE IT FROM ME. ALL CHICKS IS DAMN CRAZY.
NOTHIN' 'GAINST THEM THO'. WE ALL OF US CRAZY. WE ALL DAMN CRAZY.
ALL DAMN CRAZY.

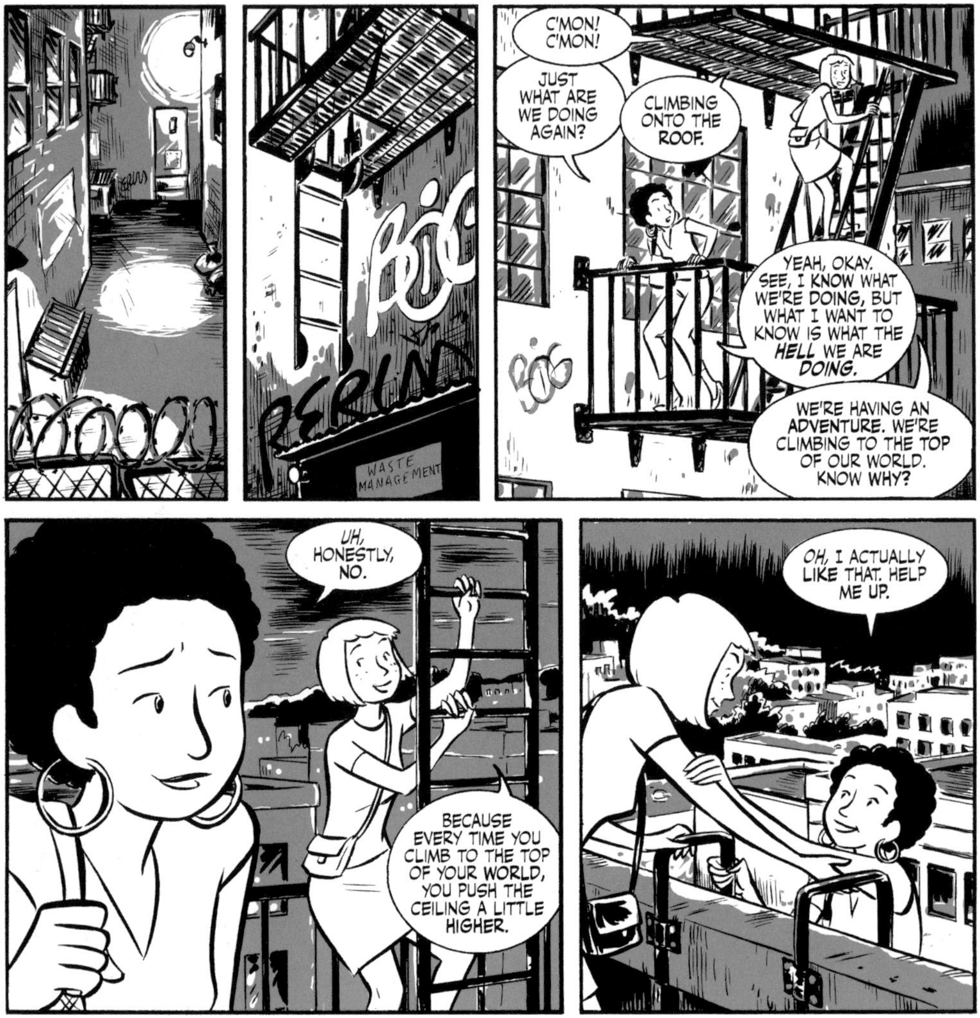
WASTE MANAGEMENT
C'MON! C'MON!
JUST WHAT ARE WE DOING AGAIN?
CLIMBING ONTO THE ROOF.
YEAH, OKAY. SEE, I KNOW WHAT WE'RE DOING, BUT WHAT I WANT TO KNOW IS WHAT THE HELL WE ARE DOING.
WE'RE HAVING AN ADVENTURE. WE'RE CLIMBING TO THE TOP OF OUR WORLD. KNOW WHY?
UH, HONESTLY, NO.
BECAUSE EVERY TIME YOU CLIMB TO THE TOP OF YOUR WORLD, YOU PUSH THE CEILING A LITTLE HIGHER.
OH, I ACTUALLY LIKE THAT. HELP ME UP.

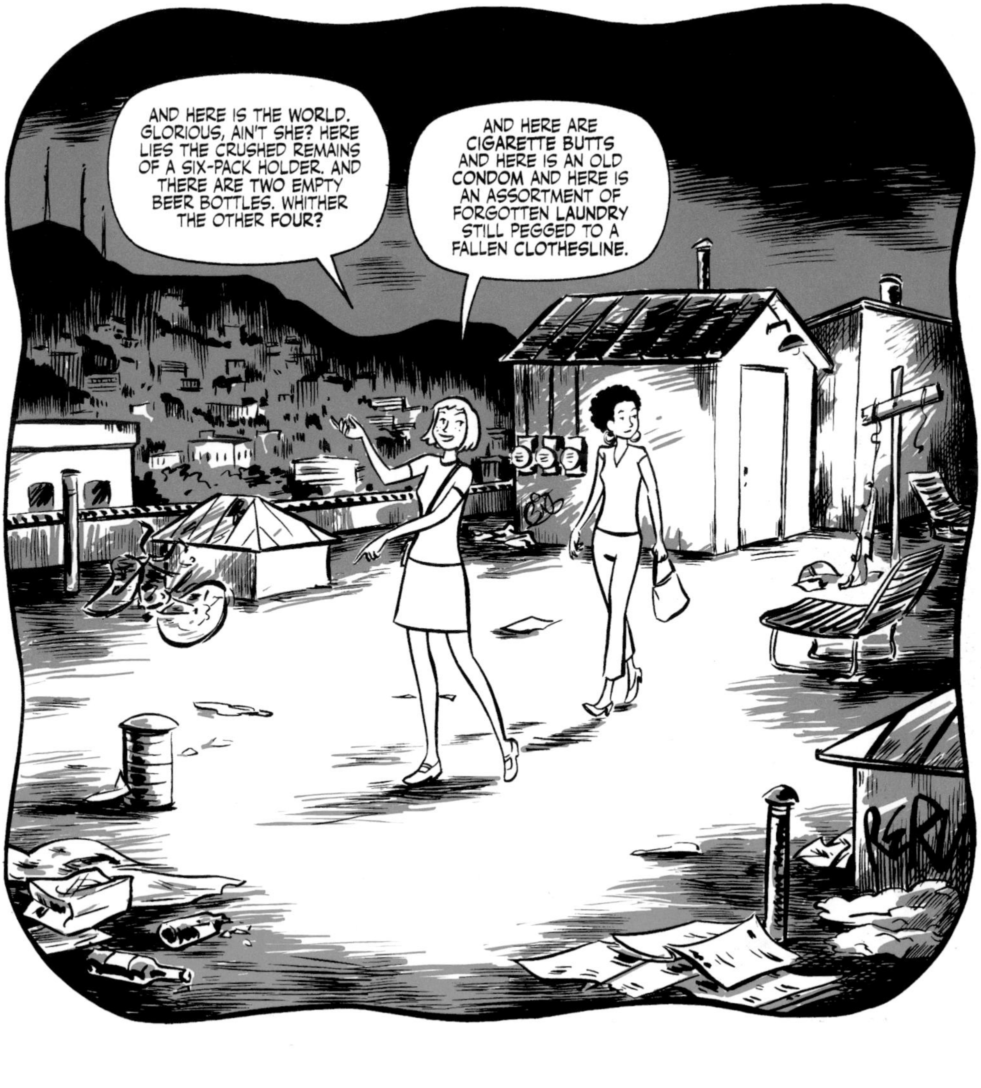
AND HERE IS THE WORLD. GLORIOUS, AIN'T SHE? HERE LIES THE CRUSHED REMAINS OF A SIX-PACK HOLDER. AND THERE ARE TWO EMPTY BEER BOTTLES. WHITHER THE OTHER FOUR?
AND HERE ARE CIGARETTE BUTTS AND HERE IS AN OLD CONDOM AND HERE IS AN ASSORTMENT OF FORGOTTEN LAUNDRY STILL PEGGED TO A FALLEN CLOTHESLINE.

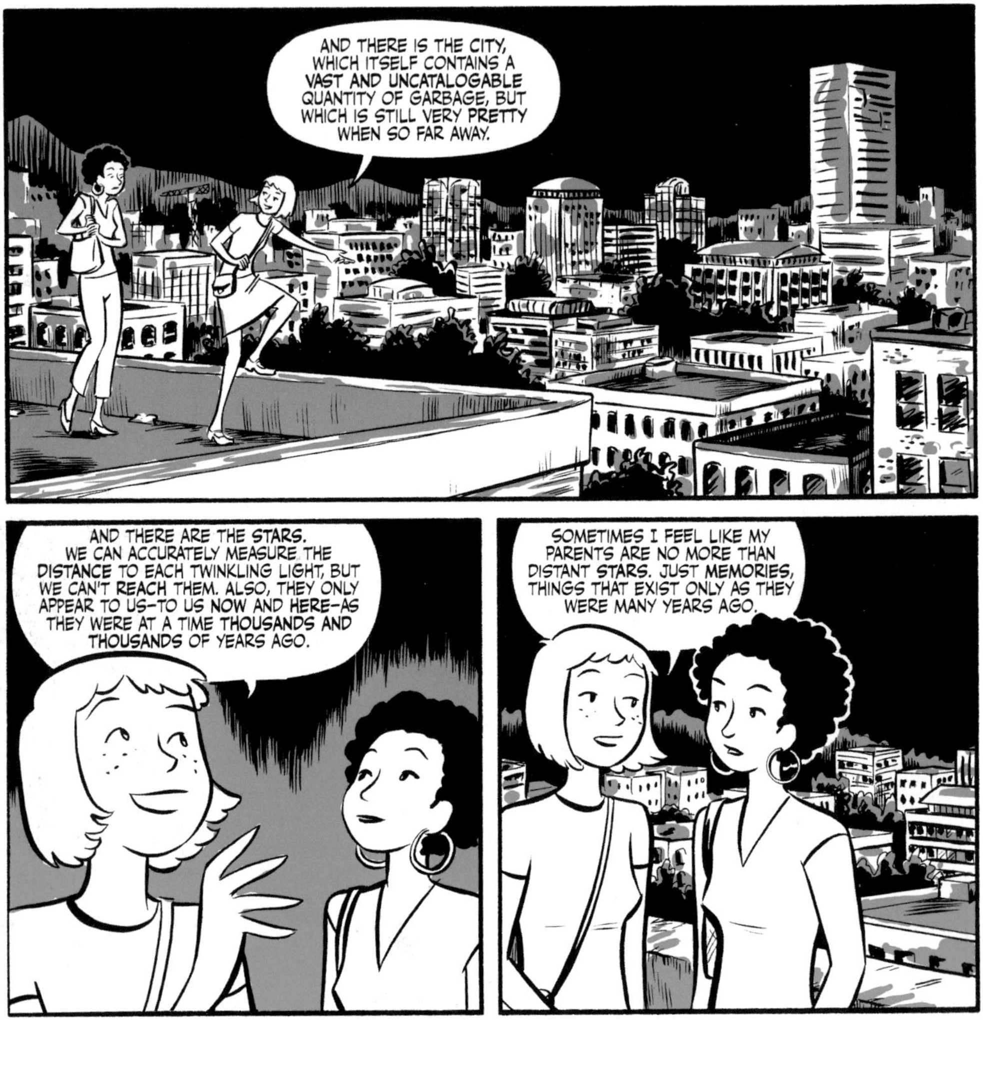
AND THERE IS THE CITY, WHICH ITSELF CONTAINS A VAST AND UNCATALOGABLE QUANTITY OF GARBAGE, BUT WHICH IS STILL VERY PRETTY WHEN SO FAR AWAY.
AND THERE ARE THE STARS. WE CAN ACCURATELY MEASURE THE DISTANCE TO EACH TWINKLING LIGHT, BUT WE CAN'T REACH THEM. ALSO, THEY ONLY APPEAR TO US–TO US NOW AND HERE–AS THEY WERE AT A TIME THOUSANDS AND THOUSANDS OF YEARS AGO.
SOMETIMES I FEEL LIKE MY PARENTS ARE NO MORE THAN DISTANT STARS. JUST MEMORIES, THINGS THAT EXIST ONLY AS THEY WERE MANY YEARS AGO.

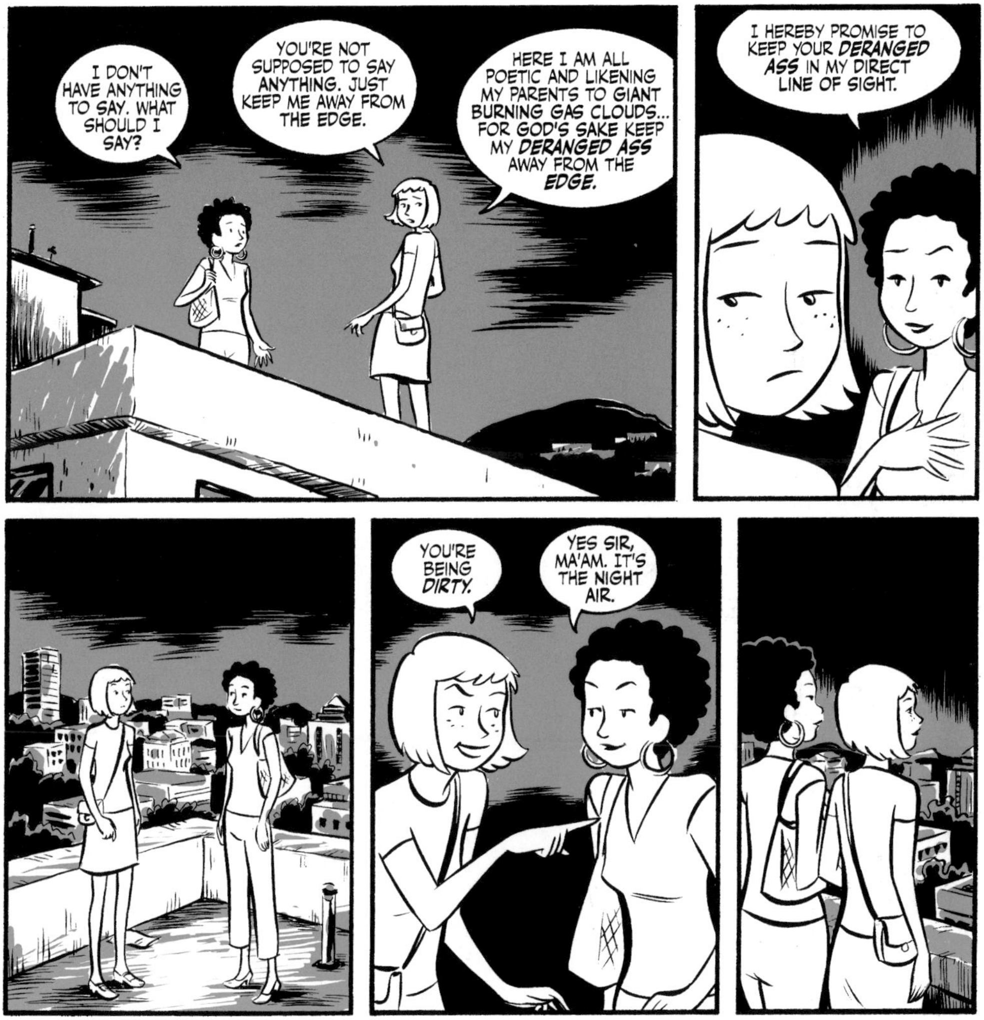
I DON'T HAVE ANYTHING TO SAY. WHAT SHOULD I SAY?
YOU'RE NOT SUPPOSED TO SAY ANYTHING. JUST KEEP ME AWAY FROM THE EDGE.
HERE I AM ALL POETIC AND LIKENING MY PARENTS TO GIANT BURNING GAS CLOUDS... FOR GOD'S SAKE KEEP MY *DERANGED ASS* AWAY FROM THE *EDGE.*
I HEREBY PROMISE TO KEEP YOUR *DERANGED ASS* IN MY DIRECT LINE OF SIGHT.
YOU'RE BEING *DIRTY.*
YES SIR, MA'AM. IT'S THE NIGHT AIR.

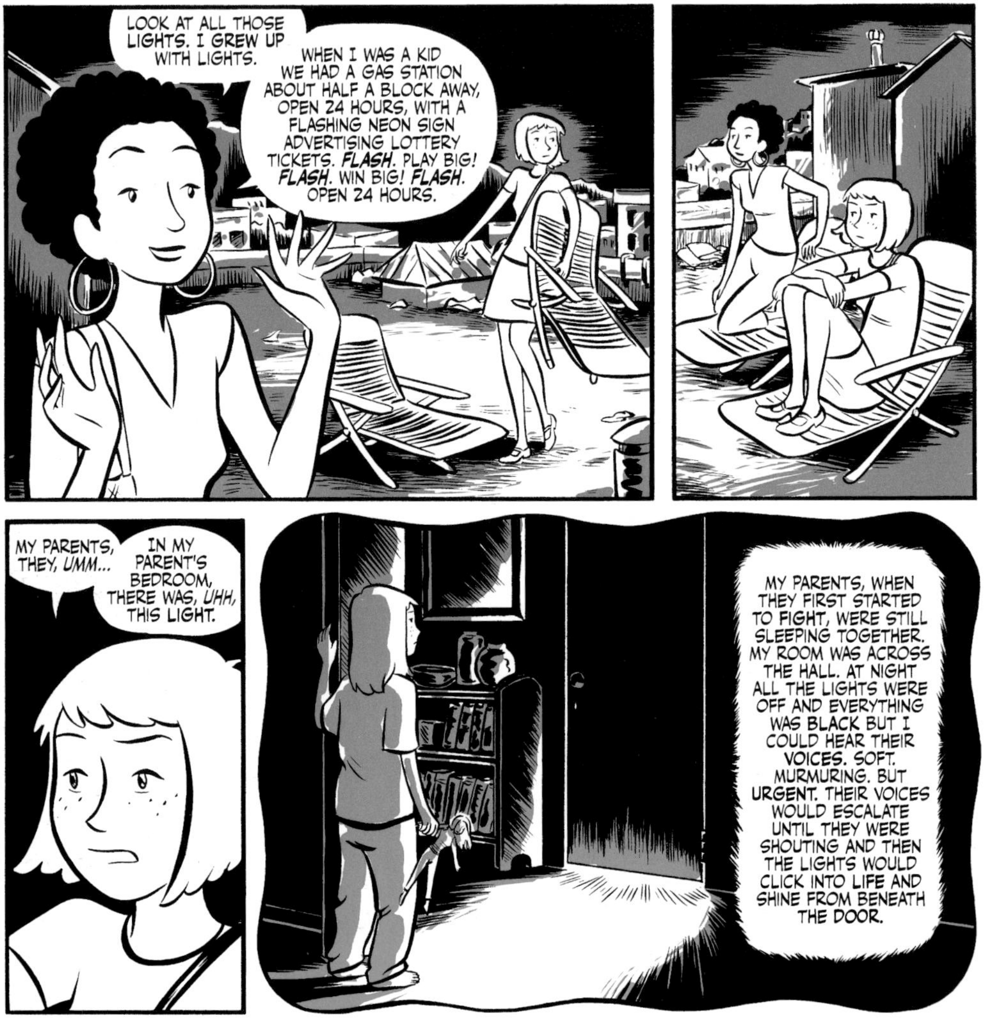
LOOK AT ALL THOSE LIGHTS. I GREW UP WITH LIGHTS.
WHEN I WAS A KID WE HAD A GAS STATION ABOUT HALF A BLOCK AWAY, OPEN 24 HOURS, WITH A FLASHING NEON SIGN ADVERTISING LOTTERY TICKETS. *FLASH*. PLAY BIG! *FLASH*. WIN BIG! *FLASH*. OPEN 24 HOURS.
MY PARENTS, THEY, *UMM*...
IN MY PARENT'S BEDROOM, THERE WAS, *UHH*, THIS LIGHT.
MY PARENTS, WHEN THEY FIRST STARTED TO FIGHT, WERE STILL SLEEPING TOGETHER. MY ROOM WAS ACROSS THE HALL. AT NIGHT ALL THE LIGHTS WERE OFF AND EVERYTHING WAS BLACK BUT I COULD HEAR THEIR VOICES. SOFT. MURMURING. BUT URGENT. THEIR VOICES WOULD ESCALATE UNTIL THEY WERE SHOUTING AND THEN THE LIGHTS WOULD CLICK INTO LIFE AND SHINE FROM BENEATH THE DOOR.

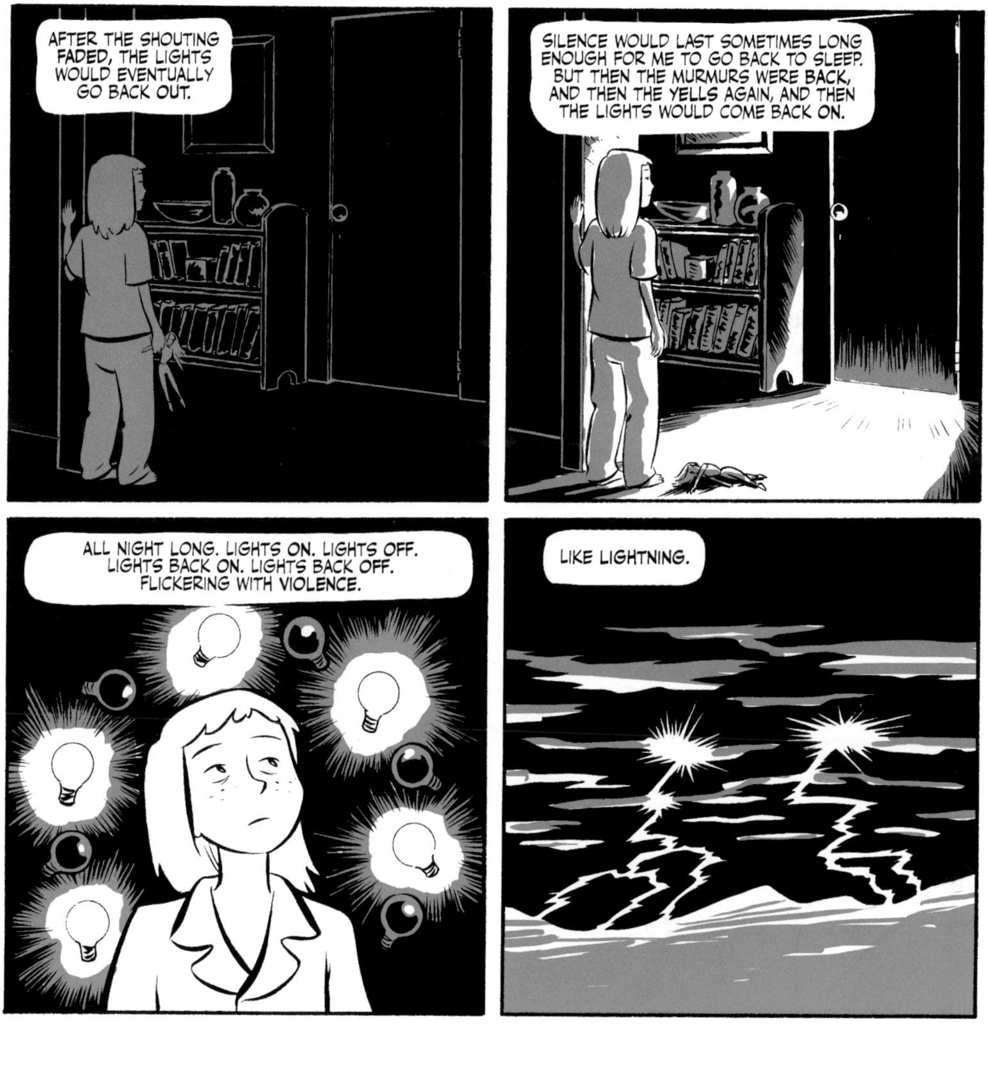
AFTER THE SHOUTING FADED, THE LIGHTS WOULD EVENTUALLY GO BACK OUT.
SILENCE WOULD LAST SOMETIMES LONG ENOUGH FOR ME TO GO BACK TO SLEEP. BUT THEN THE MURMURS WERE BACK, AND THEN THE YELLS AGAIN, AND THEN THE LIGHTS WOULD COME BACK ON.
ALL NIGHT LONG. LIGHTS ON. LIGHTS OFF. LIGHTS BACK ON. LIGHTS BACK OFF. FLICKERING WITH VIOLENCE.
LIKE LIGHTNING.

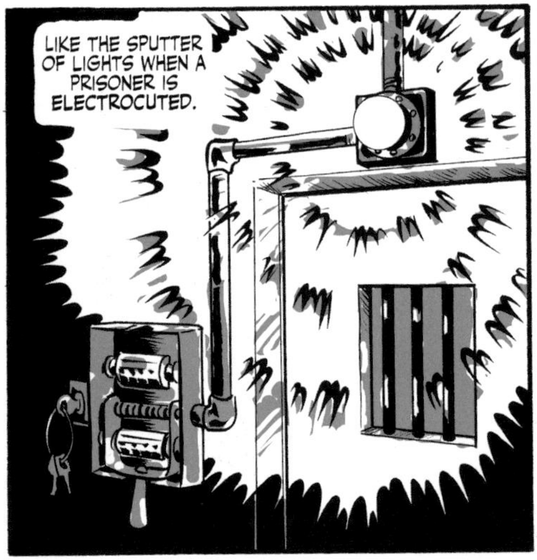
LIKE THE SPUTTER OF LIGHTS WHEN A PRISONER IS ELECTROCUTED.

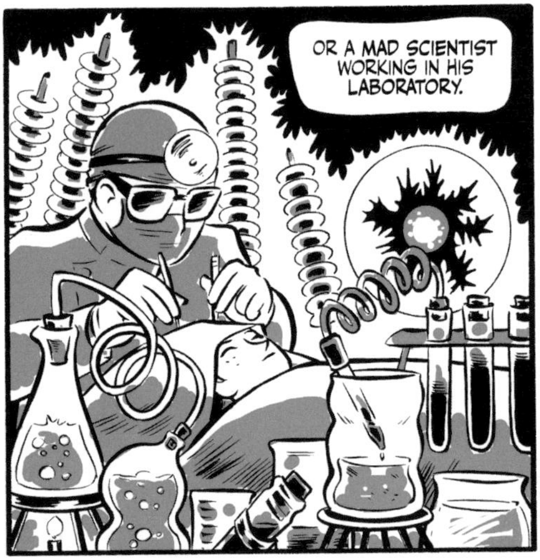
OR A MAD SCIENTIST WORKING IN HIS LABORATORY.

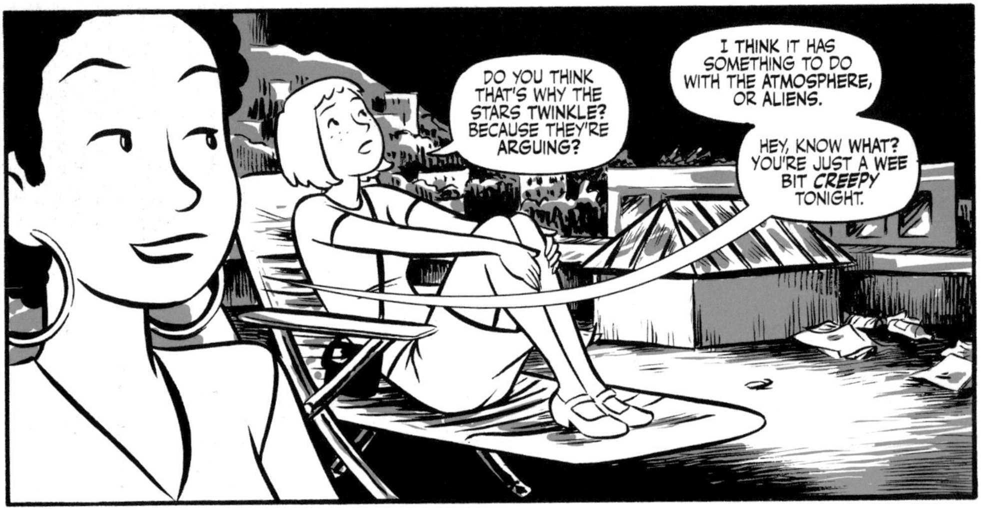
DO YOU THINK THAT'S WHY THE STARS TWINKLE? BECAUSE THEY'RE ARGUING?
I THINK IT HAS SOMETHING TO DO WITH THE ATMOSPHERE, OR ALIENS.
HEY, KNOW WHAT? YOU'RE JUST A WEE BIT *CREEPY* TONIGHT.

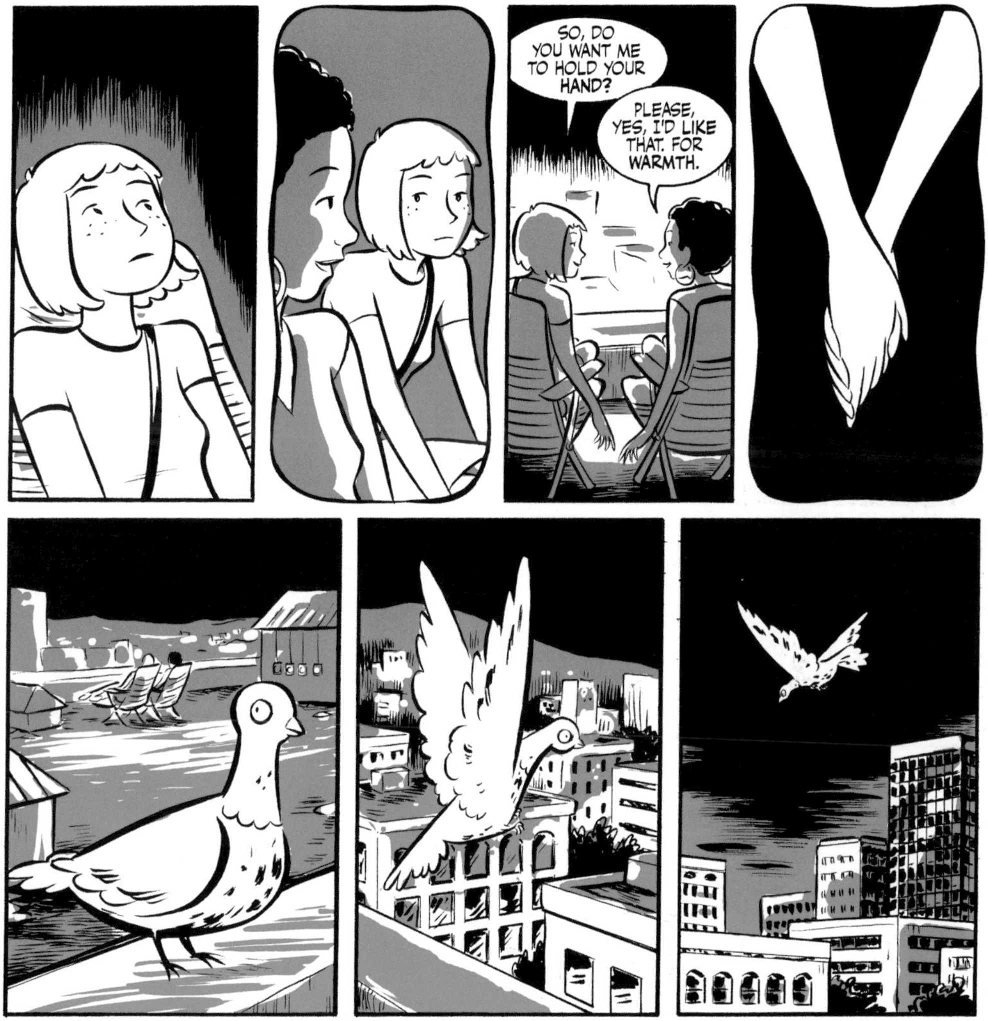
SO, DO YOU WANT ME TO HOLD YOUR HAND?
PLEASE, YES, I'D LIKE THAT. FOR WARMTH.

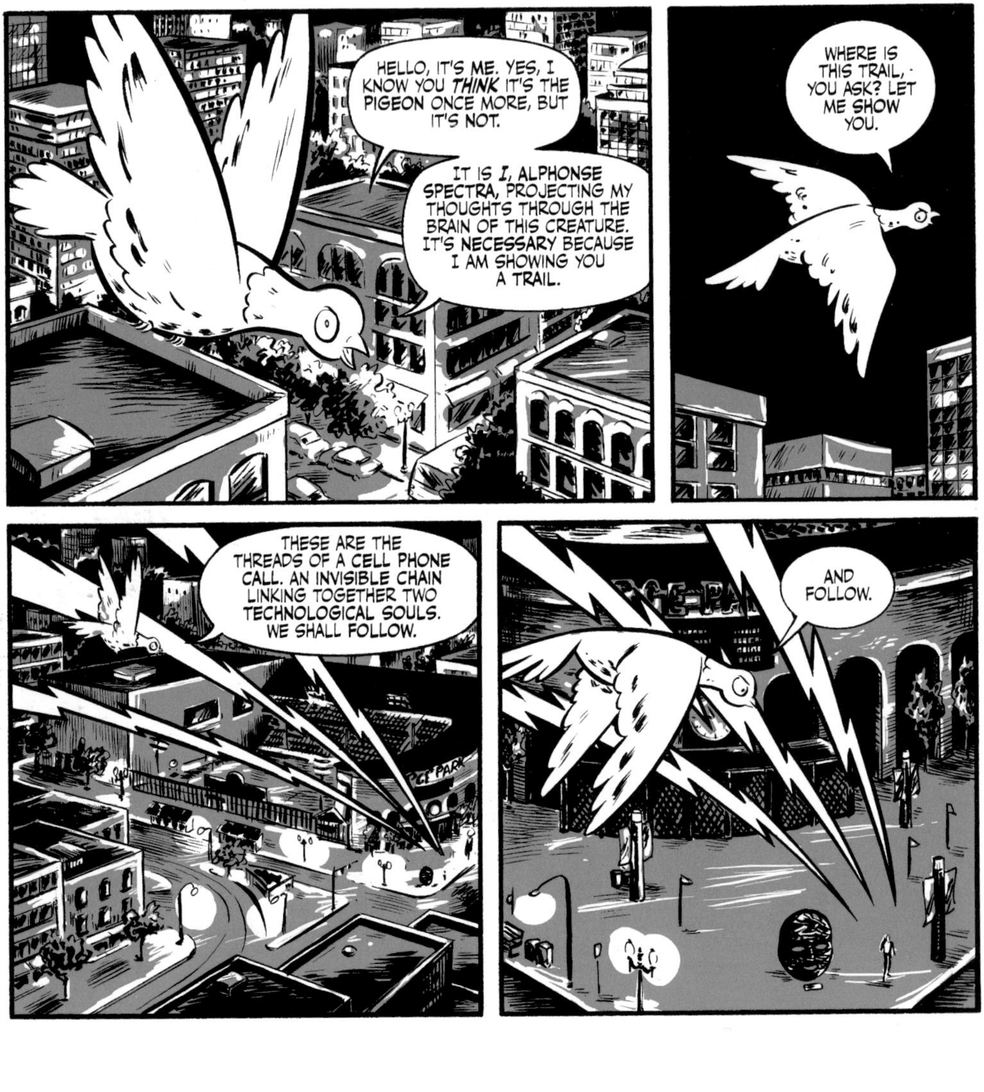
HELLO, IT'S ME. YES, I KNOW YOU *THINK* IT'S THE PIGEON ONCE MORE, BUT IT'S NOT.
IT IS *I*, ALPHONSE SPECTRA, PROJECTING MY THOUGHTS THROUGH THE BRAIN OF THIS CREATURE. IT'S NECESSARY BECAUSE I AM SHOWING YOU A TRAIL.
WHERE IS THIS TRAIL, YOU ASK? LET ME SHOW YOU.
THESE ARE THE THREADS OF A CELL PHONE CALL. AN INVISIBLE CHAIN LINKING TOGETHER TWO TECHNOLOGICAL SOULS. WE SHALL FOLLOW.
PARK
AND FOLLOW.

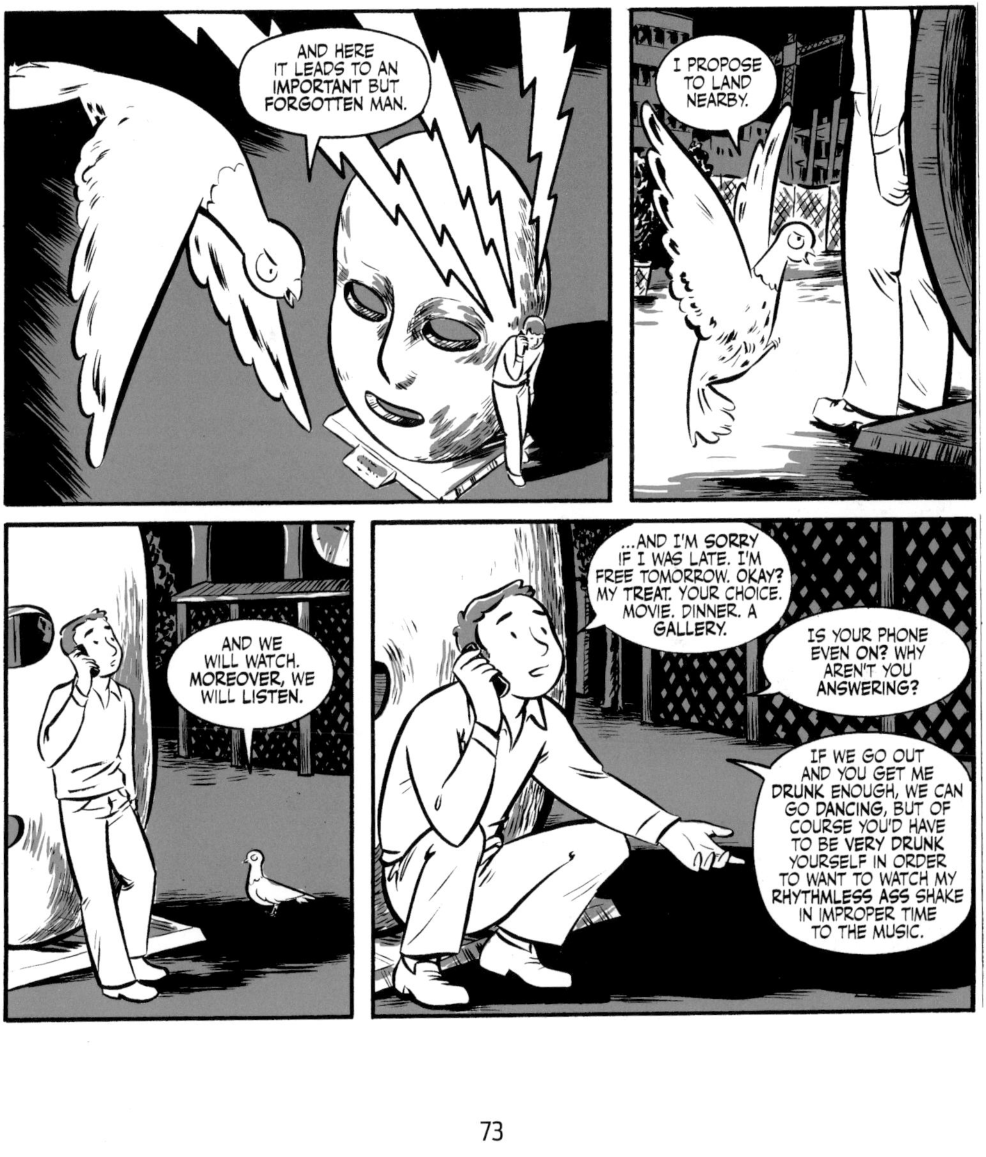
AND HERE IT LEADS TO AN IMPORTANT BUT FORGOTTEN MAN.
I PROPOSE TO LAND NEARBY.
AND WE WILL WATCH. MOREOVER, WE WILL LISTEN.
...AND I'M SORRY IF I WAS LATE. I'M FREE TOMORROW. OKAY? MY TREAT. YOUR CHOICE. MOVIE. DINNER. A GALLERY.
IS YOUR PHONE EVEN ON? WHY AREN'T YOU ANSWERING?
IF WE GO OUT AND YOU GET ME DRUNK ENOUGH, WE CAN GO DANCING, BUT OF COURSE YOU'D HAVE TO BE VERY DRUNK YOURSELF IN ORDER TO WANT TO WATCH MY RHYTHMLESS ASS SHAKE IN IMPROPER TIME TO THE MUSIC.

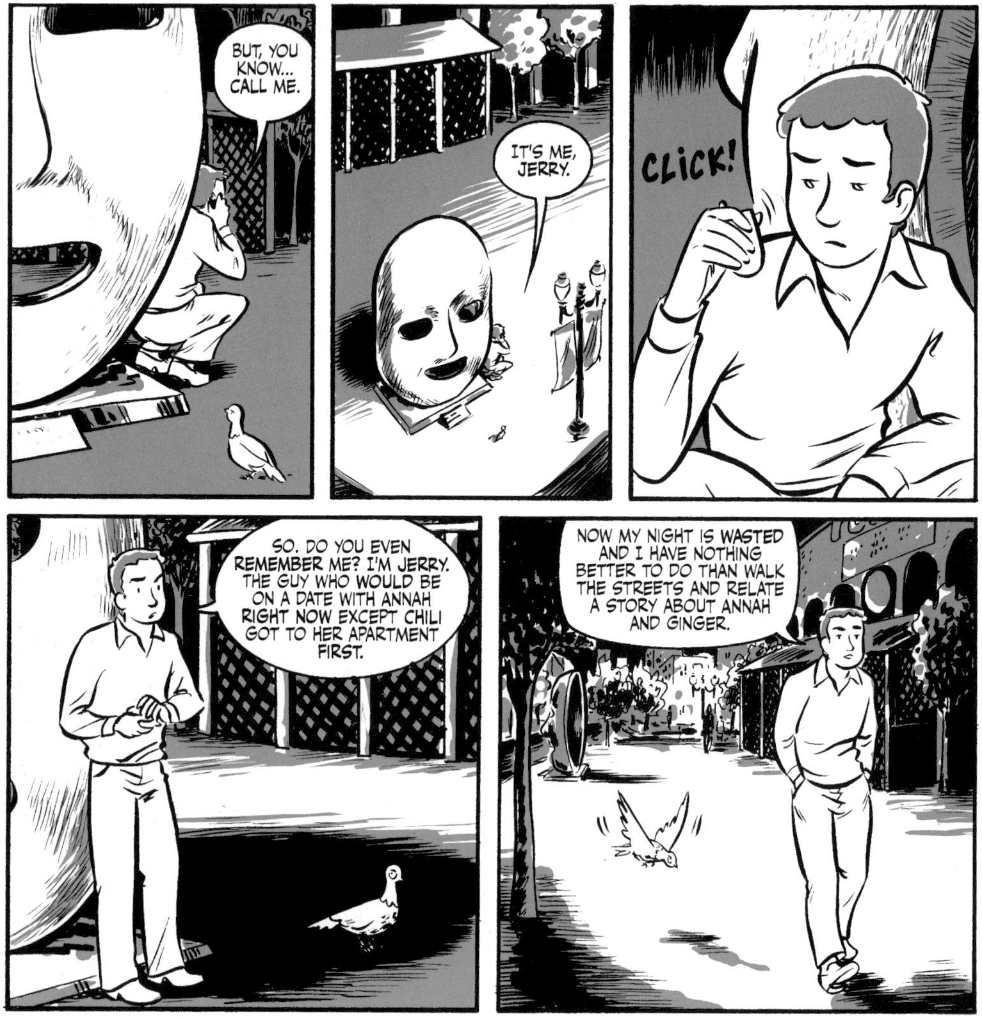
BUT, YOU KNOW... CALL ME.
IT'S ME, JERRY.
CLICK!
SO. DO YOU EVEN REMEMBER ME? I'M JERRY. THE GUY WHO WOULD BE ON A DATE WITH ANNAH RIGHT NOW EXCEPT CHILI GOT TO HER APARTMENT FIRST.
NOW MY NIGHT IS WASTED AND I HAVE NOTHING BETTER TO DO THAN WALK THE STREETS AND RELATE A STORY ABOUT ANNAH AND GINGER.

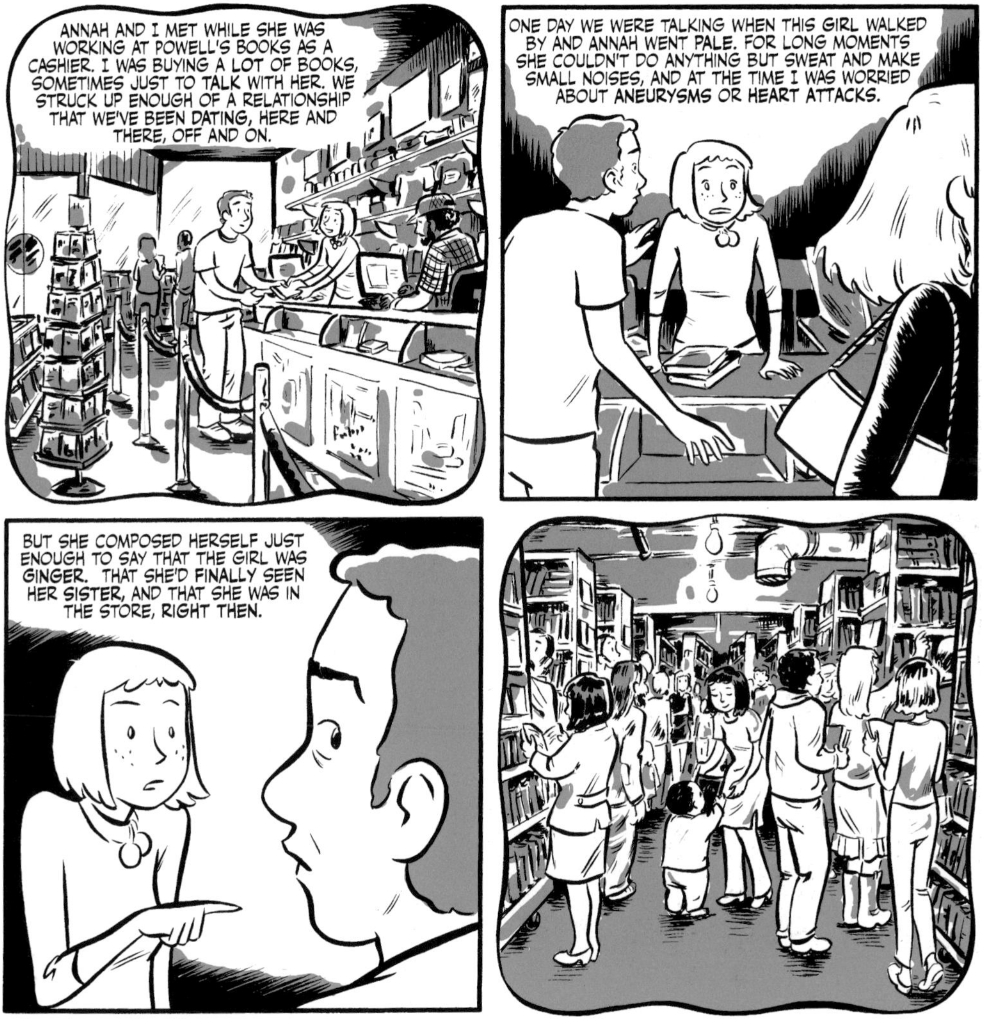
ANNAH AND I MET WHILE SHE WAS WORKING AT POWELL'S BOOKS AS A CASHIER. I WAS BUYING A LOT OF BOOKS, SOMETIMES JUST TO TALK WITH HER. WE STRUCK UP ENOUGH OF A RELATIONSHIP THAT WE'VE BEEN DATING, HERE AND THERE, OFF AND ON.
ONE DAY WE WERE TALKING WHEN THIS GIRL WALKED BY AND ANNAH WENT PALE. FOR LONG MOMENTS SHE COULDN'T DO ANYTHING BUT SWEAT AND MAKE SMALL NOISES, AND AT THE TIME I WAS WORRIED ABOUT ANEURYSMS OR HEART ATTACKS.
BUT SHE COMPOSED HERSELF JUST ENOUGH TO SAY THAT THE GIRL WAS GINGER. THAT SHE'D FINALLY SEEN HER SISTER, AND THAT SHE WAS IN THE STORE, RIGHT THEN.

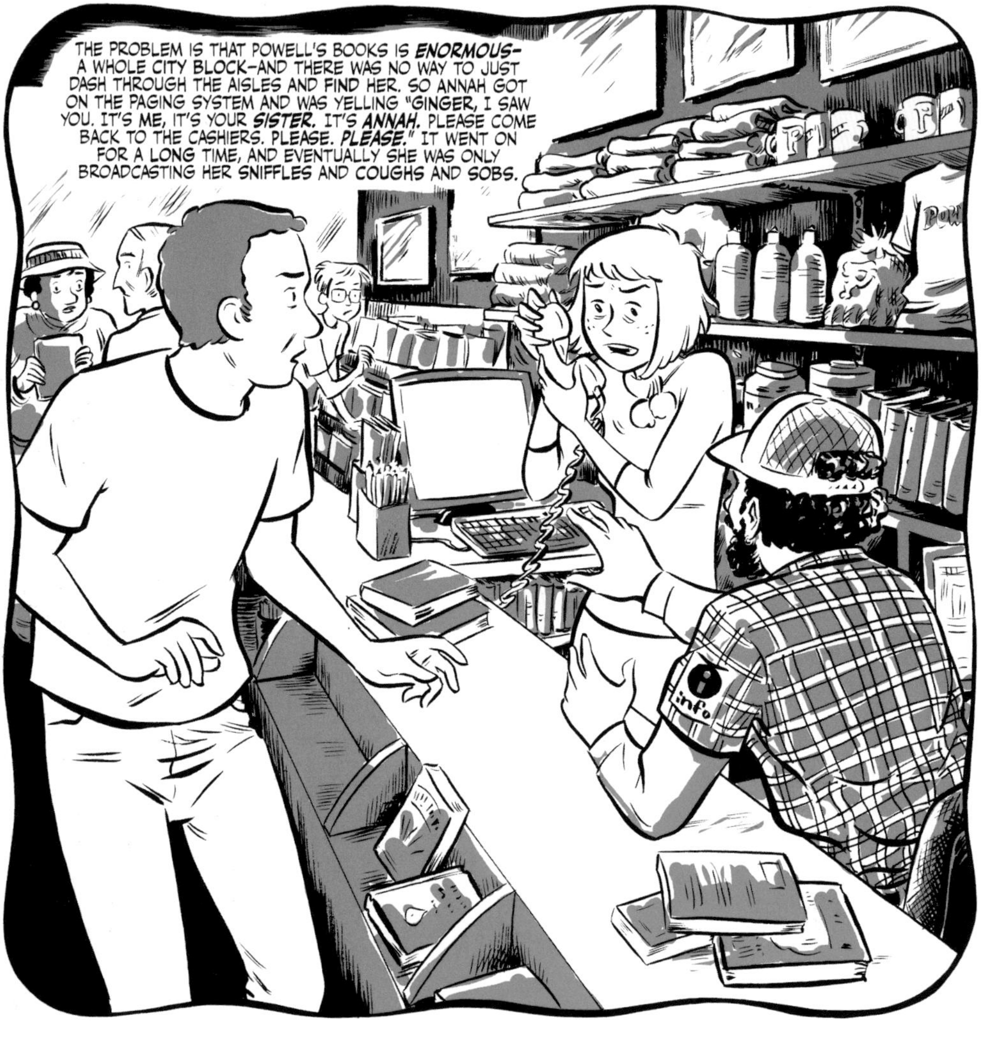
THE PROBLEM IS THAT POWELL'S BOOKS IS ***ENORMOUS***– A WHOLE CITY BLOCK–AND THERE WAS NO WAY TO JUST DASH THROUGH THE AISLES AND FIND HER. SO ANNAH GOT ON THE PAGING SYSTEM AND WAS YELLING "GINGER, I SAW YOU. IT'S ME, IT'S YOUR ***SISTER.*** IT'S ***ANNAH.*** PLEASE COME BACK TO THE CASHIERS. PLEASE. ***PLEASE.***" IT WENT ON FOR A LONG TIME, AND EVENTUALLY SHE WAS ONLY BROADCASTING HER SNIFFLES AND COUGHS AND SOBS.
info

ONE OF THE MANAGERS LED HER AWAY AND SHE WAS ALMOST FIRED.

ONCE ANNAH WAS GONE, I STOOD NEAR THE EXIT AND WAITED FOR THE GIRL WE'D SEEN, VERY CONSCIOUSLY AWARE THAT THERE WAS ANOTHER EXIT ON THE OTHER SIDE OF THE BLOCK.

BUT IT DIDN'T TAKE LONG BEFORE THE GIRL WAS BACK. HER OWN COMPOSURE WAS VERY BAD, LIKE SHE'D BEEN CRYING, AND SHE HURRIED OUT OF THE STORE.

I COULD HAVE STOPPED HER, BUT I DIDN'T. AND I'M STILL NOT SURE IF I MADE THE RIGHT OR WRONG CHOICE.

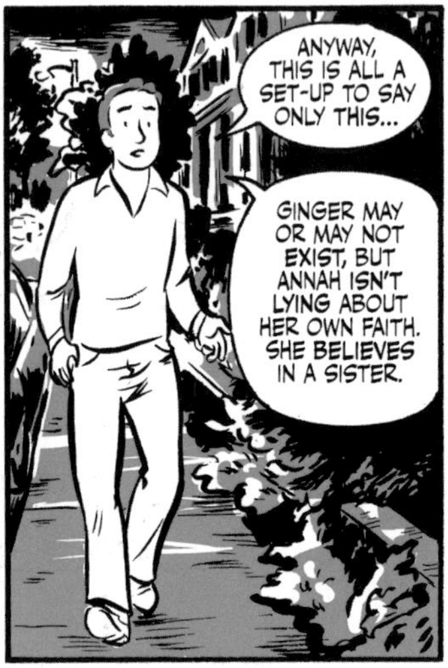
ANYWAY, THIS IS ALL A SET-UP TO SAY ONLY THIS...
GINGER MAY OR MAY NOT EXIST, BUT ANNAH ISN'T LYING ABOUT HER OWN FAITH. SHE BELIEVES IN A SISTER.

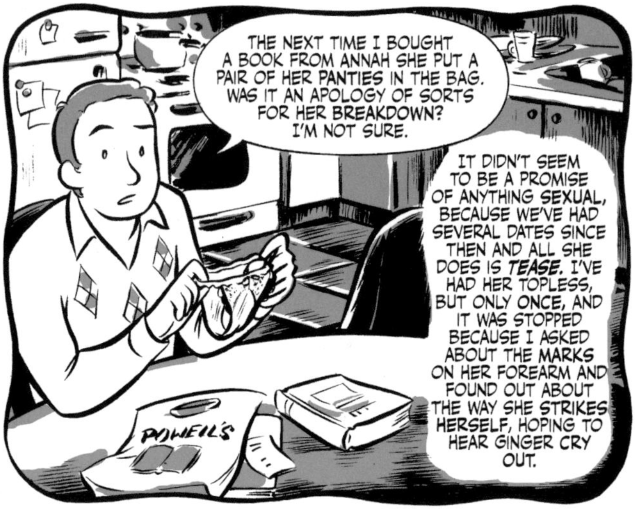
THE NEXT TIME I BOUGHT A BOOK FROM ANNAH SHE PUT A PAIR OF HER PANTIES IN THE BAG. WAS IT AN APOLOGY OF SORTS FOR HER BREAKDOWN? I'M NOT SURE.
IT DIDN'T SEEM TO BE A PROMISE OF ANYTHING SEXUAL, BECAUSE WE'VE HAD SEVERAL DATES SINCE THEN AND ALL SHE DOES IS TEASE. I'VE HAD HER TOPLESS, BUT ONLY ONCE, AND IT WAS STOPPED BECAUSE I ASKED ABOUT THE MARKS ON HER FOREARM AND FOUND OUT ABOUT THE WAY SHE STRIKES HERSELF, HOPING TO HEAR GINGER CRY OUT.
POWELL'S

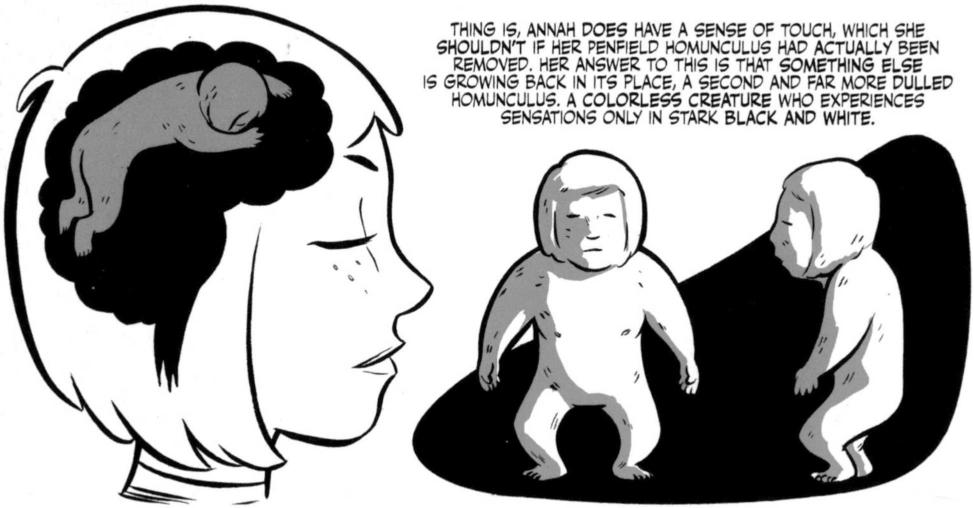
THING IS, ANNAH DOES HAVE A SENSE OF TOUCH, WHICH SHE SHOULDN'T IF HER PENFIELD HOMUNCULUS HAD ACTUALLY BEEN REMOVED. HER ANSWER TO THIS IS THAT SOMETHING ELSE IS GROWING BACK IN ITS PLACE, A SECOND AND FAR MORE DULLED HOMUNCULUS. A COLORLESS CREATURE WHO EXPERIENCES SENSATIONS ONLY IN STARK BLACK AND WHITE.

I'M DATING A CRAZY WOMAN. BUT I CAN'T STOP.
GOOD EVENING.
PUB
NO MINORS UNDER 21
THIS POINT
FIRST, BEFORE I BEGIN, A QUESTION. WHEN DATING A CRAZY PERSON, BUT FACED WITH AN INABILITY TO STOP, DOES THAT MEAN YOU'RE CRAZY, TOO?
NO, DON'T ANSWER. IT'S TOO REVEALING A QUESTION.
WE ALL FEEL OUR LOVERS ARE MODERATELY INSANE, AT MINIMUM, AND WITNESSES SHOULD NOT HAVE TO INCRIMINATE THEMSELVES.

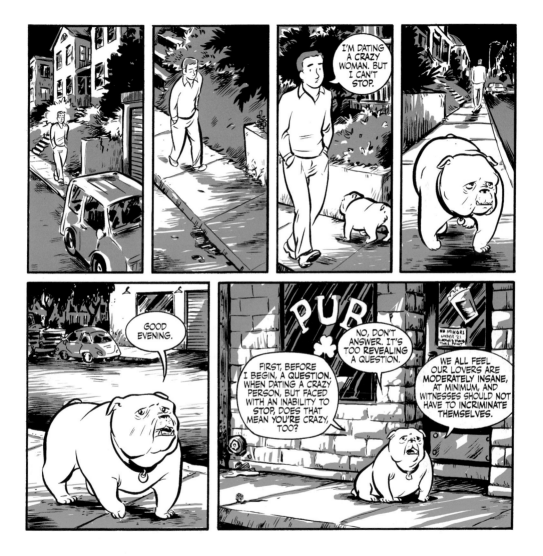

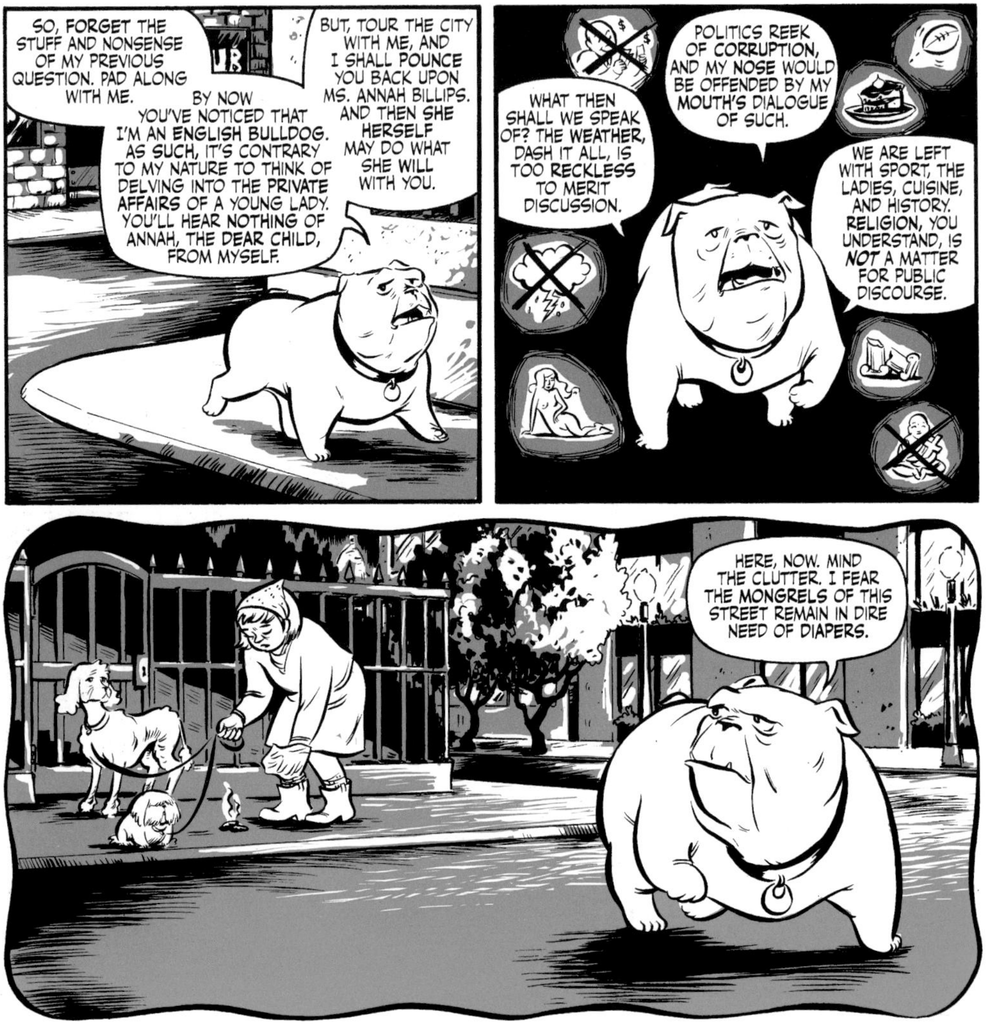
SO, FORGET THE STUFF AND NONSENSE OF MY PREVIOUS QUESTION. PAD ALONG WITH ME.
BY NOW YOU'VE NOTICED THAT I'M AN ENGLISH BULLDOG. AS SUCH, IT'S CONTRARY TO MY NATURE TO THINK OF DELVING INTO THE PRIVATE AFFAIRS OF A YOUNG LADY. YOU'LL HEAR NOTHING OF ANNAH, THE DEAR CHILD, FROM MYSELF.
BUT, TOUR THE CITY WITH ME, AND I SHALL POUNCE YOU BACK UPON MS. ANNAH BILLIPS. AND THEN SHE HERSELF MAY DO WHAT SHE WILL WITH YOU.
POLITICS REEK OF CORRUPTION, AND MY NOSE WOULD BE OFFENDED BY MY MOUTH'S DIALOGUE OF SUCH.
WHAT THEN SHALL WE SPEAK OF? THE WEATHER, DASH IT ALL, IS TOO RECKLESS TO MERIT DISCUSSION.
WE ARE LEFT WITH SPORT, THE LADIES, CUISINE, AND HISTORY. RELIGION, YOU UNDERSTAND, IS NOT A MATTER FOR PUBLIC DISCOURSE.
HERE, NOW. MIND THE CLUTTER. I FEAR THE MONGRELS OF THIS STREET REMAIN IN DIRE NEED OF DIAPERS.

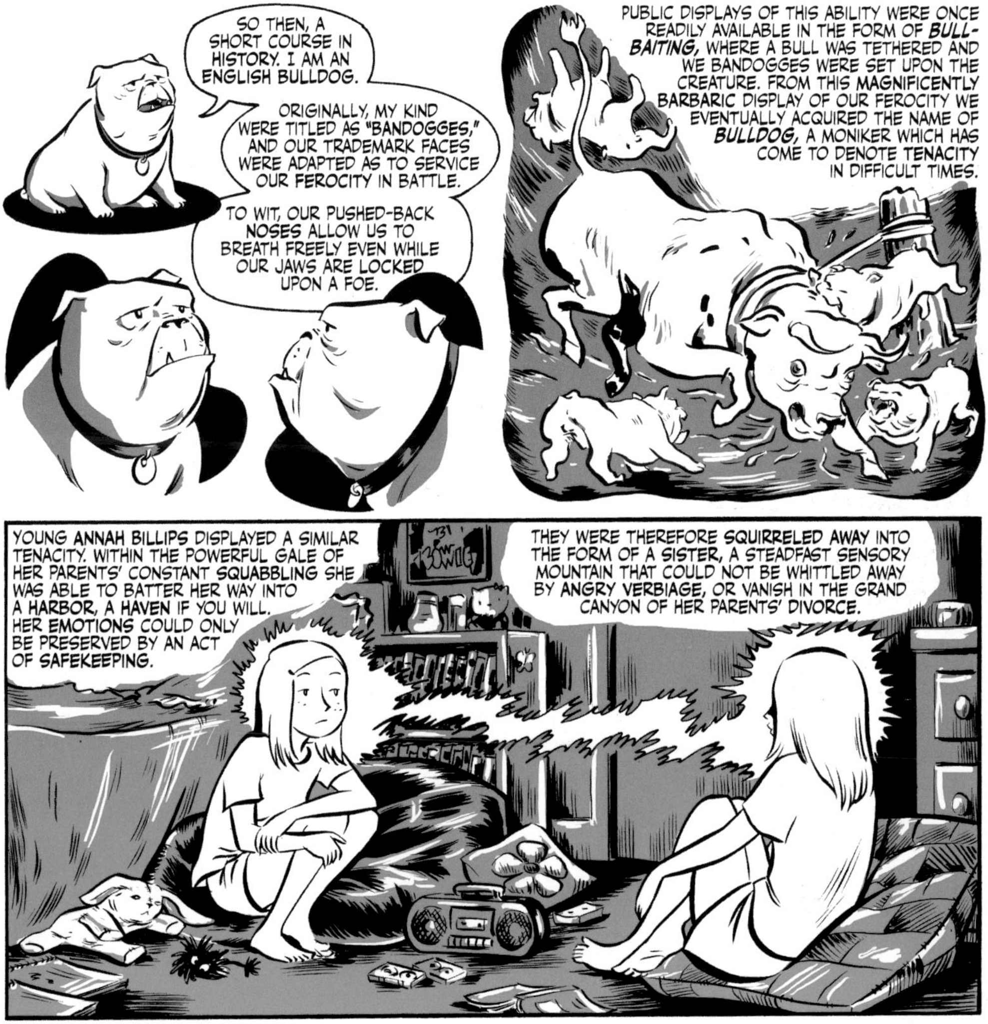
SO THEN, A SHORT COURSE IN HISTORY. I AM AN ENGLISH BULLDOG.
ORIGINALLY, MY KIND WERE TITLED AS "BANDOGGES," AND OUR TRADEMARK FACES WERE ADAPTED AS TO SERVICE OUR FEROCITY IN BATTLE.
TO WIT, OUR PUSHED-BACK NOSES ALLOW US TO BREATH FREELY EVEN WHILE OUR JAWS ARE LOCKED UPON A FOE.
PUBLIC DISPLAYS OF THIS ABILITY WERE ONCE READILY AVAILABLE IN THE FORM OF BULL-BAITING, WHERE A BULL WAS TETHERED AND WE BANDOGGES WERE SET UPON THE CREATURE. FROM THIS MAGNIFICENTLY BARBARIC DISPLAY OF OUR FEROCITY WE EVENTUALLY ACQUIRED THE NAME OF BULLDOG, A MONIKER WHICH HAS COME TO DENOTE TENACITY IN DIFFICULT TIMES.
YOUNG ANNAH BILLIPS DISPLAYED A SIMILAR TENACITY. WITHIN THE POWERFUL GALE OF HER PARENTS' CONSTANT SQUABBLING SHE WAS ABLE TO BATTER HER WAY INTO A HARBOR, A HAVEN IF YOU WILL. HER EMOTIONS COULD ONLY BE PRESERVED BY AN ACT OF SAFEKEEPING.
THEY WERE THEREFORE SQUIRRELED AWAY INTO THE FORM OF A SISTER, A STEADFAST SENSORY MOUNTAIN THAT COULD NOT BE WHITTLED AWAY BY ANGRY VERBIAGE, OR VANISH IN THE GRAND CANYON OF HER PARENTS' DIVORCE.

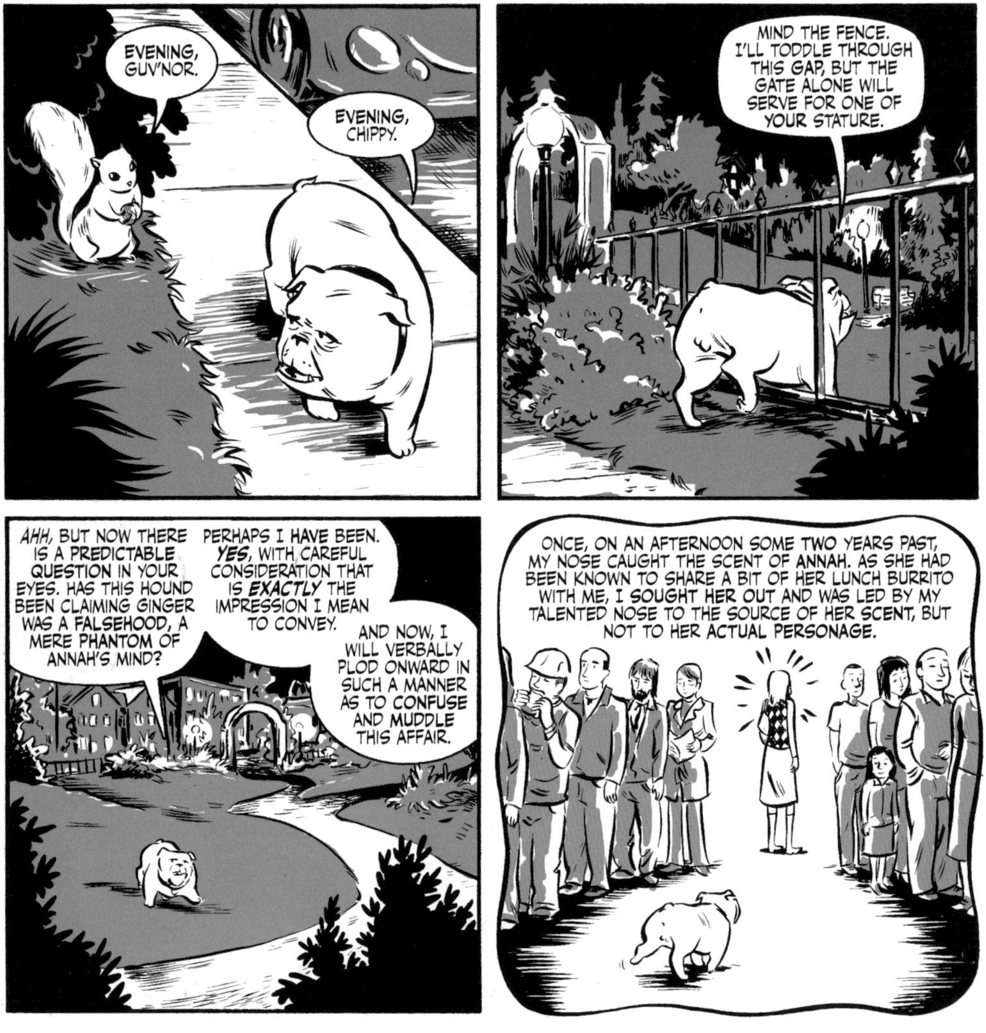
EVENING, GUV'NOR.
EVENING, CHIPPY.
MIND THE FENCE. I'LL TODDLE THROUGH THIS GAP, BUT THE GATE ALONE WILL SERVE FOR ONE OF YOUR STATURE.
AHH, BUT NOW THERE IS A PREDICTABLE QUESTION IN YOUR EYES. HAS THIS HOUND BEEN CLAIMING GINGER WAS A FALSEHOOD, A MERE PHANTOM OF ANNAH'S MIND?
PERHAPS I HAVE BEEN. YES, WITH CAREFUL CONSIDERATION THAT IS EXACTLY THE IMPRESSION I MEAN TO CONVEY.
AND NOW, I WILL VERBALLY PLOD ONWARD IN SUCH A MANNER AS TO CONFUSE AND MUDDLE THIS AFFAIR.
ONCE, ON AN AFTERNOON SOME TWO YEARS PAST, MY NOSE CAUGHT THE SCENT OF ANNAH. AS SHE HAD BEEN KNOWN TO SHARE A BIT OF HER LUNCH BURRITO WITH ME, I SOUGHT HER OUT AND WAS LED BY MY TALENTED NOSE TO THE SOURCE OF HER SCENT, BUT NOT TO HER ACTUAL PERSONAGE.

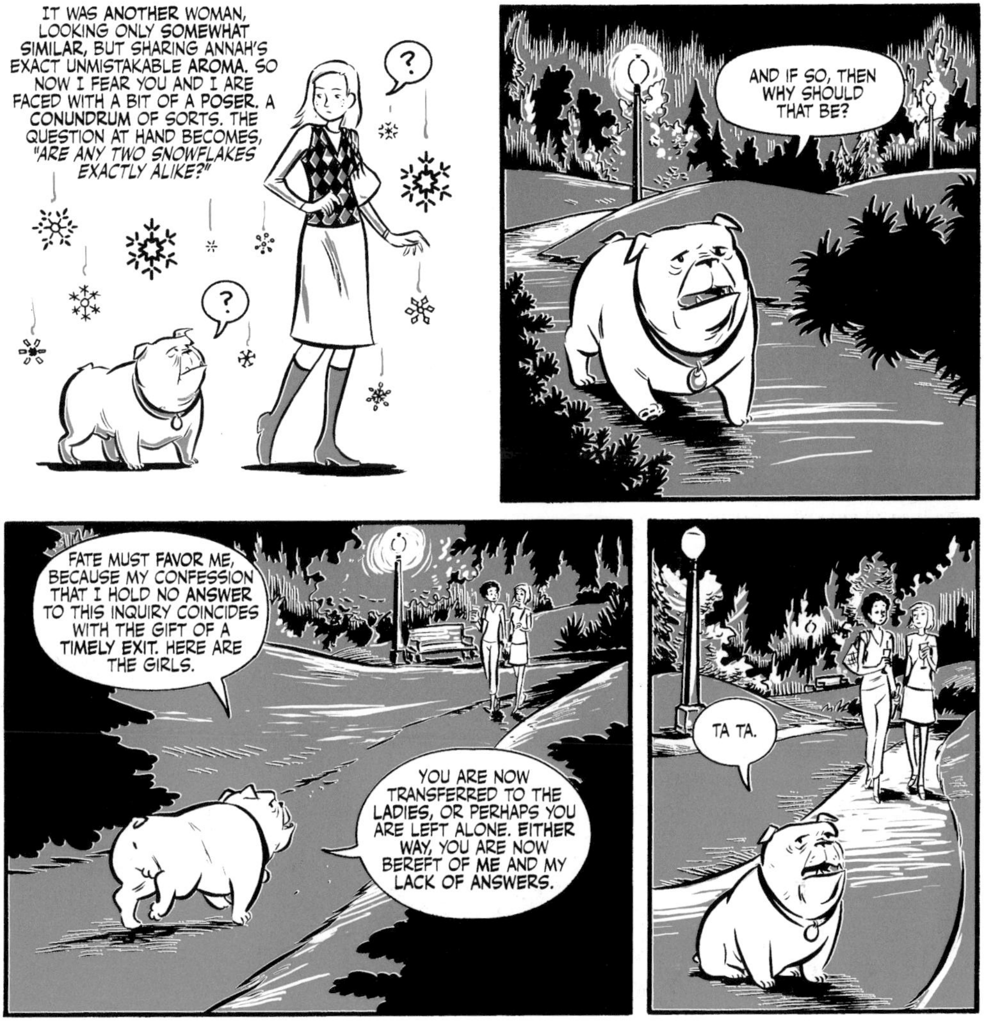
IT WAS **ANOTHER** WOMAN, LOOKING ONLY **SOMEWHAT SIMILAR**, BUT SHARING ANNAH'S EXACT UNMISTAKABLE **AROMA**. SO NOW I FEAR YOU AND I ARE FACED WITH A BIT OF A **POSER**. A **CONUNDRUM** OF SORTS. THE QUESTION AT HAND BECOMES, *"ARE ANY TWO SNOWFLAKES EXACTLY ALIKE?"*
?
?
AND IF SO, THEN WHY SHOULD THAT BE?
FATE MUST FAVOR ME, BECAUSE MY CONFESSION THAT I HOLD NO **ANSWER** TO THIS INQUIRY COINCIDES WITH THE GIFT OF A **TIMELY EXIT**. HERE ARE THE GIRLS.
YOU ARE NOW TRANSFERRED TO THE **LADIES**, OR PERHAPS YOU ARE LEFT **ALONE**. EITHER WAY, YOU ARE NOW BEREFT OF **ME** AND MY LACK OF **ANSWERS**.
TA TA.

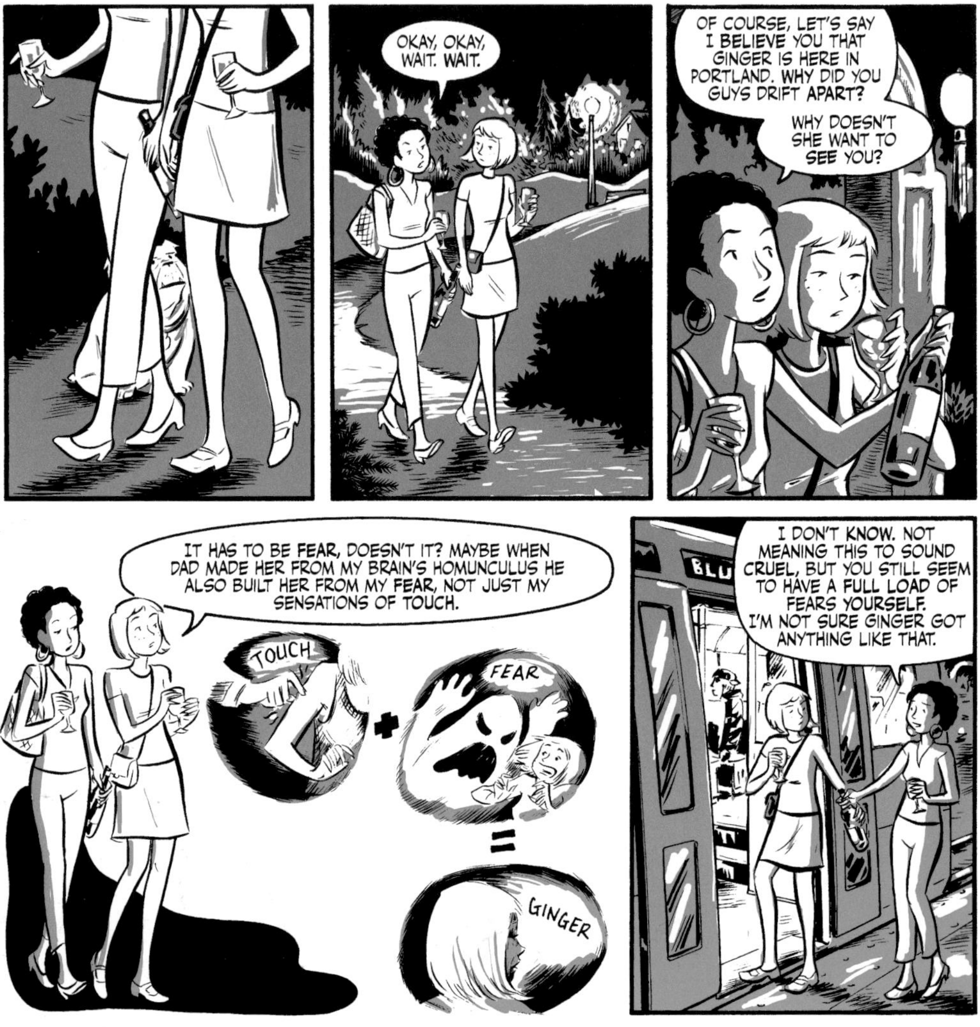
OKAY, OKAY, WAIT. WAIT.
OF COURSE, LET'S SAY I BELIEVE YOU THAT GINGER IS HERE IN PORTLAND. WHY DID YOU GUYS DRIFT APART?
WHY DOESN'T SHE WANT TO SEE YOU?
IT HAS TO BE FEAR, DOESN'T IT? MAYBE WHEN DAD MADE HER FROM MY BRAIN'S HOMUNCULUS HE ALSO BUILT HER FROM MY FEAR, NOT JUST MY SENSATIONS OF TOUCH.
TOUCH
FEAR
GINGER
I DON'T KNOW. NOT MEANING THIS TO SOUND CRUEL, BUT YOU STILL SEEM TO HAVE A FULL LOAD OF FEARS YOURSELF. I'M NOT SURE GINGER GOT ANYTHING LIKE THAT.

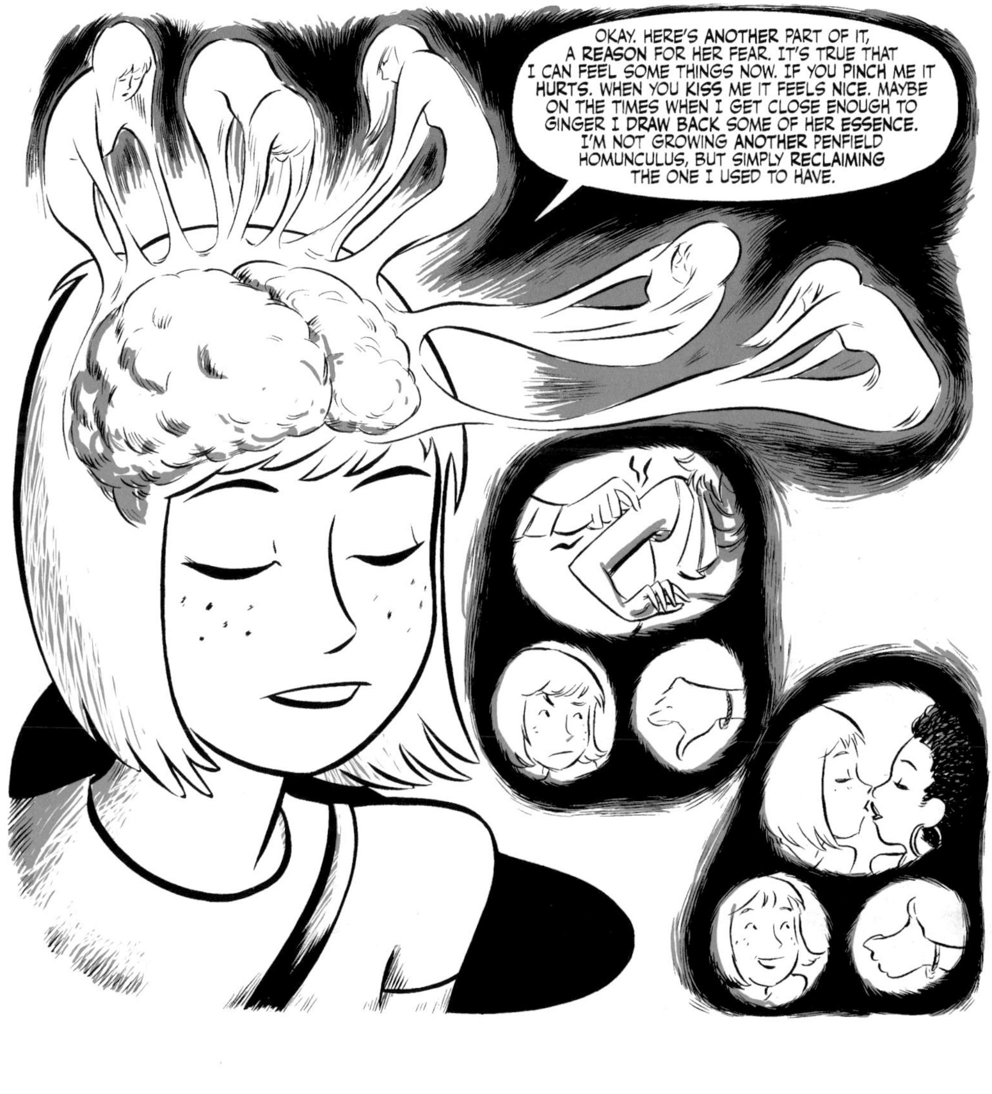
OKAY. HERE'S ANOTHER PART OF IT, A REASON FOR HER FEAR. IT'S TRUE THAT I CAN FEEL SOME THINGS NOW. IF YOU PINCH ME IT HURTS. WHEN YOU KISS ME IT FEELS NICE. MAYBE ON THE TIMES WHEN I GET CLOSE ENOUGH TO GINGER I DRAW BACK SOME OF HER ESSENCE. I'M NOT GROWING ANOTHER PENFIELD HOMUNCULUS, BUT SIMPLY RECLAIMING THE ONE I USED TO HAVE.

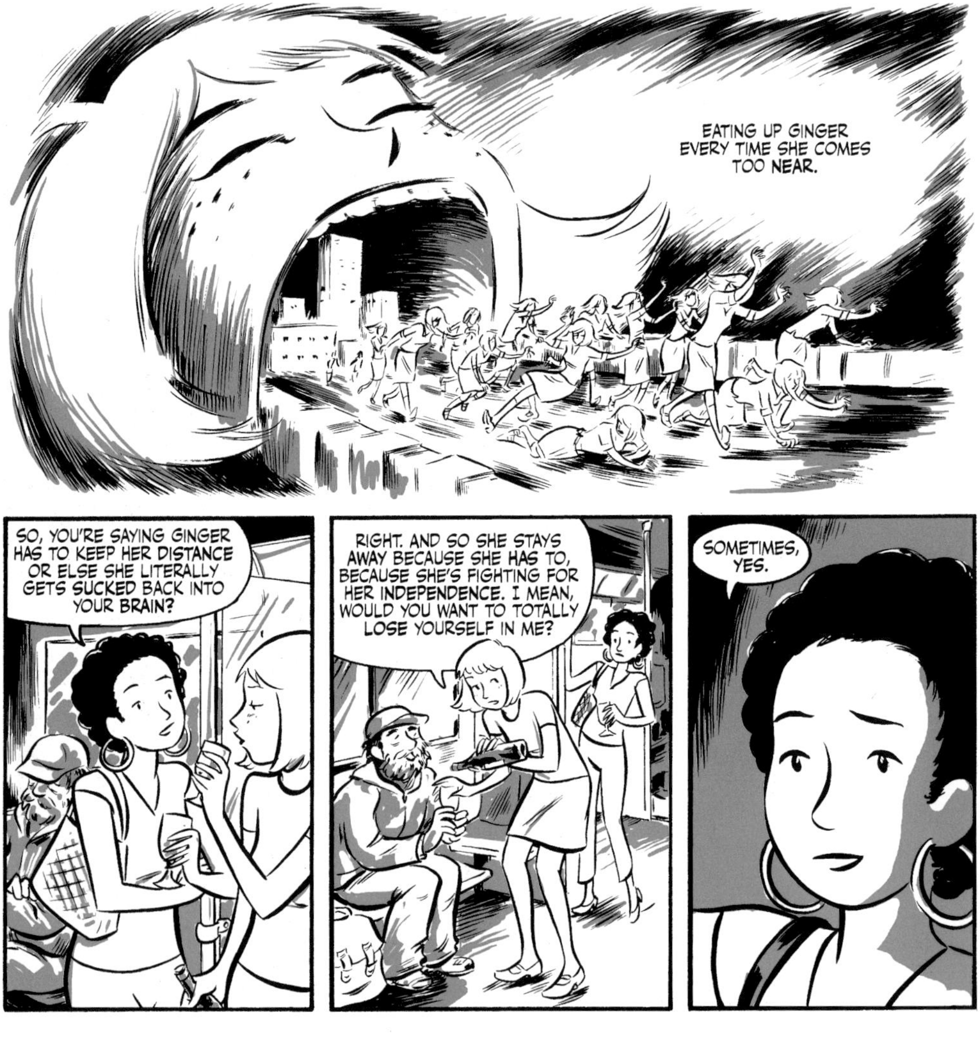
EATING UP GINGER EVERY TIME SHE COMES TOO NEAR.
SO, YOU'RE SAYING GINGER HAS TO KEEP HER DISTANCE OR ELSE SHE LITERALLY GETS SUCKED BACK INTO YOUR BRAIN?
RIGHT. AND SO SHE STAYS AWAY BECAUSE SHE HAS TO, BECAUSE SHE'S FIGHTING FOR HER INDEPENDENCE. I MEAN, WOULD YOU WANT TO TOTALLY LOSE YOURSELF IN ME?
SOMETIMES, YES.

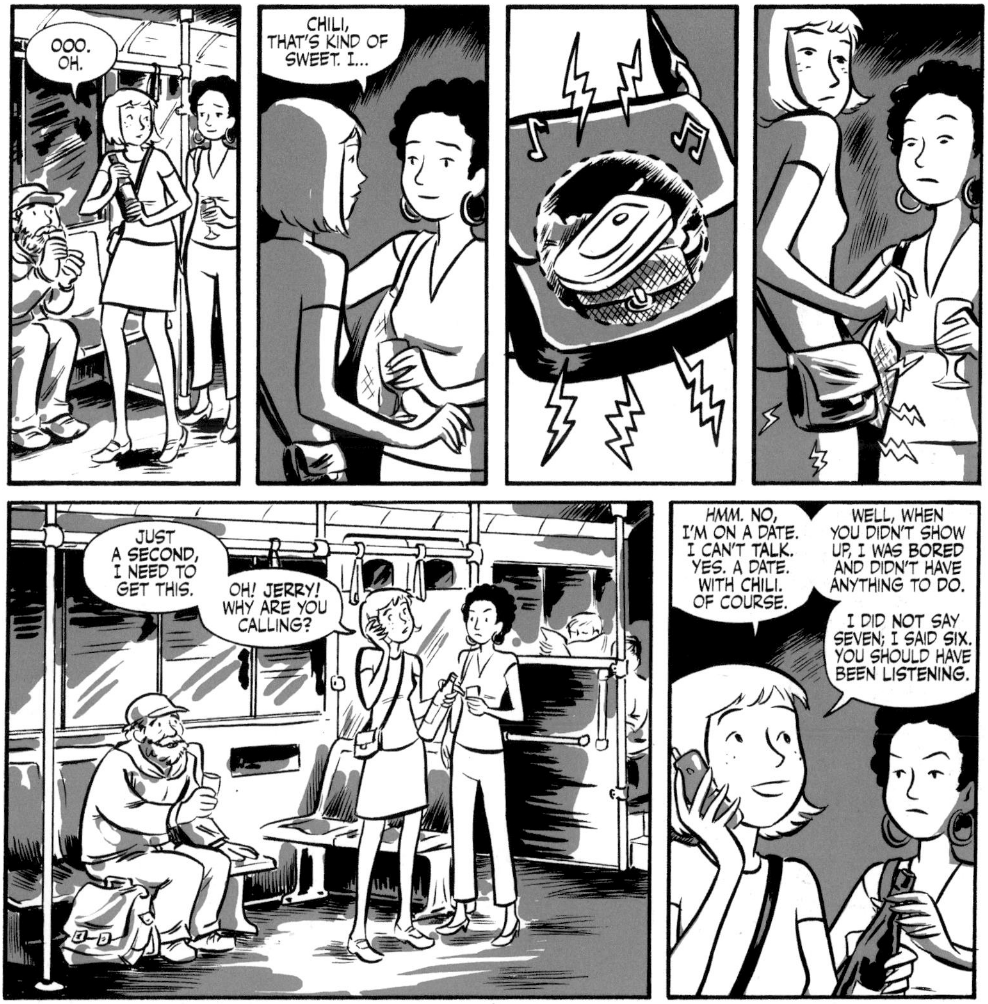
OOO. OH.
CHILI, THAT'S KIND OF SWEET. I...
JUST A SECOND, I NEED TO GET THIS.
OH! JERRY! WHY ARE YOU CALLING?
HMM. NO, I'M ON A DATE. I CAN'T TALK. YES. A DATE. WITH CHILI. OF COURSE.
WELL, WHEN YOU DIDN'T SHOW UP, I WAS BORED AND DIDN'T HAVE ANYTHING TO DO.
I DID NOT SAY SEVEN; I SAID SIX. YOU SHOULD HAVE BEEN LISTENING.

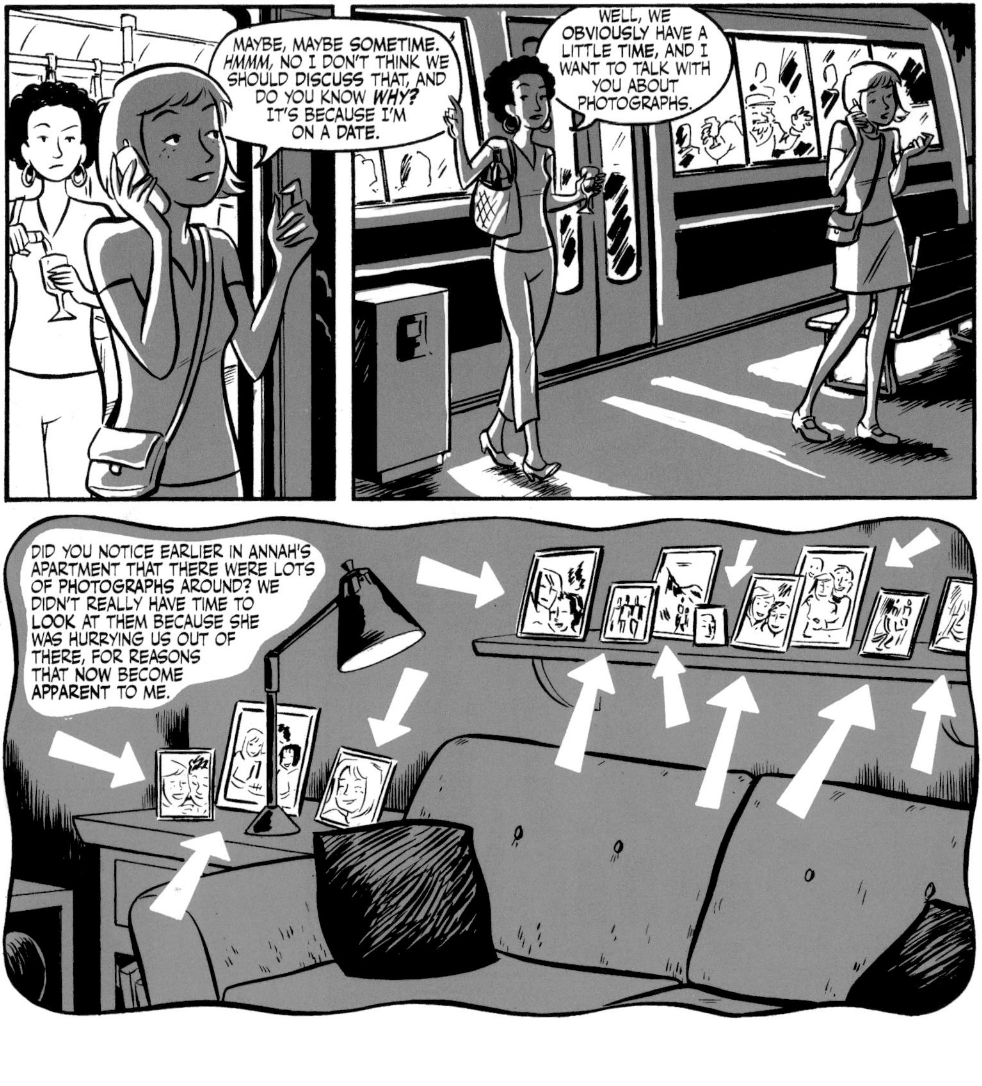
MAYBE, MAYBE SOMETIME. HMMM, NO I DON'T THINK WE SHOULD DISCUSS THAT, AND DO YOU KNOW WHY? IT'S BECAUSE I'M ON A DATE.
WELL, WE OBVIOUSLY HAVE A LITTLE TIME, AND I WANT TO TALK WITH YOU ABOUT PHOTOGRAPHS.
DID YOU NOTICE EARLIER IN ANNAH'S APARTMENT THAT THERE WERE LOTS OF PHOTOGRAPHS AROUND? WE DIDN'T REALLY HAVE TIME TO LOOK AT THEM BECAUSE SHE WAS HURRYING US OUT OF THERE, FOR REASONS THAT NOW BECOME APPARENT TO ME.

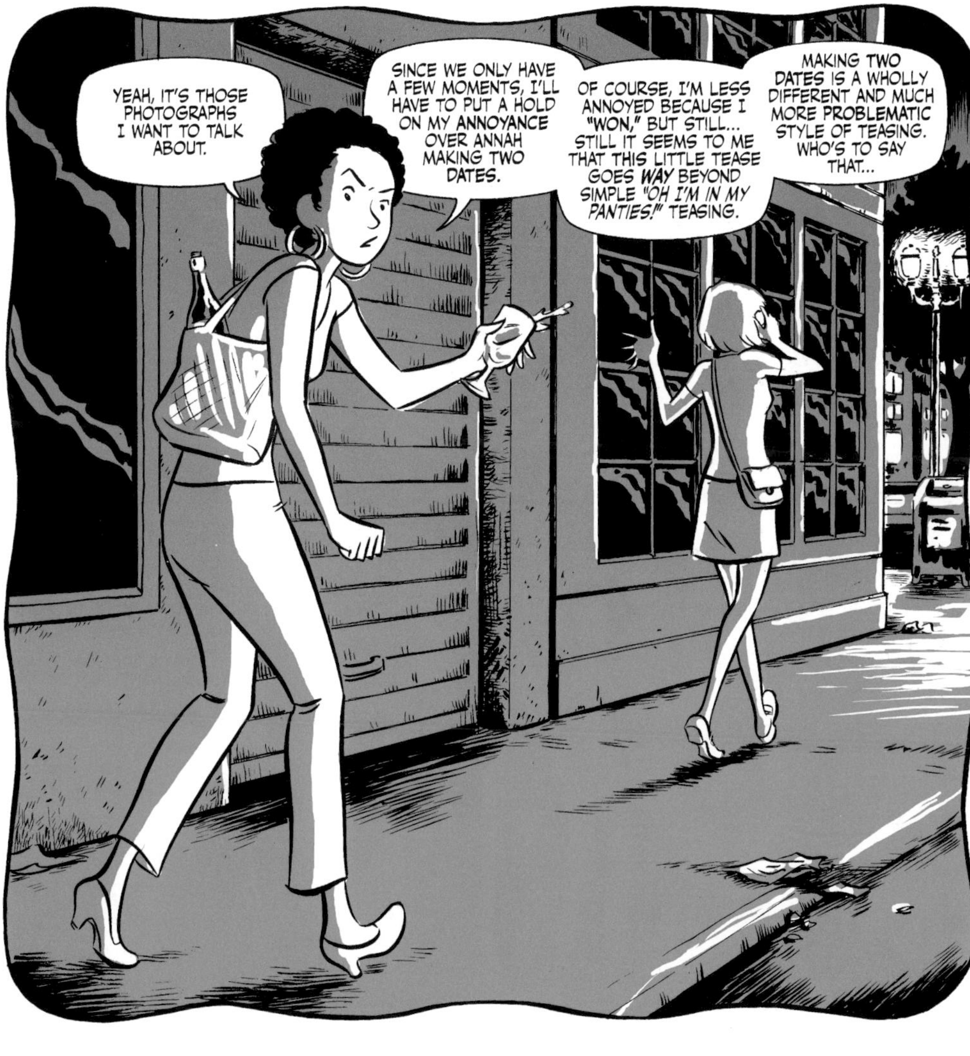
YEAH, IT'S THOSE PHOTOGRAPHS I WANT TO TALK ABOUT.
SINCE WE ONLY HAVE A FEW MOMENTS, I'LL HAVE TO PUT A HOLD ON MY **ANNOYANCE** OVER ANNAH MAKING TWO **DATES.**
OF COURSE, I'M LESS ANNOYED BECAUSE I **"WON,"** BUT STILL... STILL IT SEEMS TO ME THAT THIS LITTLE TEASE GOES ***WAY*** BEYOND SIMPLE *"OH I'M IN MY PANTIES!"* TEASING.
MAKING **TWO** DATES IS A WHOLLY DIFFERENT AND MUCH MORE **PROBLEMATIC** STYLE OF TEASING. WHO'S TO SAY THAT...

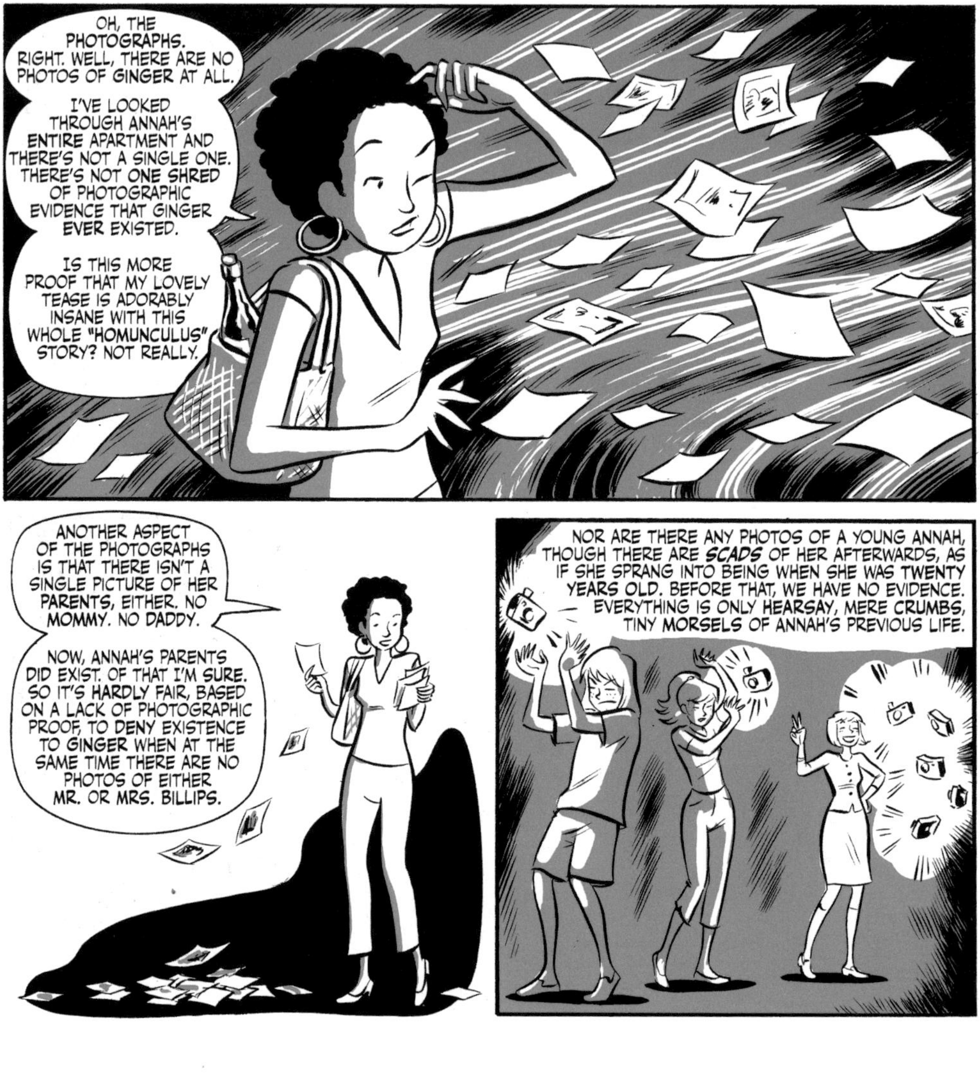
OH, THE PHOTOGRAPHS. RIGHT. WELL, THERE ARE NO PHOTOS OF GINGER AT ALL.
I'VE LOOKED THROUGH ANNAH'S ENTIRE APARTMENT AND THERE'S NOT A SINGLE ONE. THERE'S NOT ONE SHRED OF PHOTOGRAPHIC EVIDENCE THAT GINGER EVER EXISTED.
IS THIS MORE PROOF THAT MY LOVELY TEASE IS ADORABLY INSANE WITH THIS WHOLE "HOMUNCULUS" STORY? NOT REALLY.
ANOTHER ASPECT OF THE PHOTOGRAPHS IS THAT THERE ISN'T A SINGLE PICTURE OF HER PARENTS, EITHER. NO MOMMY. NO DADDY.
NOW, ANNAH'S PARENTS DID EXIST. OF THAT I'M SURE. SO IT'S HARDLY FAIR, BASED ON A LACK OF PHOTOGRAPHIC PROOF, TO DENY EXISTENCE TO GINGER WHEN AT THE SAME TIME THERE ARE NO PHOTOS OF EITHER MR. OR MRS. BILLIPS.
NOR ARE THERE ANY PHOTOS OF A YOUNG ANNAH, THOUGH THERE ARE *SCADS* OF HER AFTERWARDS, AS IF SHE SPRANG INTO BEING WHEN SHE WAS TWENTY YEARS OLD. BEFORE THAT, WE HAVE NO EVIDENCE. EVERYTHING IS ONLY HEARSAY, MERE CRUMBS, TINY MORSELS OF ANNAH'S PREVIOUS LIFE.

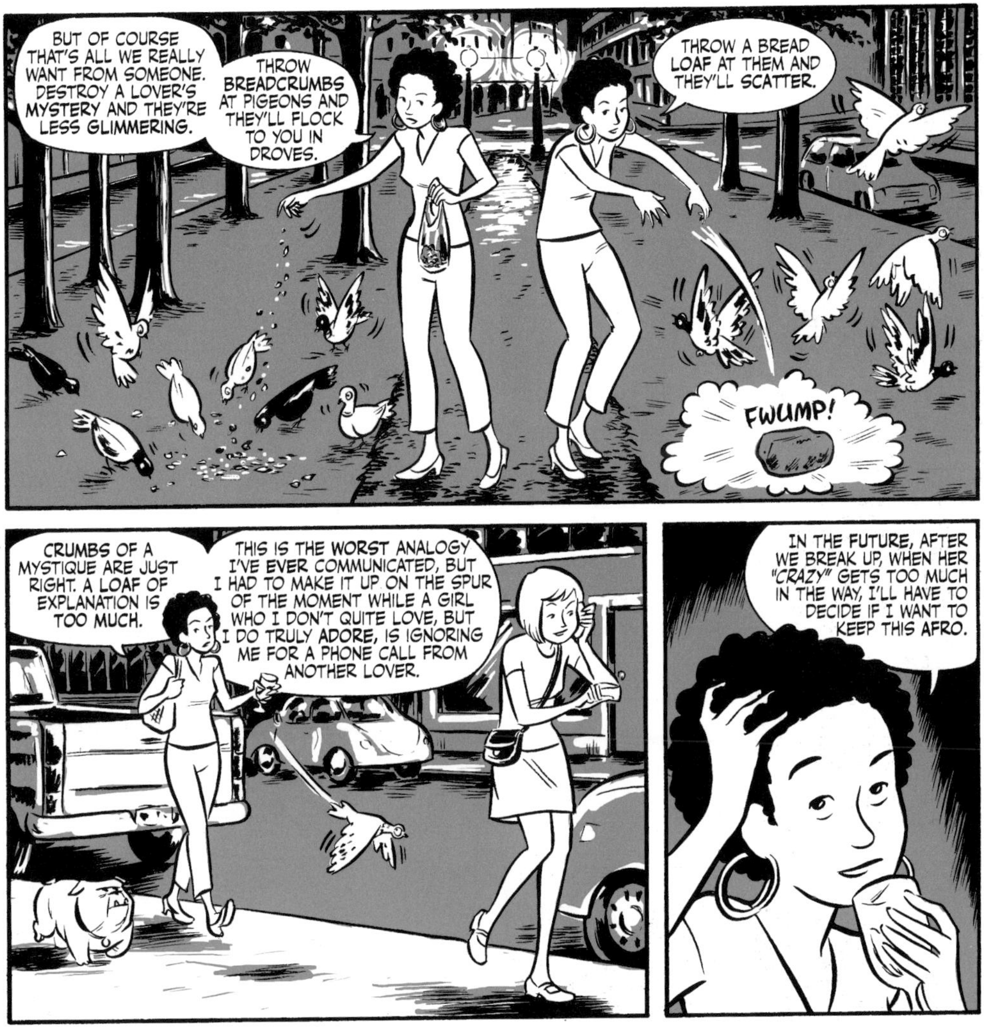
BUT OF COURSE THAT'S ALL WE REALLY WANT FROM SOMEONE. DESTROY A LOVER'S MYSTERY AND THEY'RE LESS GLIMMERING.
THROW BREADCRUMBS AT PIGEONS AND THEY'LL FLOCK TO YOU IN DROVES.
THROW A BREAD LOAF AT THEM AND THEY'LL SCATTER.
FWUMP!
CRUMBS OF A MYSTIQUE ARE JUST RIGHT. A LOAF OF EXPLANATION IS TOO MUCH.
THIS IS THE WORST ANALOGY I'VE EVER COMMUNICATED, BUT I HAD TO MAKE IT UP ON THE SPUR OF THE MOMENT WHILE A GIRL WHO I DON'T QUITE LOVE, BUT I DO TRULY ADORE, IS IGNORING ME FOR A PHONE CALL FROM ANOTHER LOVER.
IN THE FUTURE, AFTER WE BREAK UP, WHEN HER "CRAZY" GETS TOO MUCH IN THE WAY, I'LL HAVE TO DECIDE IF I WANT TO KEEP THIS AFRO.

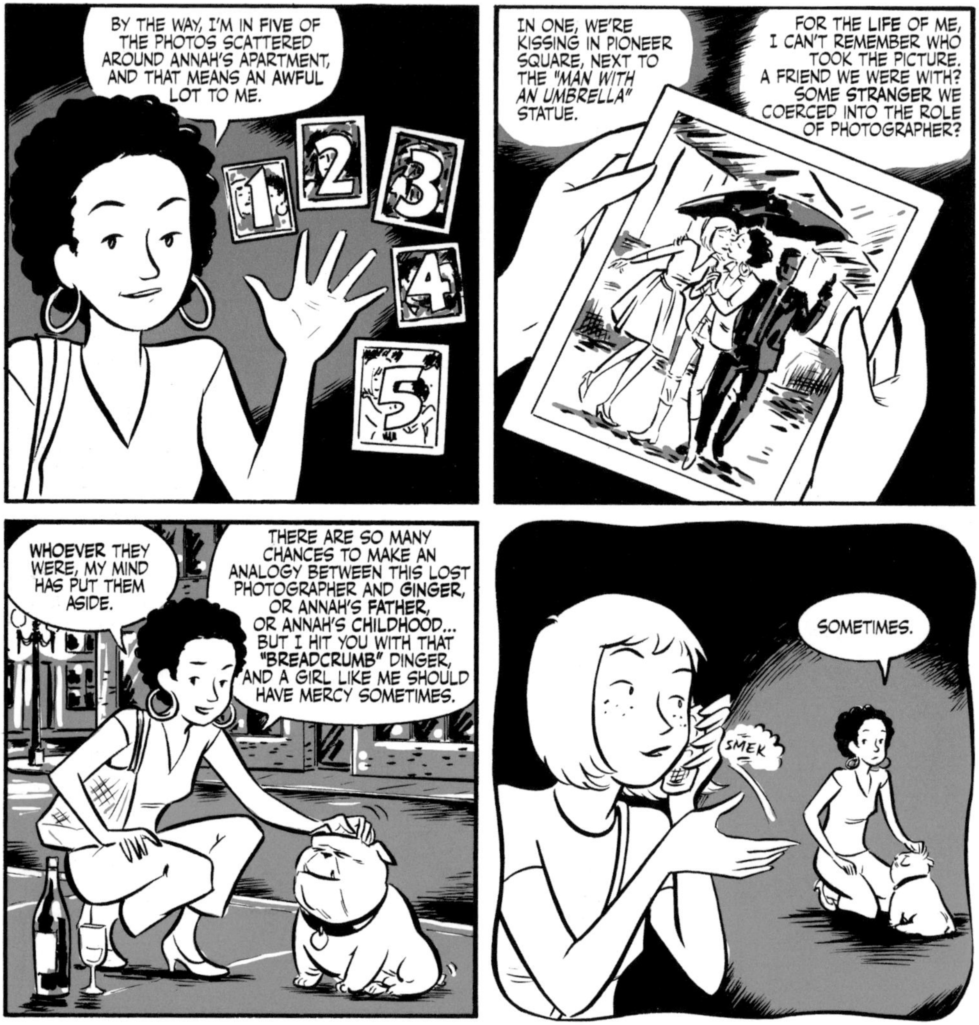
BY THE WAY, I'M IN FIVE OF THE PHOTOS SCATTERED AROUND ANNAH'S APARTMENT, AND THAT MEANS AN AWFUL LOT TO ME.
1
2
3
4
5
IN ONE, WE'RE KISSING IN PIONEER SQUARE, NEXT TO THE "MAN WITH AN UMBRELLA" STATUE.
FOR THE LIFE OF ME, I CAN'T REMEMBER WHO TOOK THE PICTURE. A FRIEND WE WERE WITH? SOME STRANGER WE COERCED INTO THE ROLE OF PHOTOGRAPHER?
WHOEVER THEY WERE, MY MIND HAS PUT THEM ASIDE.
THERE ARE SO MANY CHANCES TO MAKE AN ANALOGY BETWEEN THIS LOST PHOTOGRAPHER AND GINGER, OR ANNAH'S FATHER, OR ANNAH'S CHILDHOOD... BUT I HIT YOU WITH THAT "BREADCRUMB" DINGER, AND A GIRL LIKE ME SHOULD HAVE MERCY SOMETIMES.
SOMETIMES.
SMEK

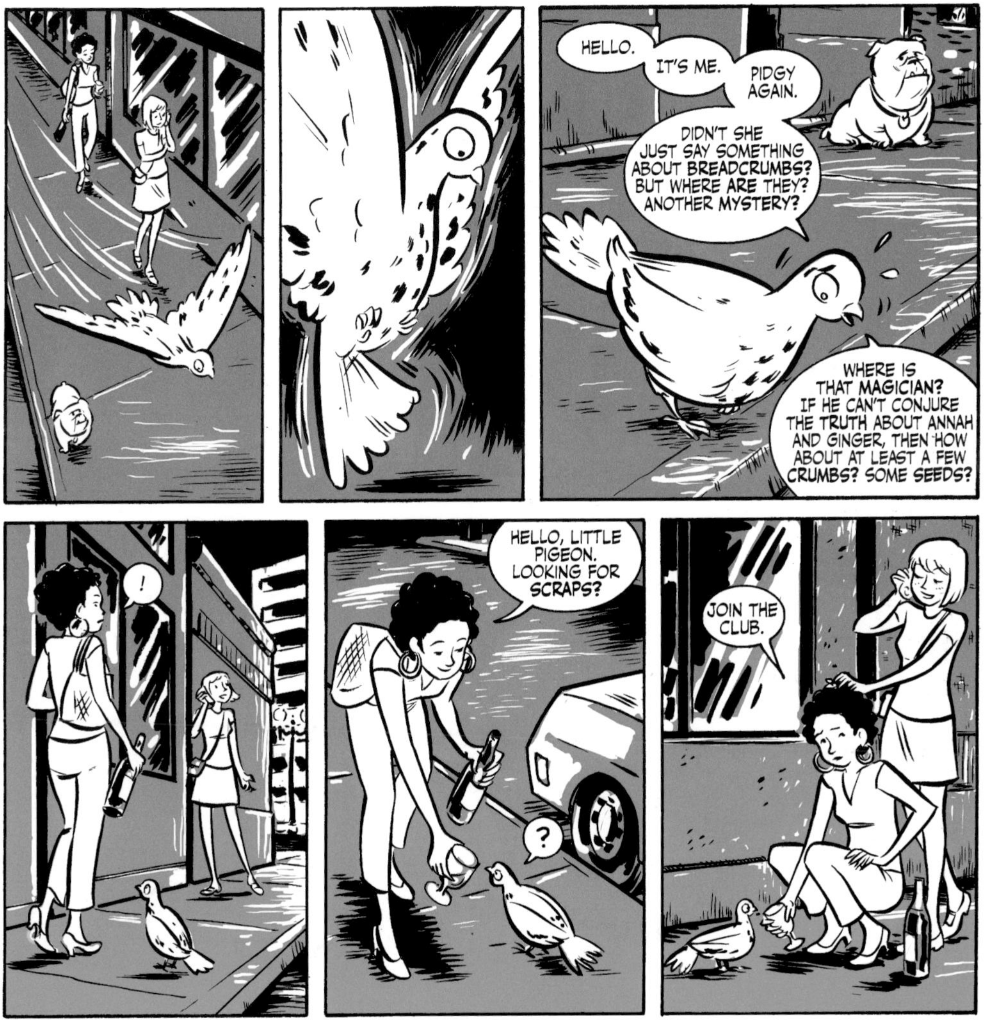
HELLO.
IT'S ME.
PIDGY AGAIN.
DIDN'T SHE JUST SAY SOMETHING ABOUT BREADCRUMBS? BUT WHERE ARE THEY? ANOTHER MYSTERY?
WHERE IS THAT MAGICIAN? IF HE CAN'T CONJURE THE TRUTH ABOUT ANNAH AND GINGER, THEN HOW ABOUT AT LEAST A FEW CRUMBS? SOME SEEDS?
!
HELLO, LITTLE PIGEON. LOOKING FOR SCRAPS?
?
JOIN THE CLUB.

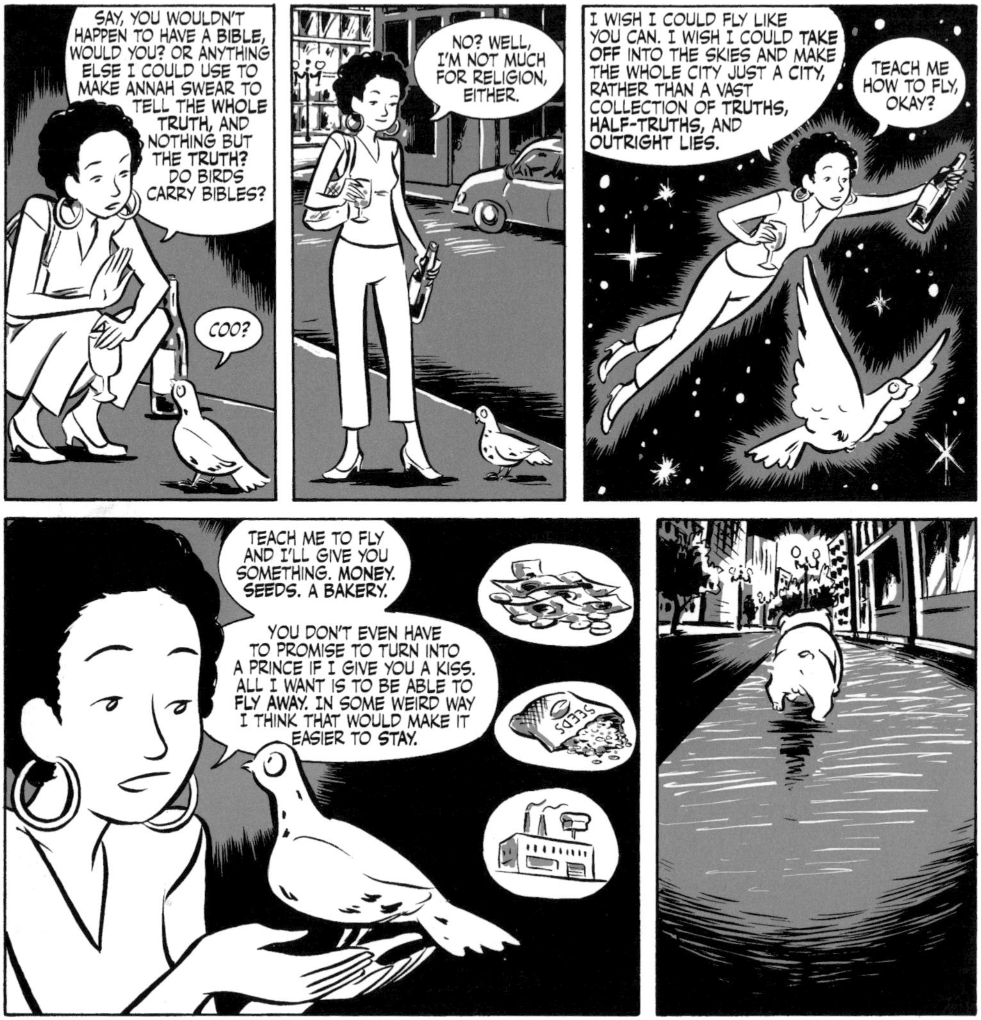
SAY, YOU WOULDN'T HAPPEN TO HAVE A BIBLE, WOULD YOU? OR ANYTHING ELSE I COULD USE TO MAKE ANNAH SWEAR TO TELL THE WHOLE TRUTH, AND NOTHING BUT THE TRUTH? DO BIRDS CARRY BIBLES?
COO?
NO? WELL, I'M NOT MUCH FOR RELIGION, EITHER.
I WISH I COULD FLY LIKE YOU CAN. I WISH I COULD TAKE OFF INTO THE SKIES AND MAKE THE WHOLE CITY JUST A CITY, RATHER THAN A VAST COLLECTION OF TRUTHS, HALF-TRUTHS, AND OUTRIGHT LIES.
TEACH ME HOW TO FLY, OKAY?
TEACH ME TO FLY AND I'LL GIVE YOU SOMETHING. MONEY. SEEDS. A BAKERY.
YOU DON'T EVEN HAVE TO PROMISE TO TURN INTO A PRINCE IF I GIVE YOU A KISS. ALL I WANT IS TO BE ABLE TO FLY AWAY. IN SOME WEIRD WAY I THINK THAT WOULD MAKE IT EASIER TO STAY.
SEEDS

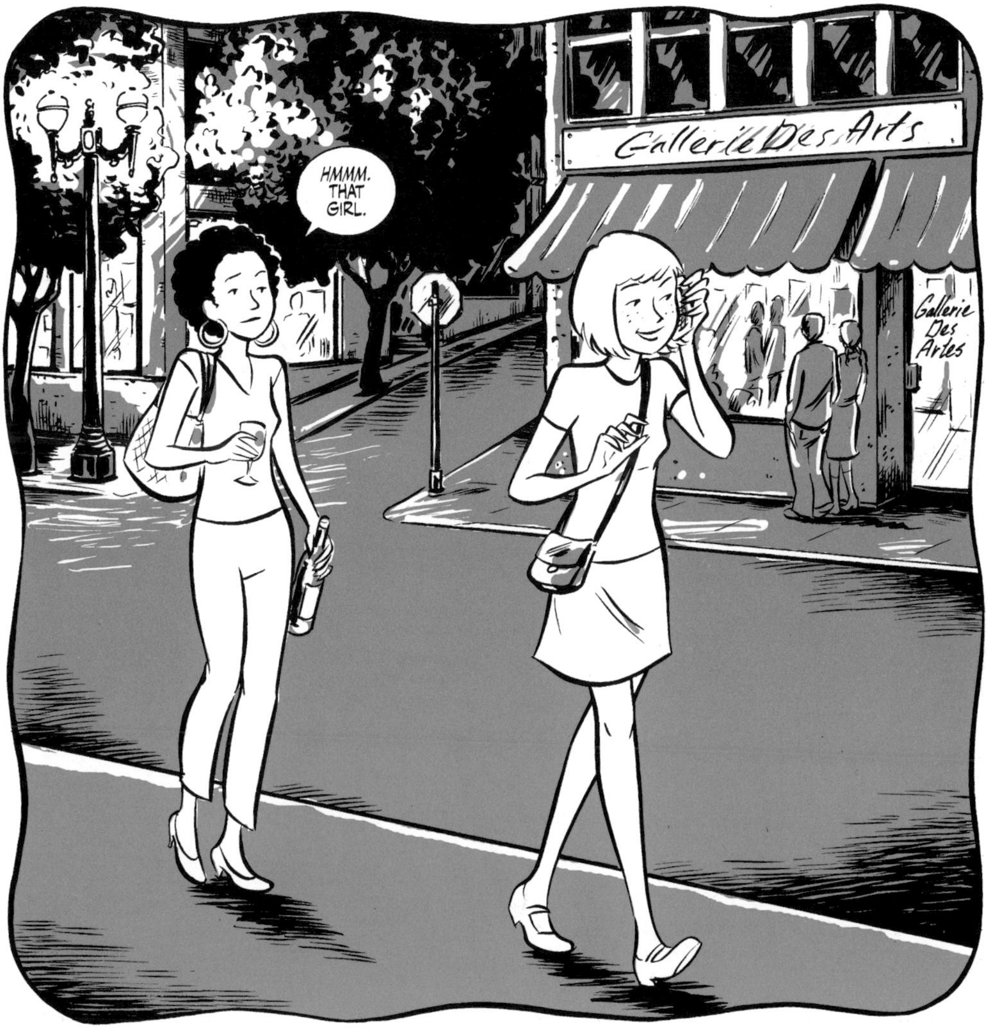
Gallerie Des Arts
HMMM. THAT GIRL.
Gallerie Des Artes

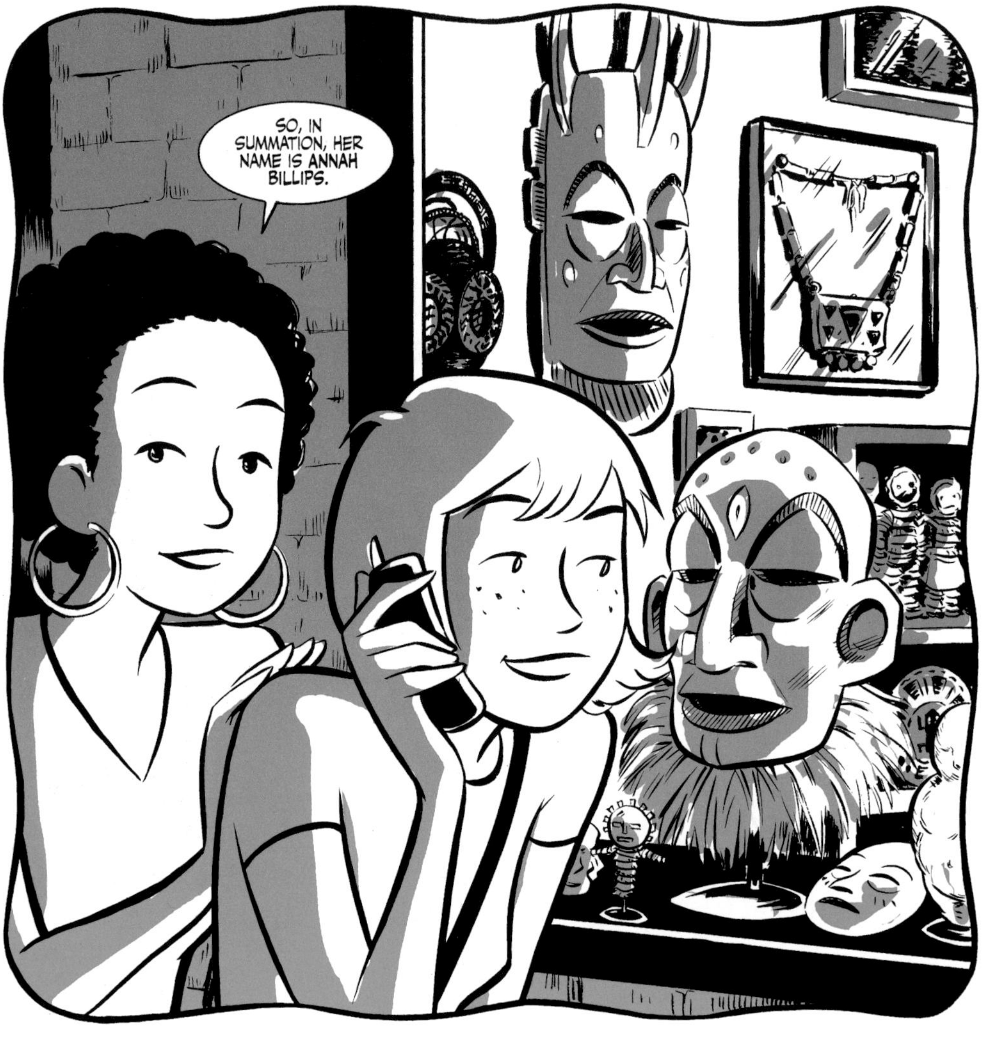
SO, IN SUMMATION, HER NAME IS ANNAH BILLIPS.

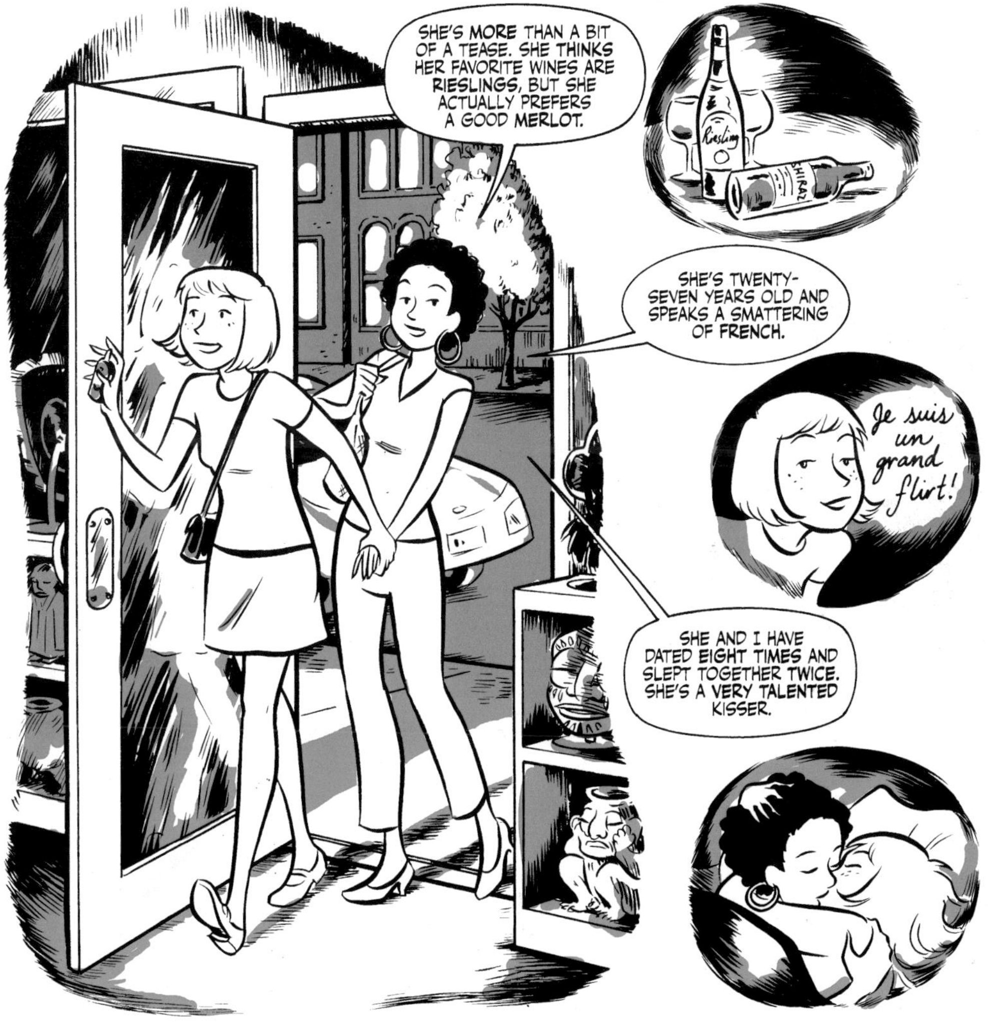
SHE'S MORE THAN A BIT OF A TEASE. SHE THINKS HER FAVORITE WINES ARE RIESLINGS, BUT SHE ACTUALLY PREFERS A GOOD MERLOT.
Riesling
SHIRAZ
SHE'S TWENTY-SEVEN YEARS OLD AND SPEAKS A SMATTERING OF FRENCH.
Je suis un grand flirt!
SHE AND I HAVE DATED EIGHT TIMES AND SLEPT TOGETHER TWICE. SHE'S A VERY TALENTED KISSER.

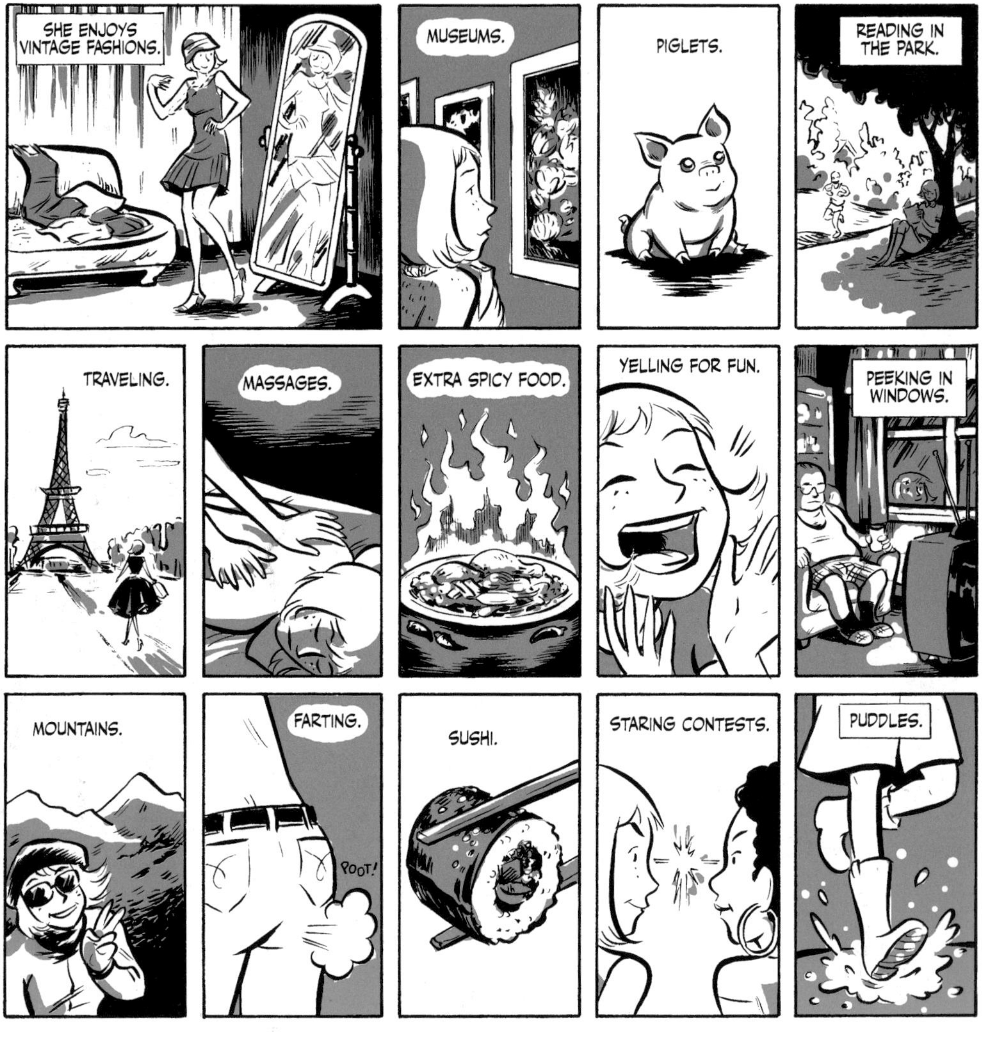
SHE ENJOYS VINTAGE FASHIONS.
MUSEUMS.
PIGLETS.
READING IN THE PARK.
TRAVELING.
MASSAGES.
EXTRA SPICY FOOD.
YELLING FOR FUN.
PEEKING IN WINDOWS.
MOUNTAINS.
FARTING.
POOT!
SUSHI.
STARING CONTESTS.
PUDDLES.

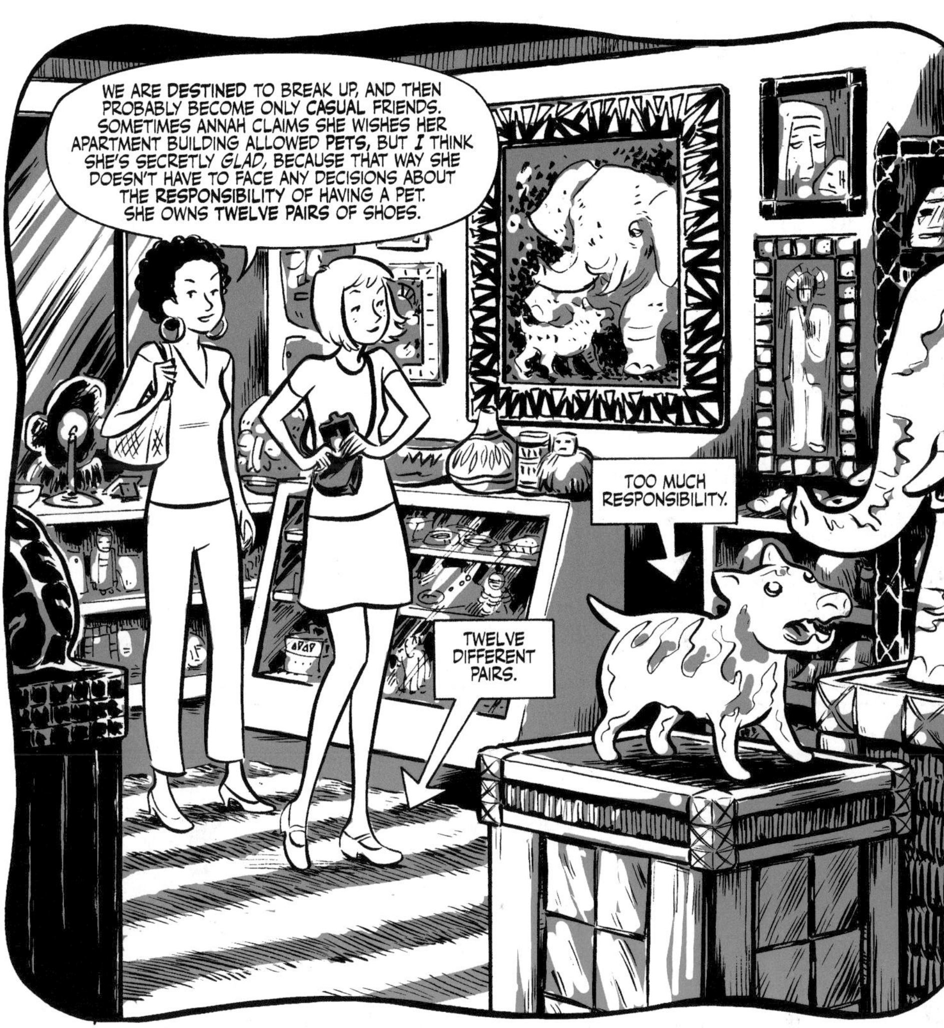
WE ARE DESTINED TO BREAK UP, AND THEN PROBABLY BECOME ONLY CASUAL FRIENDS. SOMETIMES ANNAH CLAIMS SHE WISHES HER APARTMENT BUILDING ALLOWED PETS, BUT I THINK SHE'S SECRETLY GLAD, BECAUSE THAT WAY SHE DOESN'T HAVE TO FACE ANY DECISIONS ABOUT THE RESPONSIBILITY OF HAVING A PET. SHE OWNS TWELVE PAIRS OF SHOES.
TOO MUCH RESPONSIBILITY.
TWELVE DIFFERENT PAIRS.

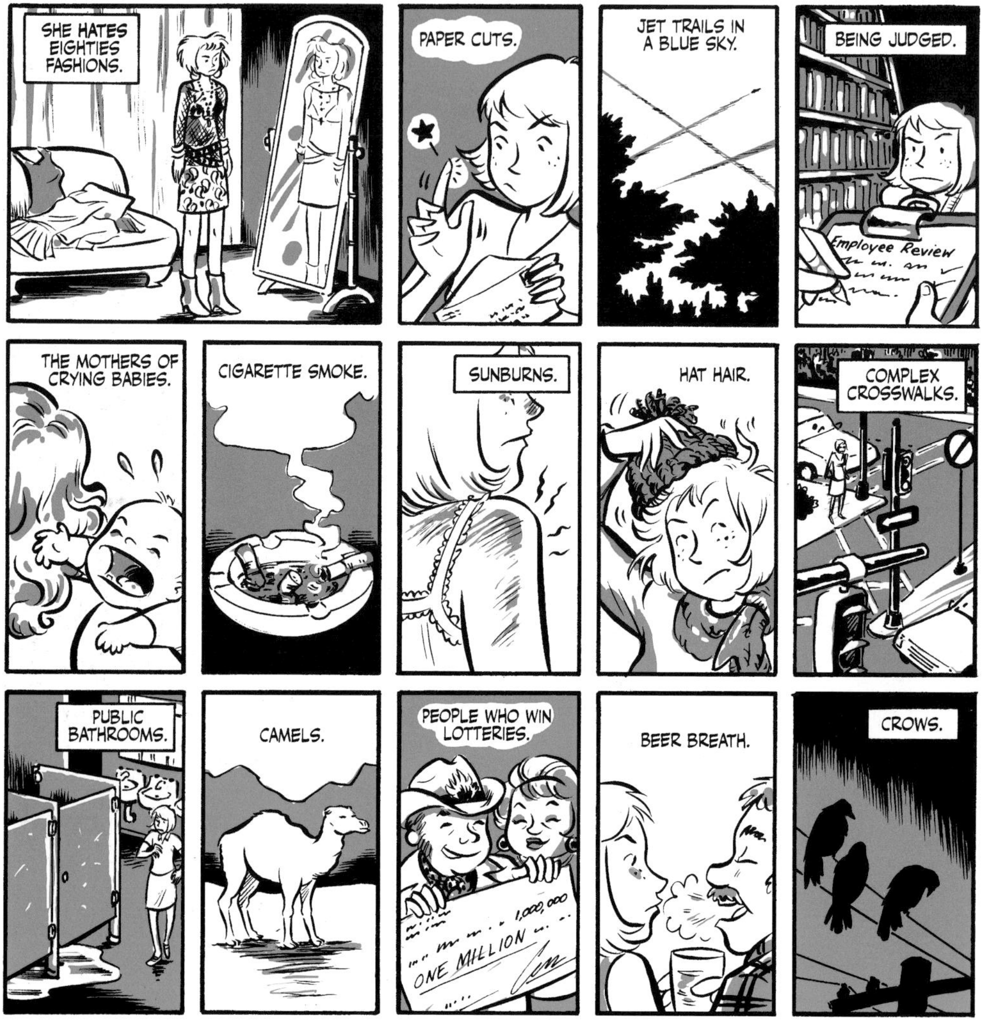
SHE HATES EIGHTIES FASHIONS.
PAPER CUTS.
JET TRAILS IN A BLUE SKY.
BEING JUDGED.
Employee Review
THE MOTHERS OF CRYING BABIES.
CIGARETTE SMOKE.
SUNBURNS.
HAT HAIR.
COMPLEX CROSSWALKS.
PUBLIC BATHROOMS.
CAMELS.
PEOPLE WHO WIN LOTTERIES.
1,000,000
ONE MILLION
BEER BREATH.
CROWS.

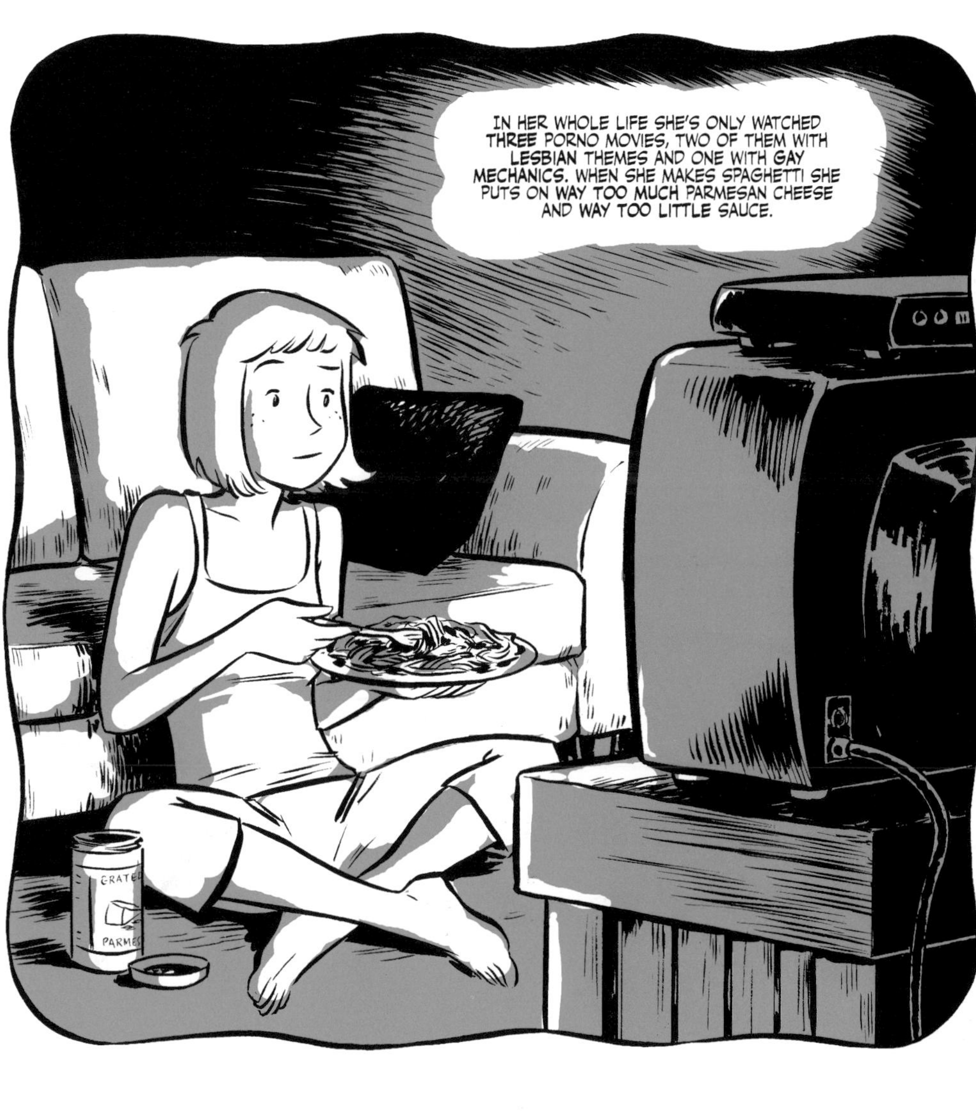
IN HER WHOLE LIFE SHE'S ONLY WATCHED THREE PORNO MOVIES, TWO OF THEM WITH LESBIAN THEMES AND ONE WITH GAY MECHANICS. WHEN SHE MAKES SPAGHETTI SHE PUTS ON WAY TOO MUCH PARMESAN CHEESE AND WAY TOO LITTLE SAUCE.
GRATED
PARMES

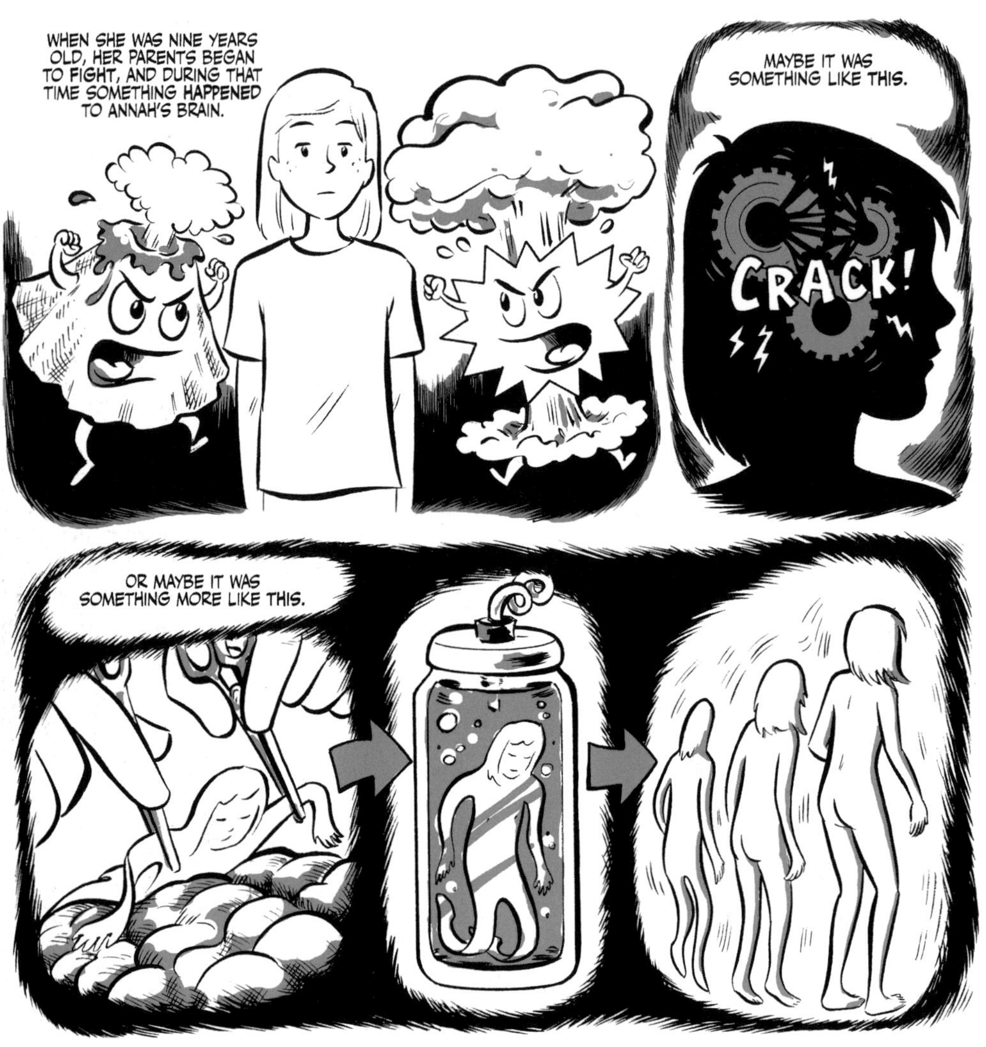
WHEN SHE WAS NINE YEARS OLD, HER PARENTS BEGAN TO FIGHT, AND DURING THAT TIME SOMETHING HAPPENED TO ANNAH'S BRAIN.
MAYBE IT WAS SOMETHING LIKE THIS.
CRACK!
OR MAYBE IT WAS SOMETHING MORE LIKE THIS.

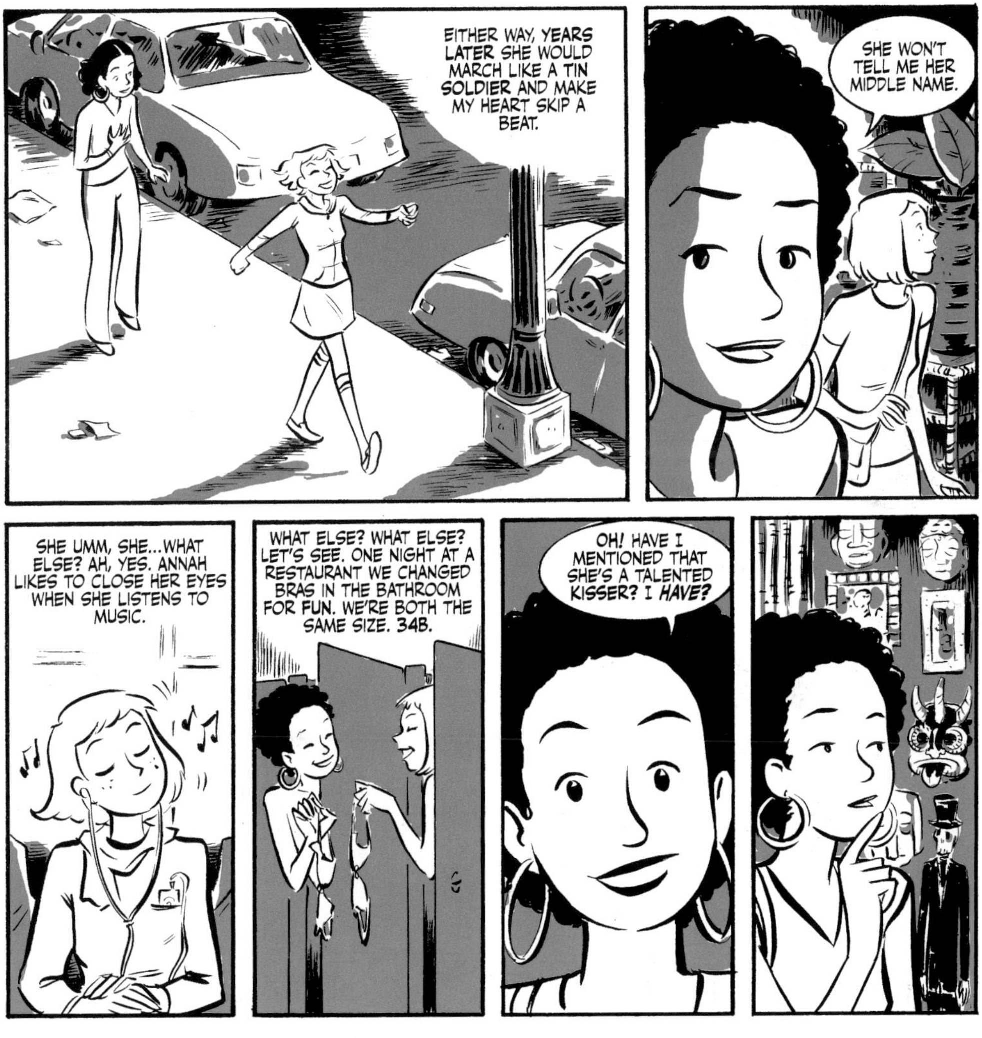
EITHER WAY, YEARS LATER SHE WOULD MARCH LIKE A TIN SOLDIER AND MAKE MY HEART SKIP A BEAT.
SHE WON'T TELL ME HER MIDDLE NAME.
SHE UMM, SHE...WHAT ELSE? AH, YES. ANNAH LIKES TO CLOSE HER EYES WHEN SHE LISTENS TO MUSIC.
WHAT ELSE? WHAT ELSE? LET'S SEE. ONE NIGHT AT A RESTAURANT WE CHANGED BRAS IN THE BATHROOM FOR FUN. WE'RE BOTH THE SAME SIZE. 34B.
OH! HAVE I MENTIONED THAT SHE'S A TALENTED KISSER? I HAVE?

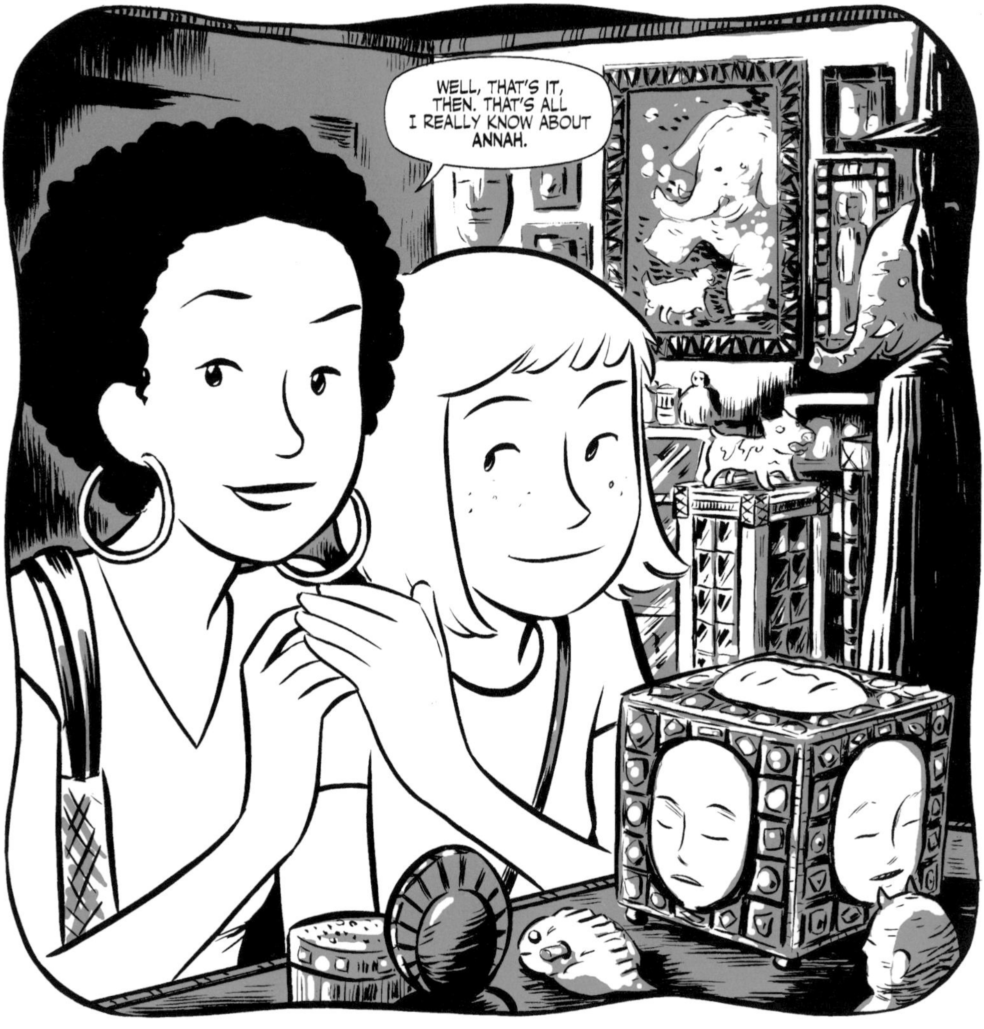
WELL, THAT'S IT, THEN. THAT'S ALL I REALLY KNOW ABOUT ANNAH.

Paul Tobin is an oft-mustachioed writer living in Portland, Oregon. He has written for Marvel Comics, DC Comics, Dark Horse, Oni Press, Fantagraphics and many other clients. He is working on a pair of novels and also occasionally pens notes that he passes to young ladies with a certain type of eyes.

Paul likes storms, girls on bicycles, vintage clothing, girls that rub his head, burlesque, soccer, vaudevillian circuses, proper men's hats, dogs, the art of the Impressionists, and the Flapper era.

Paul hates public bathrooms, spicy foods, most popular music, trash on streets, poetry, modern art, boys that rub his head, and people whose kung-fu is better than his.

PaulTobin.Net
Follow Paul on Twitter @PaulTobin

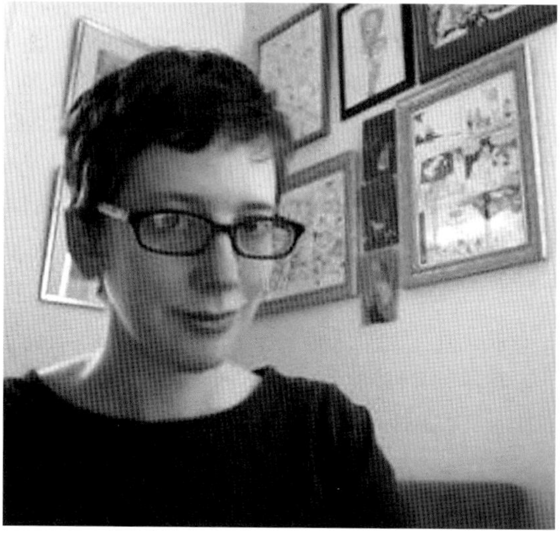

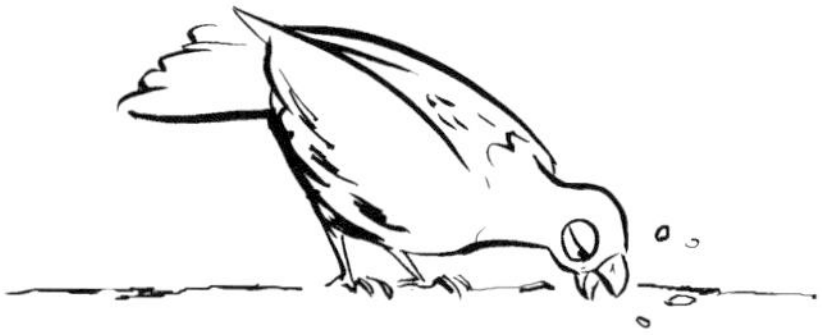

Colleen Coover is a comic book artist and illustrator living in Portland, Oregon. She is the creator of the popular erotic comic SMALL FAVORS, and artist of the all ages comedy BANANA SUNDAY. She has worked for Marvel Comics, DC Comics, Dark Horse, Oni Press, Fantagraphics, and many others.

Colleen likes bunnies, cheese, romance novels, her iPad, mashed potatoes, giving her opinion on a variety of topics, console single-player RPGs, mustard, warm slippers, and Bollywood movies.

Colleen hates terriers, maraschino cherries, being asked to do basic math on short notice, reality television, artists' statements, black licorice, MMORPGs, cold feet, Nashville corporate country music, being embarrassed.

ColleenCoover.Net
Follow Colleen on Twitter @ColleenCoover

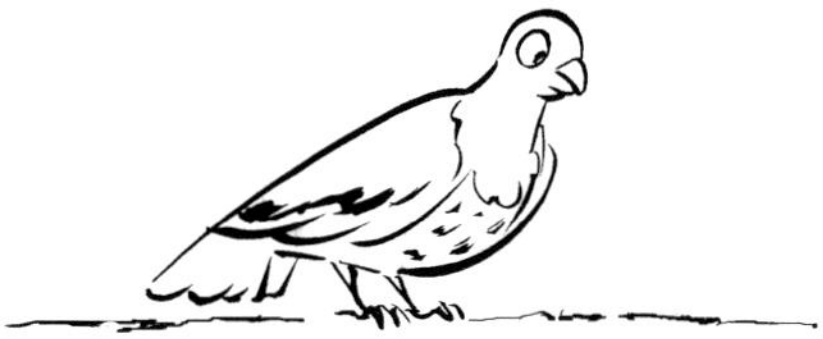